Hey Ram to Jai Shri Ram

20 dates that changed the course of India

AF661609

Anand Vardhan Singh

Foreword by

Dr. Shashi Tharoor

Prologue by

Satish Jha

ANAMIKA PUBLISHERS & DISTRIBUTORS (P) LTD.
4697/3, 21A, Ansari Road, Daryaganj, New Delhi 110002
Phones: 011-23281655, 011-43708938
E-mail: anamikapublishers@yahoo.co.in

First Published 2022
First reprint 2022

© Anand Vardhan Singh

ISBN 978-93-91524-25-8

PRINTED IN INDIA

Published by Anamika Publishers & Distributors (P) Ltd., 4697/3, 21A, Ansari Road, Daryaganj, New Delhi 110002. Typeset by Shivani Compuers, Delhi 110093 and Printed at Vikas Computer & Printers, Tronica City, Ghaziabad

Contents

Foreword

Anand Vardhan Singh's *Hey Ram to Jai Shri Ram* looks at a wide sweep of recent Indian history, examining both the soaring triumphs and crippling low points of our nearly 75 years of independence. The historical episodes within contain examples of incredible bravery, wondrous innovation, and formidable strength in the face of adversity. At the same time, they force us to confront the darkest annals of our past: the erosion of civil liberties, our struggles with foreign policy, and, both at the outset and as the narrative arcs toward the present day, the stain of religious fundamentalism.

Nations are destined to be plagued with questions of identity–perhaps none more than India, with its unique congeries of religious and ethnic groups that combine to form a place like no other, built on the premise that we are united, not divided, by our diversity. Many observers abroad have been astonished by India's survival as a pluralist state, but in reality India could hardly have survived as anything else. Pluralism is a reality that emerges from the very nature of the country; it is a choice made inevitable by India's geography and reaffirmed by its history.

Pluralism and inclusiveness have long marked the essence of India. It is the erosion of this essence that marks much of the story told in this book, from the ghastly crime of Gandhi's assassination to the more recent horrors of communal violence emerging from Ayodhya and Gujarat.

Today, more than ever before, we are in danger of retreating into a shell of religious isolation. This departs from the fundamental tenets of India. Hinduism, as Swami Vivekananda pointed out, teaches the acceptance of difference as a basic credo. Hindutva is not Hinduism; it is a political doctrine, not a religious one. A "Hindu Pakistan" would not be Hindu at all, but a Sanghi Hindutva state. That would be a state system many thinking Hindus cannot accept–and it is one that rears its ugly head time and time again in Hey Ram to Jai Shri Ram.

Singh closes by expressing his wish that "the nation moves from Jai Shri Ram, which is being used like a war cry these days, to Jai Sia Ram, the sound of peace and tranquility for all". I echo his desire for peace, tolerance, and unity: that is the sole path to a brighter future for the country we all love.

Shashi Tharoor

Prologue

Independent of its British colonial past, India is 75 years young now. Young because democracies take time aging. Their half-life is fairly long. The "oldest democracy", as we refer to the United States of America, still shows little signs of maturing on some of the most basic aspects of being a democratic republic. Little wonder then that 17 general elections to its parliament and 16 prime ministers later, India continues to be full of promises in providing a democratic governance to every fifth human being on the planet that make it India.

Our history is rich with folks who greatly contributed to human civilization, with its influence millenniums ago spreading from west Asia to the far East, particularly in spreading the messages of peace, world as a family, good for all mankind as also in early holistic understanding of nature and science. However, globally, it continues to draw most respect because of two great Indians, both called Mahatma, Buddha and Gandhi. Their message cuts across all geographical, national or political boundaries.

Capturing the evolution of a nation of more than a billion people, almost since the second world war, is a huge endeavor. To connect the dots across thousands of significant events that left their mark on the nation in this journey is not for the faint hearted or deletants when not a day goes by without stirring the conscience of any observer interested in betterment of our lives, social fabric and the way we contribute to building our future.

Anand Vardhan Singh is one of the rare observers in these times who has been keeping his wide open, commenting, standing up and finding innovative ways to let his viewers understand the ground realities. This is what we look for in a vibrant media in a thriving democracy. Lately, however, these attributes in independent media are a rarity and the mainstream media is being seen mostly as courtiers, a lapdog of powers that be. Anand Vardhan has been editing a prominent Hindi daily published from Lucknow for over a decade and recognized that when readers choose the digital medium, journalists must also become adept in reaching the readers and viewers wherever they may be. A couple of years ago he founded Public India that got quickly recognized for its straightforwardness, standing up to the powers that be, speaking truth to them in ways that may be a role model for others. His programs engage the participants and the viewers, bring in a variety of contemporary issues and have developed a substantial viewership. Moreover, Public India is beginning to be widely seen as exemplifying what citizens wish journalism to be.

This book traces the long journey since independence through some incidents that stand out in India's recent evolution as a society and as a nation. With the help of twenty specific incidents that changed the course of history of India since1947, the book narrates a brief account of lot of known, forgotten and unknown facts that highlight the trials and tribulations of becoming a defined geography, a union of various states within, a nation everyone identifies as India that is Bharat. The author places his understanding of how these dates and facts are so essential in discovering who we are as nation.

Anand Vardhan Singh draws greatly on his upbringing in a politically active family, that offered him the privilege to share, listen, witness and participate in many incidents, small, trivial, significant and tectonic in impact that have shaped the country. Starting from the assassination of Mahatma Gandhi to the laying of foundation stone of Ram Mandir in Ayodhya, this book travels through various stories in every chapter that not everyone may be aware of.

The title of the book cleverly captures the journey of 75

years, a whole generation, about the life expectancy of an average Indian. It was one of the cruelest irony that within months of gaining independence from the British rule, India saw the "father of the nation", the leader of her nonviolent freedom struggle, by any measure one of the greatest Indians who taught the world the virtues of nonviolence, peace, truth and higher values as a citizen, who didn't wear any more clothes on his body than the poorest could afford, who embodied greatness in the simplest of physical forms fell prey to the bullets pumped into him by a right wing, fundamentalist who conspired to silence the voice of the nation. The life of the most nonviolent man the world knew was taken away most violently. That event has continued to divide the nation ever since. Gandhi's assassin continues to be portrayed as a hero by the majoritarian right-wing Hindutva, as distinct from Hindu, forces that currently run the Union government.

Starting out with the assassination of Gandhi, Anand Vardhan does not confine himself to the political episodes alone. He weaves through how India adopted its constitution and became a republic to the diplomatic, military, sports, mass movements, militaristic questions, economy, development, riots, corruption and several others to conclude with what the rise of Narendra Modi has wrought on one of the two most populous nations on the planet. He sees these events through the lenses that he refined along his journey of several decades, being an insider in some events, having a ring side view of some others, outside observer of some and as a student of distant moments in India's recent history.

It's a gripping book by any measure and brings in insights that may not have been penned or available outside the few who may have been privy to how these events evolved, erupted or were shaped by the forces of history.

Satish Jha
Boston, USA
Former Editor—*Dinmaan*
Founding Editor—*Jansatta*

Acknowledgement

I was encouraged to question status quo, as a child and over time it became a part of my being - to seek answers and analyse individual events that often come together to create history.

I must begin by acknowledging the late George Fernandes who played a key role in shaping my world view and political perspective from a socialist prism. The year 1969 when he came to address rickshaw pullers & horse-cart (Tonga) owners on the invitation of my brother who was being baptized by the socialist leaders of his time stands out as the big event that drew me to real politics.

I must thank my late brother, Harsh Vardhan who dedicated his life to fight for the rights of the less privileged and against injustice. He was twice elected to the Lok Sabha and once to the state assembly, and it is through him I got an insight into electoral politics since 1977. My brother gave me complete freedom to organize the campaign and had absolute faith in the strategies I put to use for over four decades.

The freewheeling discussions at home about politics and the encouragement to hold independent views is the biggest contribution that my parents made that shaped me into the man I am today.

My mother Savitri Singh's in-depth knowledge of

literature, history and her story telling skill had a huge influence on me as a child. She was a freedom fighter who spent years at Mahatma Gandhi's Sevagram—it wasn't just my siblings and me but even our next generation were greatly enriched by her huge depository of mythological stories besides the first-hand account of freedom movement and Gandhi.

My father Yogendra Pal Singh was born with a silver spoon but he chose to make his own mark. He didn't just play a crucial role in banning the ghastly practice of buffalo slaughter during Dussehra in Basgaon (Uttar Pradesh) but also ushered in a revolution by ploughing fields in defiance of caste based conservative practices that barred Thakurs and Brahmans from doing so.

I must acknowledge the contribution of each of my siblings who stood by all my tough choices—some of which may have gone wrong - but it is their implicit Main Hun Na confidence that made decisions simple.

My wife Pratibha deserves not only my acknowledgement but my deepest appreciation and love for being my biggest support during our bond over the last 40-years. During my long periods of absence because of extensive traveling, I never had to worry about household responsibilities and my children. It will be unfair to not mention one of her most extraordinary capabilities - through the years whenever I was in dire need of money, she has always been my financier. It continues to be a mystery how she manages to make it all so simple and easy.

For my children Nikhil and Nidhi I have been the hero who could do no wrong- and that was my moral compass to always make the right decisions.

We are a joint family - and I must thank our next generation for treating me as an older friend—which has helped me remain inquisitive and energetic. My fondest memories are the festivals celebrated at my family home in Daliganj, Lucknow—led by me and ably supported by my nephew Rajan.

It may not be possible to thank all the activists who I greatly admire but I must assert, your compassion and belief in your cause is inspiring. My large circle of friends and colleagues make every day bright.

Pranita Lele deserves my special thanks for being my first editor and for raising critical questions that helped in putting together essential details.

Gyanesh didn't just take care of the technical aspects but has been my sounding board for many of my initiatives including the story I narrate here.

My staff gave me the comfort to not bother about anything else while putting together this book and no words are enough to appreciate their commitment. Mushaif, thank you for creating the cover which truly reflects the text and events that follow.

I must thank Supriya, my niece who insisted on the need for this book to chronicle and put together a history that is being greatly distorted.

My sincere thanks to Pankaj Sharma of Anamika publishers for his faith in the book and publishing it without any change in the script.

In the end I must acknowledge an all new love that I discovered through my granddaughter Jia— I fondly call Kuchi-Kuchi—a love that keeps the heart warm and is almost divine.

Finally, the awe inspiring Indians - who despite all the adversity, fake news and hate spewing politics around—keep the soul and idea of India alive. It's over to you now...

Anand Vardhan Singh

Chapter-1

Hey Ram
The Assassination of Mahatma Gandhi
30 January 1948, Friday

'Hey Ram!'–these were the last words of the man who was riddled with three bullets by a fellow Indian at point-blank range on 30 January 1948. The mortal Mahatma Gandhi was made immortal by these bullets. The nation lost the Father of the Nation, the honorific title given to him by Netaji Subhash Chandra Bose; and this is the way he is remembered by India.

In Hindu philosophy, it is said that if you utter the magical word 'Ram' while dying, you will achieve *moksha* (salvation). Here, a Hindu shot by the Hindu, Nathu Ram Godse, died with Ram on his lips. The self-proclaimed protector of Hindu religion Nathu Ram Godse chose Friday to shoot the Mahatma. Friday is the most revered day for Muslims to offer prayers to the almighty. *Jumme ki namaaz* was over but Gandhi was not allowed to complete his evening prayers. Gandhi was in a way crucified like Christ by his people to whom he had dedicated his entire life.

The Journey from Mohandas to Mahatma Gandhi

After completing his education of law in England, Mohandas Karamchand Gandhi came back to India for a brief period before going to South Africa. There he experimented with his ideas of non-violence, satyagraha, truth, etc. One can safely say that South Africa was his primary lab where he sharpened his basic tools to oppose a foreign government that was not working for the welfare of the people. During his entire life, he worked at being strong mentally and spiritually to build a strong society and in turn, a strong nation to strive for their rights.

Mahatma Gandhi not only gave us the weapon to fight the Britishers but also gave us the idea of *Swaraj* or self-rule. He knew that driving the Britishers out of India was achieving only partial freedom but to give to his fellow countrymen *azaadi* from hunger, unemployment, gender bias and untouchability was a gigantic task.

Mahatma Gandhi was never in favour of a two-nation theory but the Congress leadership wanted the British to leave India immediately even if it was at the cost of partition. Jinnah's demand for a separate state for Muslims suited the British purpose. On 15 August 1947, Gandhi was not celebrating Independence but fasting in Calcutta for communal peace and harmony. There are numerous articles, writings, etc. of Mahatma Gandhi regarding the partition of India. We are not going into the details because the purpose of this book is to understand the impact of Mahatma Gandhi's murder on Indian politics. After partition, Mahatma Gandhi toyed with the idea of an India and Pakistan Confederation. The idea was later manifested by Dr Ram Manohar Lohia as the Bharat-Pak Mahasangh.

Gandhi was always confident that someday, some working arrangement between the two nations would be in place so that both could progress together.

Once or twice, Mahatma Gandhi went to the Rashtriya Swayamsevak Sangh (RSS) camp upon the invitation of the then head of the institution; he praised the discipline of the RSS but advised them about changing the definition of 'Hindu' as propagated by the RSS. The Hinduism practised by Mahatma Gandhi was inclusive and not exclusive as propagated by the RSS. It is widely believed that Nathu Ram Godse was an RSS sympathizer. It is also believed that the Hindu Mahasabha was involved in the conspiracy to kill Gandhi. Savarkar was the strategist and the material support was provided by Mahant Digvijaynath of Gorakhnath Matt.[1]

Mahatma Gandhi–Congress–Nehru–Sardar Patel

According to a letter, Mahatma Gandhi wanted to disband the Congress since it had achieved its role of attaining freedom.[2] Mahatma Gandhi's idea of *Purna Swaraj* was never limited only to driving out the Britishers but also to uplift the last man of society–*antyodaya* (welfare of the poorest). What I understand is that Mahatma Gandhi wanted Congress to remain an ideological and social body, and not involve directly in elections. To make understanding easier, perhaps he wanted something like the RSS and BJP (the Bharatiya Janta Party), where RSS only works on spreading its ideology and BJP participates in elections. So, he visualized a clear-cut demarcation between the Congress movement and the Congress party. The party could participate in elections. The Congress movement would have been separate from various political parties pursuing the Congress ideology like the Congress party, the Socialist party, etc.

Mahatma Gandhi always worked to strengthen the Congress. He always acted as a coach of the team as it were and never the captain of the Congress party, not even a non-playing captain. Gandhi was of the opinion that vision of Nehru and administrative skills of Patel were equally important for India. Sardar Patel was 15 years older than Jawaharlal Nehru. He never challenged Nehru on any issue. Sardar Patel knew that in elections votes were needed and that Nehru was a darling of the people. He was a vote-puller. Sardar also knew that India needed a firm start and Nehru had to engage himself on the developmental front. One needed to have an efficient and reliable partner, and Sardar always played the role of a sheet anchor. There are numerous occasions in history where we see that the determination and will of Sardar prevailed and Nehru accepted it. The affection and respect of Nehru towards Sardar was that of an elder brother.

On the advice of Gopal Krishna Gokhale, Mahatma Gandhi returned to India from South Africa in January 1915. Gokhale died on 19 February 1915 but as suggested by Gokhale, Gandhi travelled the length and breadth of India to understand the country, the people living there, their diversity and above all their suffering. One has to appreciate the understanding and larger plans of Gandhi to free the country not only from British Rule but also to free the society from its evil practices and traditions. The power of youth was well understood by him and he left no opportunity to address the students. The first opportunity was provided by Mahamana Madan Mohan Malviya. The Foundation Stone of Banaras Hindu University (BHU) was laid on Basant Panchmi in 1916 by Lord Hardinge, viceroy and governor-general of India. A galaxy of academicians and rulers of princely states were invited to grace the occasion. Gandhi was requested to address the gathering. The audience was primarily students. Annie Besant—another moving force along with Malviya—tried to persuade Gandhi to check his words. The romance of Gandhi especially with the youth and students was obvious from BHU. He spoke, touching various subjects and insisted on the importance and need for freedom.

St Stephens was his place of residence in Delhi in the initial years. The Principal of the college Sushil Kumar Rudra used to be his host. Birla House and St Stephens are both in Delhi. Gandhi took his last breath in Birla House and issued the first call of non-cooperation while addressing the students at St Stephen's. The rulers were annoyed with Principal Rudra who stood firm in his decision of hosting Gandhi in the future too. There are not one but numerous incidents during the freedom struggle when not only Indians but also British heads of institutions, vice-chancellors, principals, stood as a shield for the agitating students. Police or administration was not allowed to enter the institutions. This hangover of the British Raj was enjoyed by the student leaders for quite some time. In today's India, this protection to students is denied. The rules of the game have changed. In the second innings of Modi with Amit Shah in command as Home Minister, police entering universities and academic institutions is a common phenomenon. In the closing months of 2019, Jawaharlal Nehru University, Jamia Millia Islamia University, Aligarh Muslim University witnessed police frequently entering their premises.

Last 144 days of Mahatama Gandhi

Gandhi reached Delhi in the first week of September 1947 on his way to Pakistan. The events at Delhi made him stay back. After Partition, Delhi became the epicentre not only of power but also of hatred. Along with the top leadership of Congress, Viceroy Lord Mountbatten also understood the role and importance of Gandhi in tackling the charged emotions of Hindus and Muslims because of Partition. The environment was getting more vitiated with news of violence coming from across the border. The gory stories of refugees coming from Pakistan added fuel to the fire. Gandhi was able to visualize the sufferings across the border. He understood that the sufferings of the people in Pakistan and India were similar. H. S. Suhrawardy, after losing control of the Muslim League in East Pakistan (East Bengal) to K. Nazimuddin, stayed back in Calcutta and worked with Mahatma Gandhi in various parts of Bengal. He shifted to Pakistan very late on 5 March 1949. K. Nazimuddin became the chief minister of East Pakistan. It was 18 September when Suhrawardy called on Mahatma Gandhi in Delhi on his way to Pakistan. Gandhi told Suhrawardy to convey to Jinnah that he had failed to keep his promise about taking care of the rights and safety of minorities in Pakistan. It was reported in the *Hindustan Times* that the same day while addressing a gathering of Hindus and Sikhs, Gandhi asked them to show respect and honour to their Muslim brothers,[3] further added that he would be going to Pakistan soon to protect the rights of the minorities (Hindus and Sikhs) and was ready to sacrifice his life for that. Mahatma Gandhi had planned to visit Pakistan to bring peace and harmony to both countries. India and Pakistan both were burning due to Partition and the communal hatred it triggered. This was something that was not foreseen by leaders of either India or Pakistan at the time of Partition.

It looked like the efforts of Gandhi were paying dividends as for a very brief period, riots came to an end and it looked like peace had been restored. In the first week of January 1948, a fresh round of violence broke out against Muslims. Gandhi announced his decision to fast. He met Mountbatten and also informed him about his decision. Nehru had a long discussion with Gandhi lasting more than two hours one day before his fast. On the morning of 13 January, Sardar Patel had a one-to-one discussion with Gandhi. Gandhi started his fast on the 13th itself which lasted for six days. The reason for this fast is not very clear as there seems to have been many reasons. Gandhi had stated that the purpose of fasting was to bring peace and harmony and to end the violence against Muslims. But many people including Godse believed that Mahatma Gandhi fasted to pressurize the Indian government to give Rs 550 million (55 crores) to Pakistan. At the time of Partition under the terms of division of assets and resources, India was to pay Rs 750 million to Pakistan. The first instalment of Rs 200 million (20 crores) was paid. But the invasion of Kashmir by self-styled liberators with the covert support of the Pakistani Army took place before the second instalment was paid. Due to this attack, the Government of India decided to withhold the balance amount of Rs 550 million. India was apprehensive that this money would be used against India.

Mahatma Gandhi was baffled by the stand of the Indian government and termed it as a breach of trust. He took up the matter with Sardar Patel and the then Governor-General Lord Mountbatten. Mountbatten agreed that this was the only mistake that the Indian government had committed. Sardar who was supposed to be a man of words was told by Mahatma Gandhi that he (Sardar) had changed and he was not the Sardar whom Gandhi had once known. Since Pakistan was having acute resource crunch, Mahatma Gandhi was also apprehensive that Jinnah in his desperation might attack India on the pretext of non-payment of the balance amount, terming it as a breach of trust. Both nations were not in a position to cope with war. India had too many internal problems and did not want to give an impression to the world that they were incapable of governance. Also, the image of India would have been tarnished on moralistic grounds as someone who could not honour their words.

On 14 January, Nehru, Patel and Azad again met Gandhi to assure him that the government was trying its level best to keep their word. The general perception was that Sardar Patel was anti-Muslim. Regarding this Gandhi made important comments in one of his prayer meetings. He said, 'The Sardar is blunt of speech. What he says sometimes sounds bitter. The fault is in his tongue.'[4] Showing the amount of faith he had in Patel, he told Muslims, 'Bring to the Sardar's notice any mistake which in their opinion he commits.' Gandhi was not able to complete his speech on 15 January owing to weakness and his secretary Pyarelal read out the text. Gandhi emphasized that his fast was in solidarity with the sufferings of minorities both in India and Pakistan. Gandhi after talking to Maulana Azad put seven conditions to end his fast, all related to end the sufferings of Muslims. A Peace Pledge signed by about two lakh people in Delhi—mainly Hindus, Sikhs and Christians—assured Gandhi that no Muslim would be harassed or tortured. On the morning of 18 January, after a meeting in the house of Rajendra Prasad, the government agreed to all the seven demands and Gandhi broke his fast without knowing that this was going to be his last experiment with truth. The cabinet had cleared the pending payment to Pakistan on 15 January itself.

Nathuram Godse

Nathuram Vinayrao Godse was a Chitpawan Brahmin. His original name was Ramchandra Godse. Three brothers who were born before him had died whereas his three sisters survived. The family considered this as some curse on the male child and decided to bring up Godse as a girl child. The tradition of piercing the nose, which is done for girls, was performed for Godse too and even a nose ring (*nath*) was put on him. From this *nath*, he derived his name Nathu Ram. Only after his younger brothers were born and survived, was he treated as a male child.

Born in 1910, he joined RSS in 1932 in Sangli as Boudhik Karywah (ground worker). He was fascinated by the idea of Hindu nationalism. He was also a member of the Hindu Mahasabha. In 1942, on Vijaydashmi day, he formed his outfit 'Hindu Rashtra Dal' but continued to be a member of the RSS and Hindu Mahasabha. Godse started the Marathi magazine and came into contact with Golwarkar of RSS. Both of them translated the Marathi version of *Rashtra Mimansa,* a book written by Ganesh Damodar Savarkar in English. Godse broke away when Golwarkar took the entire credit of translating the book.

On the fateful evening of 30 January 1948, Godse, wearing a khaki bush shirt and blue trousers, pumped in three bullets from his 38 calibre Beretta M 1934 semi-automatic Italian pistol into Mahatma Gandhi. After half an hour at 1740 hours, the nation lost its Bapu. Godse shot the fourth shot but was overpowered by a sergeant of the Royal Indian Air force, who had come to pay his respect to Mahatma Gandhi.

Nehru, Patel and Lord Mountbatten worked successfully to contain riots and unrest in the country. Bombay witnessed riots where people were killed and injured. The trial of Godse went on for a year and he was sentenced to death on 8 November 1949. Mahatma Gandhi's sons Manilal Gandhi and Ramlal Gandhi in line with the lifelong philosophy of Mahatma Gandhi—'hate the sin not the sinner'—made a petition for commutation of a life sentence for Godse instead of hanging. The petition was turned down by Prime Minister Nehru, Deputy Prime Minister and Home Minister Patel and Governor-General Rajgopalachari. On 15 November 1949, Godse was hanged in Ambala jail.

Impact and Consequence

Due to the murder of Mahatma Gandhi, the proposed visit to Pakistan never happened. India certainly needed Gandhi for at least five to six years more so that the initial consolidation of state and direction of the country could be steered in a better way. Mahatma Gandhi's killing snatched the opportunity of the Indian subcontinent to lead the world for a few decades. Under the able guidance of Gandhi, the hatred between India and Pakistan would not have scaled the present heights, sacrificing invaluable lives and resources.

Mahatma Gandhi's murder gave some sort of approval to radicals. In other words, it was the first act in free India that proclaimed, 'if I don't agree with your views/ philosophy I will silence your voice by killing you.' During the freedom struggle, the act of violence was always against Britishers or against someone who sympathized with their policies but Mahatma Gandhi's murder was by an individual who practised and advocated a philosophy based on religion. The making of the Godse temple after more than seventy years of his murder is testimony that a group not only sanctions his act of murdering but worships him. In a way, Nathuram is a role model for that organization.

Due to the death of Gandhi, he had no role in the making of the Indian Constitution. The role of Mahatma Gandhi in framing the Constitution of India was very limited due to his early death. Moreover, in the early days of Partition, the focus of the government and country was more on handling Partition problems than the framing of the Constitution. The Constituent Assembly was in place but the real drafting was yet to start.

There were irreconcilable differences between Gandhi and Ambedkar but Gandhi had an important role in bringing Ambedkar to the Constituent Assembly. Both Gandhi and Ambedkar had a vision for the emancipation of the oppressed. Therefore, rightly one is called the 'Father of the Nation' and the other, 'Father of the Constitution'. From time to time the world has seen the emergence of noble souls who have shown us the path of goodness and taught us how to try to live an honest and ideal life. Perhaps these two stalwarts, Mahatma Gandhi and Ambedkar, with their basic philosophy of the welfare of the poor and the downtrodden, are a part of our rich heritage.

Gandhi advocated the theory of Hind Swarajya and documented his thoughts. But the concept of Hind Swarajya is completely missing in the Constitution. There is no doubt that the concept of Mahatma Gandhi regarding local self-government should have been the central theme of our Constitution. But Gandhi and Ambedkar had differences regarding the approach for India's path of development itself. Gandhi wanted a village-centred model of development which he called 'Ram Rajya', an idealized traditional village community. He did not believe in industrialization. Ambedkar, in contrast, wanted economic development which was based on industrialization as the basic prerequisite for the abolition of poverty.

Mahatma Gandhi could always balance two extremely opposite philosophies. That was his unique trait. The socialist group always looked at him as their leader, the communists had constant dialogues with him, and the group led by Subhash Chandra Bose that thought that only a violent army action could drive the British from India had faith in his leadership. His capitalist followers like Ghanshyam Das Birla and Jamnalal Bajaj were active freedom fighters and also funded the freedom struggle. Mahatma Gandhi always had a larger picture of the country and the world before him.

Somehow just as a coincidence, the gory act of killing a politician, which changed the destiny of the country, had one thing common in the name—Gandhi. Mahatma Gandhi, Indira Gandhi and Rajeev Gandhi—killing is the testimony that we are not ready to live in peaceful coexistence in free India.

Notes

1. Founded by Matsyendranath, it is located in Gorakhpur district of Uttar Pradesh. It is the citadel of the Nath Sect and got its name from Guru Gorakhnath. The matt came into prominence recently when the sitting head Yogi Adityanath became Chief Minister of the BJP government in Uttar Pradesh.
2. An article published in *Harijan* on 2 February 1948, titled 'His Last Will and Testament'; also *Gandhi Literature: Collected Works of Mahatma Gandhi*, vol. 98, 333, the Draft Constitution of the Congress, available at: https://www.gandhiashramseva gram.org/gandhi-literature/collected-works-of-mahatma-

gandhi-volume-1-to-98.php (accessed on 1 February 2020).

3. Ramachandra Guha, 2018, *Gandhi: The Years That Changed the World, 1914-1948*. Knopf Doubleday Publishing Group, Apple Books.
4. Speech at the prayer meeting, 13 January 1948, New Delhi. *Gandhi Literature: Collected Works of Mahatma Gandhi*, vol. 90, 413.

CHAPTER-2

We, the People...

India Embraces the Constitution

26 January 1950, Thursday

India is governed by a written constitution. In our country, the Parliament is not supreme, it is the Constitution that is supreme as the same was written and adopted by the Constituent Assembly and not the Parliament. The Constitution was adopted by the Constituent Assembly on 26 November 1949 but implemented on 26 January 1950. To understand the significance of 26 January, we need to look into all that changed between these two dates. From the day of the adoption of the Constitution, that is 26 November 1949, India was no more a dominion of the British Crown. India, after Independence in 1947, was ruled by the Government of India Act 1935 and other Acts passed by the British before 1935. On 26 January 1950,the Government of India Act, 1935 and also the India Independence Act, 1947 was repealed. The last Article of our Constitution that is Article 395 repealed all the previous Acts passed by the British parliament. This was to ensure that the authority of the Constitution was adopted on 26 November 1949. Before moving to the main topic of framing of the Constitution, it will be interesting to understand the development of British rule regarding governing India. Several Acts and Rules were evolved from the legislation passed in Britain. The major ones are as follows.

Regulating Act of 1773

The East India Company (EIC), created by the Royal Charter of the British Crown on 31 December 1600 to trade with this part of the continent, developed a political interest to govern parts of India. To regulate the affairs of the EIC, the British government took control. A Council of Four was formed to oversee the affairs of the Company. The council was elected from the Court of Directors of the EIC. The governor of Bengal became governor-general of Bengal and Warren Hastings was the first incumbent. This Act also started the formal judiciary system by the formation of the Supreme Court of India.

East India Company Act of 1784

It was popularly known as Pitts India Act. Commercial and administrative functions were bifurcated by this Act. A six-member Board of Control was set up to supervise the military and civil activities. Members were from the government and the Company. The commercial activities were left to be governed by the Court of Directors of the Company.

Saint Helena Act of 1833

It was also known as the Charter Act of 1833. It extended the charter of the East India Company by 20 years. It redesignated the governor-general of Bengal as the governor-general of India. Lord William Bentinck became the first governor-general of India. His government was addressed as the Government of India and his council was called the India Council with powers to legislate for the whole of India. The commercial activities of the East India Company came to an end. It became a purely administrative body.

Charter Act of 1853

This charter provided a separate governor of Bengal relieving the governor-general of India from his duties of Bengal and leaving him free to look after the Government of India. The charter carried the seeds of two most important institutions in India. It saw the beginning of the parliamentary system in India, with the separation of legislative and executive functions of the governor-general council. The legislative council of the governor-general expanded to 12 members with four local representatives. It also marked the birth of the Civil Services. The entrance examination was open to all and no longer had just the nominees of the EIC. In 1858, the Indian Civil Services, which was later opened for Indians, too came into existence. After Independence, the Indian Bureaucracy in its new avatar of IAS came into existence. It is a more than one-and-a-half-century-old institution.

Government of India Act of 1858

It led to an end of the rule of the East India Company and transfer of functions and power to the British Crown. The governor-general, who was the representative of the British government in India to rule the provinces of British India, also got the title of viceroy. The governor-general thus also became the viceroy. As viceroy, he had to deal with the princely states of India. He had no relationship with the British government and showed his allegiance to the British Crown. He dealt directly with the monarch. As a governor-general, he governed the British India provinces. For convenience, the viceroy and governor-general of India was called the viceroy. A British cabinet minister who was the political head of the India office was designated the position of Secretary of State for India. A council of 15 members was appointed to assist the Secretary of State for India.

Indian Council Act of 1861

Changes were made in the composition of the governor general's council for executive and legislative purposes. The legislative council at Calcutta was given powers to pass legislation for the whole of British India. The power withdrawn earlier was given back to the Bombay and Madras legislative councils to pass legislation for their respective presidencies. It also provided for 6 to 12 members to be nominated as additional members of the central executive. At least half of them were to be non-official. It was decided that the central executive of the governor-general would have a portfolio system. Departments were to be divided and all five members were made responsible for their areas of work. The Act provided for the creation of a new legislative council for the provinces of Bengal, North West Frontier and Punjab. The governor-general enjoyed sweeping powers to veto any legislation and bring an ordinance on his own, etc.

Indian Council Act of 1909

It was also known as Morley Minto Reforms. The number of members in both the central and provincial legislative councils increased. Prasanna Satyendra Sinha became the first Indian to be included in the Viceroy Executive Council. Sinha was elected president of the Indian National Congress in 1915. He returned to England in 1917 to assist the

Secretary of State Edwin Samuel Montagu and was instrumental for the Montagu—Chelmsford Reforms. The most important decision of the Act was a grant of separate electorates for Muslims.

Government of India Act of 1919

It was also known as the Montagu–Chelmsford Reforms. The central and provincial lists were introduced by this Act. Diarchy was introduced in the province. The legislative council had no say in transferred and reserved subjects. The central council was divided into the Upper House (Council of State) and Lower House (Legislative Assembly). Separate electorates were awarded to Sikhs, Christians, Anglo Indians and Europeans.

Government of India Act of 1935

Powers were divided between the centre and provinces by way of the Federal list, Provincial list and Concurrent list. Diarchy was abolished in the provinces and was introduced at the centre. The Federal subjects were divided into two categories—the Reserved and Transferred subjects. The provincial legislatures of Bengal, Bihar, Bombay, Madras, Assam and the United Province were made bicameral. Another landmark decision was the formation of the Reserve Bank of India (RBI). World War II ended in Europe on 8 May 1945. During the war, British Prime Minister Winston Churchill had formed a wartime coalition with leaders of the Labour and Liberal parties. The coalition broke up on 23 May 1945 and England went to polls on 5 July 1945. The entire campaign of Conservatives was built around the wartime hero Churchill. After collecting ballot boxes from far-flung places, the counting was done on 25 July; the Labour Party had a landslide victory while the hero of World War II Churchill had to face a humiliating defeat. A more sympathetic government under Clement Richard Attlee was formed and the Constituent Assembly of India was implemented under the Cabinet Mission Plan on 16 May 1946.

The Constituent Assembly

When the British decided to leave India, it was decided that for a smooth transfer of power India needed a set of rules and regulations to govern herself. For more than 100 years, we were ruled by a nation 6,000 km away with 6,000 officers and 30,000 British soldiers. After World War II, the political climate changed. Clement Richard Attlee of the Labour Party became the prime minister of Britain in 1945. The Labour Party was more sympathetic to the Indian cause. They decided to withdraw from India without bloodshed. Attlee considered Indian Independence his 'finest achievement'. The division of the country was not finalized when the idea of the Constituent Assembly was first introduced. The best course of framing the Constitution would have been by electing the representatives directly by the people. But India was still under the British Rule. We had two Indias—India ruled directly by the Britishers and India ruled by the kings and taluqdars owing direct allegiance to the British Crown. The time was short and the best possible course was to elect the members of the Constituent Assembly through the elected members of the Provincial Assembly. Now, this had inherent flaws. As the voting right was not given to all the citizens, the elected representatives were from a defined voters list which was less than 20 per cent of the population. The basis of representation was roughly one member for 10 lakh population, that is, 1:10 lakh.

It was decided to have 389 members in the proposed Constituent Assembly—292 members were to be elected with proportionate representation from the Provincial Assemblies, and four from the Chief Commissioner Provinces of Delhi, Ajmer—Mewar, Coorg and British Baluchistan; 93 members were to represent the princely states. The election for the Constituent Assembly was completed by August 1946. Out of 296 seats, the Congress won 208 seats and the Muslim League got 73.

The interim government of India was formed from these elected members of the Constituent Assembly on 2 September 1946. The Viceroy Executive Council transformed into the Council of Ministers. The powers of the prime minister were entrusted to the Vice President of the Executive Council. Initially, only Congress leaders joined the government. Jawaharlal Nehru was the Vice President or in other words, the prime minister of the interim government; the Executive Council was headed by Lord Wavell till 20 February 1947 and then Lord Mountbatten from 21 February as President in his capacity as viceroy and governor-general. The interim government had 14 members including Viceroy Lord Wavell and commander-in-chief of the Supreme Commander of the British Indian Army Sir Claude Auchinleck. It also had 12 council members who were also the ministers. In the beginning, the Muslim League boycotted the interim government but subsequently on 15 October, after a lot of hard bargaining decided to be a part of the interim arrangement. Five Congress ministers had to leave to accommodate five Muslim League nominees.

Out of the five Congress ministers who were dropped, three were Muslims. The Muslim League never wanted any Muslim to be part of an interim government from the Congress side. Out of the dropped ministers, Sir Shafaat

Ahmed Khan—a scholar who was Head of the Department of History at Allahabad University—became high commissioner for India in South Africa from 1941 to 1944. He had to resign from the Muslim League in 1946 when he refused to drop his title in line with the Muslim League. The names of the members of the interim government were announced on 24 August 1946 and within five hours of the announcement, Sir Shafaat was stabbed seven times in head, neck and chest in Shimla. He was a minister for Art, Education and Health. Syed Ali Zahir, the Law minister, was the second victim of the Muslim League. He was a leading lawyer of Oudh and subsequently became an Indian Ambassador to Iran when India became independent. The third was Asaf Ali, a part of the Defence Committee of the Congress. He fought the famous Indian National Army trial from November 1945 to May 1946. He was the Minister for Railways, Transport and Communication.[1] Asaf Ali became the first Indian Ambassador to the United States of America. R.K.S. Chetty, Finance Minister, had to resign when the Muslim League decided to join the interim government. After India got independence, he became the first Finance Minister. Sarat Chandra Bose, a tall politician in his own right and pride of a lot of Indians being the elder brother of Subhash Chandra Bose, was minister for Works, Mines and Power before he had to leave to accommodate the Muslim League. Bose was a member of the All-India Congress Committee from 1936 till 1947 when he resigned in protest of the partition of Bengal.

Liaquat Ali Khan of Muslim League took over as Finance Minister of the interim government in October 1946 and subsequently became the first prime minister of Pakistan. The month of October always remained the most happening month in the life of Liaquat Ali. He was born on 1 October 1895 in Karnal (now Haryana, India). He joined the interim government on 15 October and was shot dead in Rawalpindi on 16 October 1951 by Saad Akbar Khan Babrak. The prime minister's assailant was killed on the spot by the police and the conspiracy regarding who got him killed was never solved. It is also a cruel joke of destiny that in India Father of the Nation, Mahatma Gandhi was killed by a radical Hindu and the second most influential leader after Jinnah in Pakistan, Liaquat Ali was killed by a Muslim. The main actor of the Indian partition Lord Mountbatten was also killed by an Irish group in England on 27 August 1979.

The Muslim League, on some pretext or other, was trying to postpone the inaugural session of the Constituent Assembly (CA) whereas the Congress was keen to start the process of Constitution-making. Nehru as vice president of the interim government called for the first session of the Constituent Assembly on 9 December 1946. The Constituent Assembly met for 165 days spread over eleven sessions from December 1946 to November 1949. The inaugural session started on 9 December 1946, Monday at 11 am in the Central Hall (then called the Constitution Hall) of Parliament with Acharya J.B. Kriplani introducing Dr Sachidanand Sinha, who chaired the session as temporary chairman of the Assembly. A total of 207 members including nine women members attended the session, gave their credentials and signed the register. Sinha read out congratulatory messages received from America, China and Australia. The Muslim League abstained from this session.

On 11 December 1946, Dr Rajendra Prasad was elected president of the Constituent Assembly; a prominent Christian leader of Bengal, H.C. Mukherjee was elected vice president of the Assembly. The Constituent Assembly patiently waited for the Muslim League members to join the deliberations. The most important resolution, that is the Objective Resolution (defining and detailing the scope of the Assembly) was moved by Jawaharlallal Nehru on 13 December 1946 and after deliberations were adopted on 22 January 1947. The second and third sessions of the Constituent Assembly held from 20-25 January and 28 April–2 May 1947 was also not attended by the League. In the meantime, on 3 June 1947, Lord Mountbatten announced the scrapping of the Cabinet Mission Plan. The independence of India was announced with two riders. Lord Mountbatten brought forward the date of British withdrawal to 15 August 1947. It was decided that India would be partitioned as India and Pakistan. The Indian Independence Act was passed on 18 July 1947.

The story of Dr Ambedkar is interesting and gives some idea of the functioning of the Constituent Assembly. Dr Ambedkar was from Maharashtra and so he contested from the Maharashtra Assembly where the Congress was in power. On the advice of the Congress central leadership, namely Sardar Patel and Dr Rajendra Prasad, the Congress leader in the Maharashtra Assembly Mr Kher saw to it that Dr Ambedkar lost the election. Jogendra Nath Mandal who was sharing the provincial government in Bengal with the Muslim League invited Dr Ambedkar to get elected from Bengal. Mandal got him elected from Jessore, a Muslim-dominated constituency. Ambedkar attended the first three sessions of the Constituent Assembly as an elected member of Bengal. After the announcement of Partition on 3 June 1947, it was decided that the people elected from the geographical area of Pakistan would be a part of the Pakistan Constituent Assembly and people elected from the area of India would be a part of the Indian Constituent Assembly; so, Dr Ambedkar ceased to be a member of the Indian Constituent Assembly as Jessore in Bengal was going to be a part of East Pakistan. Hence, he was now a member of the Pakistan Constituent Assembly. Jogendra Nath Mandal, one of the five ministers of the Muslim League in the interim government was to become the president of the Pakistan Constituent Assembly and later the first Law Minister of Pakistan.

Dr Ambedkar was in a very awkward situation and approached the viceroy and Mahatma Gandhi. They believed that the best brains in the country should be involved while framing the Constitution of free India irrespective of their political affiliation or political leanings. To have the best team, **30 statesmen who were not a part of the Congress party,** got elected with Congress support. **It is said that 16 of them were handpicked by Gandhi himself.** On the intervention of Gandhi and the viceroy, the Congress leadership started looking for a way out to accommodate Dr Ambedkar. Dr Rajendra Prasad, president of the Constituent Assembly, wrote a letter to the chief minister (then called prime minister) of Bombay Province, B.G. Kher on 30 June 1947, requesting him to get Ambedkar elected immediately so that he could join the fourth session of the Constituent Assembly commencing on 14 July 1947. **Dr M.R. Jayakar, first vice-chancellor of Pune University, Judge of Federal Court of India, was persuaded by Kher to resign** and Dr Ambedkar was nominated in his place as a member of the Constituent Assembly.

A total of 17 committees were formed. Rajendra Prasad was chairman of four committees, Nehru headed three and the other 10 committees were headed by different members of the Constituent Assembly. On 29 August 1947, the

Drafting Committee of seven members was constituted with Dr Bhim Rao Ambedkar as its chairman.

The strength of the Indian Constitution after Partition stood at 299 members. To understand and appreciate the humungous work done by the framers of our Constitution, it is important to go through a small brief on the Pakistani Constitution. The first formal meeting of the Constituent Assembly of Pakistan was held on 11 August 1947. After many meetings under different chairmen, it was dissolved on 24 October 1954. The second Constitution Assembly, formed on 28 May 1955, promulgated the Constitution on 23 March 1956, making Pakistan the Islamic Republic. Martial law was imposed on 7 October 1958 and the Constitution was abrogated. After the creation of Bangladesh, Bhutto managed to give Pakistan a new Constitution on 14 August 1973, which lasted for less than four years. In the military coup by General Zia on 5 July 1977, the Constitution was again suspended. It was restored in 1985 to be suspended by General Parvez Musharraf in 1999 when he overthrew the elected government of Pakistan. It is a classic example of how two nations born out of common heritage, common struggle, common aspirations at the time of Independence are poles apart as far as democracy is concerned. India stands miles ahead on the score of rule of law in line with the Constitution given by our leaders.

The logo of the Constituent Assembly of India was the map of undivided India with an elephant head, which denotes Ganesh (the Hindu god who is the first God to be remembered at the beginning of any important or auspicious event). The elephant memory proverb here denotes that no section of society is left untouched whose rights are not protected by the Constitution. The National

Flag of India was adopted by the Assembly on 22 July 1947. The five principles which guided the Constituent Assembly were: 1. republic state; 2. parliamentary form of government; 3. federal structure; 4. fundamental Rights; and 5. independent judiciary. In May 1949, the Constituent Assembly accepted and approved the membership of India to the Commonwealth.

The Constituent Assembly had eleven sessions. The last session in which the Constitution was adopted was held from 14 to 26 November 1949. Two hundred and eighty-four members again met on 24 January 1950 to sign the Hindi and English versions of the original Constitution. The first person to sign the Constitution was Dr Rajendra Prasad and the last person to put his signature was Feroze Gandhi. Maulana Hasarat Mohani (who coined the slogan *inquilab zindabad*), member of the Assembly, refused to sign the Constitution as he felt that the people who drafted the Constitution were not the true representatives of the common man. He maintained that during British rule, only the privileged had the right to franchise. Three more important decisions came into force from 24 January 1950– Dr Rajendra Prasad was elected the first President of India, and the National Anthem and National Song were adopted.

After the Constitution was ready to be printed, Nehru approached Prem Behari Narain Raizada (Saxena), a master of calligraphic art, to handwrite the entire Constitution in flowing italics style. On the issue of remuneration, Prem Behari refused to charge any money but put his condition that every page which he would handwrite would bear his name and at the end of the last page his name along with his grandfather's name should be written. This request of Prem Behari was accepted. He was allotted a room in Constitution Hall (now Constitution Club, Rafi Marg, New

Delhi); using nib 303 for the calligraphic work, he used 432 pen-holder nibs to complete the job single-handedly in six months. Famous artists Nandlal Bose and Beohar Ramchandra Sinha designed all the borders of the pages and decorated it with famous pieces of art. The original manuscript of the Constitution was written on parchment sheets so that they had a long life. The dimension of the sheet was 16×22 inches. The final copy of the Constitution had 251 pages and weighed 3.75 kg. Both the versions are kept in the Library of Parliament in a helium-filled case.

The Constitution at the time of enactment had 395 Articles spread into 22 Parts and 8 Schedules with 1,45,000 words. The Constitution of state of Alabama, United States, is the only written constitution in the world larger than the Indian Constitution. The gap of two months between the adoption and implementation of the Constitution, 26 November and 26 January 1950 is the story of emotional attachment and importance 26 January had in the heart of every Indian. During the Lahore session of the Congress in December 1929 on the bank of the river Ravi, the President of the Congress, Jawaharlal Nehru, gave a call of Purna Swaraj (complete independence) and declared 26 January the Independence Day of India. Since then, for 17 years, all the countrymen celebrated 26 January as Independence Day. But Mountbatten was emotionally attached to 15 August because the Japanese Navy had surrendered on 15 August 1945 to Lord Mountbatten, who was the Supreme Commander of Allied Forces in South East Asia. Therefore, on 3 June 1947, Mountbatten declared that the British would leave on 15 August 1947, making it the Independence Day of India. It was deemed fit to realize a 30-year-old promise of the nation to mark 26 January instead of Independence Day as Republic Day. On 26

January 1950, Thursday, the Constitutional Assembly transformed into the provisional Parliament of India till the time a new parliament was constituted in 1952.

Notes

1. After World War II, the British army captured about 20,000 soldiers who fought under the leadership of Subhash Chandra Bose as the Indian National Army (INA) along with the Japanese. To show impartiality, Major General Shah Nawaz, Lt Colonel P. K. Sehgal and Lt Colonel G. S. Dhillon—a Muslim, Hindu and Sikh—were tried for treason at the Red Fort, Delhi, by the Britishers.

CHAPTER-3

Hindi–Chini Bhai Bhai

Debacle in War and Nehru's Death

20 October 1962, Saturday

The History We Want to Forget

The war of 1962 will always be a sour point or a matter of anger and despair for our country. In 1947, at the time of Partition, India had gone to war with Pakistan but the impact of the war on the country, in general, was not felt due to the agony of Partition and consolidation of the nation during this period. We can say the nation was not at war; rather, it was the settlement of border dispute. So the taste of war or difficulties, anxiousness, valour, pride, nationhood was witnessed by the country for the first time in 1962 when China attacked India. This war was mainly fought by the Indian Army with little engagement of the Indian Airforce and no role of the Indian Navy.

Nehru was perusing the policy of *Panchsheel* and trying to revive the old vision of India—that is, *Vasudhaiv Kutumbakam.*[1] Sukarno of Indonesia, Abdul Naser of Egypt and Tito of Yugoslavia were Nehru's partners in bringing back world order and it was the starting point of the Non-Aligned Movement, which at that point of time were termed Non-Aligned countries that were not part of the cold war between America and Soviet Russia. We were a nascent nation and trying to walk on our own. On the one hand, the US was treating us as a socialist and communist country in the making and had all the goodwill and support for our neighbour Pakistan against us. On the other hand, the USSR was also suspecting us as a nation that was soon going to become a capitalist nation and was more sympathetic to communist China. The friendship and support we got from Moscow in later years were missing initially. India was having a tryst with destiny and also making her destiny.

Immediately after Independence, India wanted to build dams, power houses, steel plants, heavy industry, etc. with the limited resources under her command. India also wanted to divert a sizeable budget to modernize and upgrade the defence forces. The call was made by Nehru and he started laying the foundation of the country by focusing on rapid industrialization by diverting maximum resources in this area.

China is also one of the oldest civilizations and on 1 January 1912, the Republic of China came into existence; it was also the end of the Qing dynasty which had ruled China since 1644. The Republic of China witnessed a bitter power struggle. Civil war erupted between nationalists and communists, and this only ended in 1949. Mainland China came under the Communist Party and they named the area the People's Republic of China. It came under the leadership of Mao Zedong. Nationalists led by Chiang Kai Shek established themselves in Taiwan and named it the Republic of China. Taiwan, about 35,808 sq. km (smaller than Kerala which is about 38,000 sq. km), had ceded to Japan in 1895 and was annexed by China in 1945 after the Second World

War. India was among the first countries to give formal recognition to the People's Republic of China.

Dalai Lama also became a reason for dispute between India and China. Tibet had a long history of independence. After the Chinese occupation of their area, the freedom movement intensified. The Chinese started building pressure and Dalai Lama had to leave China. Nepal was too small a country to give him shelter and his request for asylum was heard by India. India designated land for the Dalai Lama and the Tibetan refugees in the mountainous region of Dharamsala in Himachal Pradesh. He formed a government in exile. This led to strategic discord and rivalry between China and India. Today, in retrospect, we may call it a wrong move but we must remember that we still have ITBP (Indo Tibetan Border Police), which proves that we still recognize Tibet as a country and not part of China. It gives moral strength to the demand for independent Tibet. It reflects that we were helping our neighbour and not a dissident or rebel group of China as it is perceived of presently.

To understand the genesis of the Indo-China border dispute, we need to go back to historical and geographical details to have a better understanding of the issue. There are two distinct areas of conflict at the border. The running border of India and China is touched by the border of three nations. If we consider Tibet as an independent identity and not a part of China then we have border with China in the northern part of India along with Jammu & Kashmir beyond Ladakh only. We do not have continuous borders with China, unlike Pakistan. The border is broken by the Himalayan Kingdom of Nepal. We have a common border with Bhutan that adjoins the Indian states of Assam, Arunachal Pradesh, West Bengal and Sikkim. Four northeast

Indian states share the border with Myanmar: Arunachal Pradesh, Nagaland, Mizoram and Manipur. The state of Sikkim, which has a common border with China, was ruled by the Buddhist priest-king. It became a princely state of British India in 1890. In independent India, Sikkim which had protectorate status of the Republic of India became an integral part of India after the 1975 referendum.

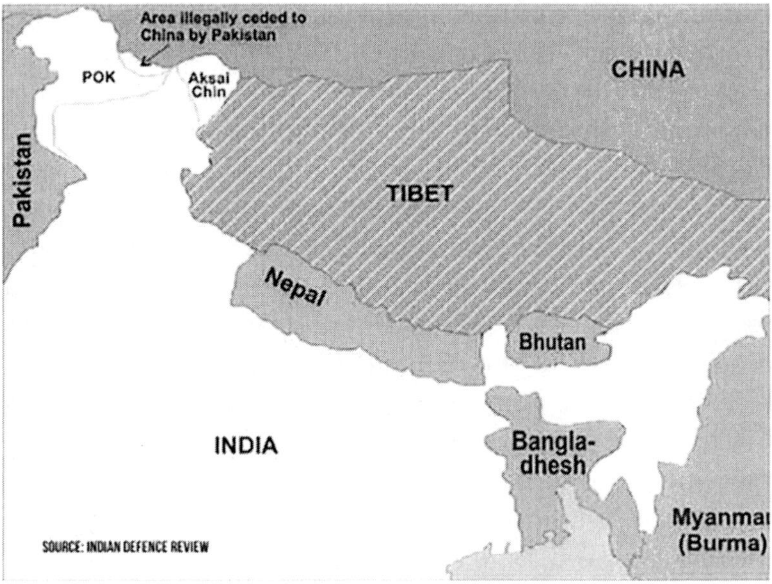

Map 3.1

In the northeast, the first Chinese province that has a common border with India is Xinjiang; then comes Indian territory Aksai Chin and then China-occupied Tibet. (See map) So on the west of Indian territory is Aksai Chin and Xinjiang and on the east is Tibet. The road which connects Tibet and Xinjiang passes through Aksai Chin, which is about 38,000 sq.km., about the size of Switzerland. Gulab Singh, the first Dogra King of Jammu and Kashmir state, was under the suzerainty of the Sikhs, won Ladakh in 1834, and signed a formal treaty with Tibet in 1842. After the first Anglo–Sikh War of 1846 in which Sikhs were defeated, Gulab Singh came under the suzerainty of the British India Rule. Since then, Aksai Chin is considered to be a part of India. The Chinese dispute this and claim it to be a part of the Xinjiang Uyghur Autonomous Region (XUAR). The state, known as East Turkestan, was annexed by China in 1949. China at times also claims it to be part of the Tibet Autonomous Region.

The states of Assam and Manipur were annexed by the British through the Treaty of Yandobe signed on 24 February 1826 after the First Anglo—Burmese War. With Assam and Manipur becoming a part of India, British India had common borders with China. In 1913 and 1914, representatives of the United Kingdom, China and Tibet met in Shimla to sort out the border dispute. The Shimla agreement was initialized by the representatives of three countries. But China changed their stand and it was never ratified by the Chinese government. British India also held direct negotiations with Tibetan officials and signed an agreement without involving China. The chief negotiator of the agreement was the Foreign Secretary of British India Sir Henry McMahon. The agreement was signed by McMahon from the British side and Lonchen Satra on behalf of Tibet. This border was named the McMahon Line demarcating the Tibetan region of China and the north east region of India. It extends 890 km from Bhutan in the west to 260 km east of the great bend of the Brahmaputra river. After the Shimla agreement, the McMahon Line was forgotten until 1935, when British civil service officer Olaf Caroe convinced the government to publish the Shimla Convention and use the McMahon Line on official maps. India regarded it as the legal international border. China says that Tibet, not being a sovereign state, was not competent to sign the treaty. The Chinese map shows the region south of the McMahon Line as South Tibet in China measuring an area of about 65,000 sq.km.

The North East Frontier Agency (NEFA) though a part of Assam till 1972 was directly administered by the governor. On the fifth anniversary of Republic Day 26 January 1954, NEFA was divided into six frontier divisions, of which one division Tuensang was separated and attached to the Naga hill districts; so, five divisions remained with NEFA. On 1 August 1965, the administration of NEFA was transferred to the Ministry of Home from the Ministry of External Affairs and the five frontier divisions became five districts under the deputy commissioner instead of the political officer. NEFA, on 27 January 1972, became Union Territory of India Arunachal Pradesh; subsequently, on 20 February 1987, it got statehood status.

The Indian defence forces of independent India were raised from the British military and it had to cope with the likes and dislikes of not only leaders but masses too. Till Partition, the Indian army were part of the British machinery, which was ruling India and the perception of people, in general, was that they are also a part and parcel of the ruler who not only oppressed but were also hostile towards native Indians. The hangover of colonial rule took some time to break. India was a democratic country not only in words but in spirit too. The army was always subservient to the legislature. China calls itself communist and the government is for the people but the military plays a major role in the governance of the country. Pakistan subsequently became a tool in the hands of military generals, who were responsible for all the major decisions and appointments. Even the prime minister has to have a nod from the bosses in uniform before taking any major decision.

Though the trial of the Indian National Army (INA) or the Azad Hind Fauj of Netaji Subhash Chandra Bose was held at Red Fort and the top leadership of the country, who happened to be the defending lawyers, also fought their case, after freedom, the INA personnel were not inducted into the Indian Army; Pakistan, on the other hand, inducted INA personnel into their ranks and files.

The army which had been part of the British army was quick to become the Indian army. As soon as we became independent, the first confrontation was in the store with our neighbour Pakistan's army. Most of them were fellow officers until yesterday. The army and political leadership, which had come out of the freedom struggle were having teething trouble and were unable to understand each other. On 17 April 1957, Kailash Nath Katju, defence minister of India, was replaced by V.K. Menon, who got elected from the Mumbai North Lok Sabha Constituency in the general elections. In about a fortnight, on 8 May 1957, General K.S. Thimayya took over as third Chief of Army Staff for a four-year tenure. General Thimayya was one of the brightest generals of the Indian army, who had the distinction of being the only Indian officer to command an infantry brigade during the Second World War. Thimayya headed the United Nation's Neutral Nations Repatriation Commission in Korea during the Korean war. He was awarded the civilian honour 'Padma Bhushan' in the very first year of the institution of the civilian awards in 1954.

The new defence minister Menon had spent about a quarter of a century in Britain. After graduating in History and Economics from Presidency College, Chennai, Menon went to England and got his masters in Psychology and Political Science in First Class. It is jokingly said that he completed his studies at the age of 37. Menon, known to be of communist leaning, served as the first High Commissioner of India in England soon after India got independence. He was the head of the Indian delegation in the United Nations from 1949 to 1962. At times, people remember Vijay Laxmi Pandit to be the Indian ambassador in the United Nations (UN), which she never was. In 1953, she was elected the first female President of the United Nations General Assembly for a one-year term. Menon is remembered for holding the record of the longest speech of eight hours inthe United Nations. Defending India's stand on Kashmir, he spoke nonstop for five hours on 23 January and he spoke for two hours forty-eight minutes on 24 January 1957. After the speech, he collapsed on the floor and was admitted to the hospital. He was also the founding member of Penguin Pelican, now a major publishing house. Menon was the defence lawyer for Udham Singh, who shot dead Michael O'Dwyer in England during his trial in 1940. He was also a staunch opponent of nuclear weapons and was active on many forums. In 1953, he was brought into Rajya Sabha and in 1956, made minister without portfolio. He was seen as the person who proposed the idea of World Order as conceived by Nehru on different diplomatic forums. One controversy which haunted Menon was the first corruption case of free India in 1948. When he was the High Commissioner of India, he signed the Jeep purchase contract worth about Rs 8 million without going as per the protocol. A feather in the cap of Menon will be the annexation of Goa in December 1961 which is described as the Liberation of Goa, ending 451 years of Portuguese rule. Menon also had a unique distinction of representing four different states in parliament. He became a Rajya Sabha member from Madras (now Chennai) in 1953 and subsequently from Kerala which was formed in 1956. He won the Lok Sabha election from North Mumbai in 1957 and 1961 on Congress ticket. After resigning from Congress, he lost the 1967 general elections as an independent candidate from North East Mumbai. As an independent candidate, he won the elections in 1969 from Midnapur in Bengal and 1971, from Trivandrum (now Thiruvananthapuram) in Kerala.

Another factor must be kept in mind before understanding the relationship between General Thimayya and political leadership. Pakistan was failing as a state. Between 14 August 1947 and 7 October 1958, Pakistan had seven different prime ministers. Finally, on 27 October 1958, General Ayub became the second president of Pakistan after a successful army coup. Some doubts in the mind of political leaders regarding the army's misadventure on the lines of our neighbours cannot be ruled out. The political leadership was always apprehensive that the armed forces could lead a coup like in neighbouring Pakistan. So, to govern politically, Nehru needed a strong defence minister and V.K. Menon was his best bet. We will be going through the course of events which led to China's attack on India in 1962. But before that, some light needs to be shed on the famous resignation of General Thimayya.

In 1956, China, without the knowledge of India, built a 1,200 km-road connecting Lhasa in Tibet with Xinjiang. It was one of the highest roads in the world and had an average height of more than 4,000 metres above sea level, the highest point being 5,500 metres. Some parts of the road passed through the Indian territory of Aksai Chin. The nation came to know about this in August 1959 when Nehru announced it in the parliament. Nehru also announced that because of the skirmish between India and China, border patrol in the NEFA region would be replaced by the deployment of the army. This was an indication of Indian readiness for war. General Thimayya, who was held in high esteem by Nehru, met him to explain the difficulties and complexities of deploying the army without additional resources. It is said that he advised the prime minister to find a way out to get out of this situation by taking back his statement in the parliament. Subsequently, defence minister Menon met Thimayya and whatever transpired between them became the cause of Thimayya's resignation. The resignation letter was received at Teen Murti (which was the prime minister's office) on 31 August 1959, and the same afternoon, after a long conversation with the prime minister, Thimayya was persuaded to withdraw his resignation letter. It was widely believed that there was friction between Prime Minister Nehru and General Thimayya. The discord among Thimayya, Nehru and Menon is one of the reasons cited by some for the low level of preparedness of the Indian Army, leading to its defeat at the hands of the Chinese. But there is hardly any evidence to prove it. On scrutiny, that doesn't hold water. It seems to be a figment of the imagination. The talks of Lt General Thorat being ignored for promotion as Chief may have some substance, but that he also had a grudge against Nehru seems to be imaginary. Just after the war, Nehru was succeeded by Y.B. Chavan as the new defence minister. A nine-member National Defence Council under the chairmanship of the defence minister was established on 25 November 1962. The committee had three serving Chiefs of the Armed Forces; the Defence Secretary; Dr D.S. Kothari Chairman, University Grant Commission; Lt General S. P. P. Thorat; the Corps Commander in NEFA and two former Chiefs of Army Staff General Rajendra Sinhji and General

Thimayya. This shows the uniqueness of Nehru as a prime minister, who could involve the best and also of former generals, who despite their differences in opinion came together without any second thoughts when the nation needed them.

One of the common myths about the People's Republic of China becoming the permanent member of the Security Council with veto power was because of Nehru. It was said that the membership was initially offered to India, and Nehru persuaded the United Nations to give it to China. For clarity, we need to examine records. The United Nations came into existence on 24 October 1945 after five permanent members of the Security Council ratified the UN Charter. The five permanent members with veto rights were France, the Republic of China, the Soviet Union, the United Kingdom and the United States. After the formation of the People's Republic of China (PRC), the Republic of China (ROC) shifted its base to Taiwan. The ROC retained the membership of the Security Council. The People's Republic of China (which we call China) became a permanent member of the UN Security Council replacing ROC in 1971. The PRC was not even a member of the United Nations till 1971, leave aside being a permanent member of the Security Council. The question of Nehru gifting a permanent seat offered to India to China has no basis. First of all, there is not a single document of the UN that can substantiate this offer of membership to India. The only country for which the US lobbied openly was Brazil but they were also denied exclusive permanent membership. It is also a fact that Nehru wanted China to be engaged with the world forum to restrain its activities. Prudence dictated that the PRC be provided a status commensurate with its power. What made it imperative to engage with the PRC and accommodate it in global power structures is aptly summarized in the lines – 'PRC is a strong country but [has an] abnormal state of mind'.[2]

This move can be interpreted in many ways. The most logical reasons appear to be that it was apparent that China with its sheer size and numbers would be a power to reckon with and in the future, any Chinese misadventure with any superpower would have repercussions on India. Secondly, surrounded by a very hostile neighbour in the west and east, south providing a natural sea barrier, Tibet already taken over by China, to have a friendly neighbour in the north certainly was not a bad idea. Between the two Chinese countries, Nehru was more inclined towards the PRC as it was a product of revolution. On the other hand, the ROC was under martial law. Nehru wanted the ROC to be replaced by the PRC in the UN and was of the view that not accommodating the PRC was not only foolish but dangerous for world peace. In his opinion, rehabilitation of the PRC was the best course to counter its aggression.

Dalai Lama, the spiritual head of Tibet was also their political head since 1750 (in the past, too, they performed the role of a ruler) until today. The present Dalai Lama is fourteenth in the order. At the age of five he became religious head in 1940 and on 17 November 1950, he was also formally enthroned as the political head. In 1951, Dalai Lama and the Central Peoples Government signed the Seventeen Point Agreement affirming the Chinese sovereignty over Tibet. It is also considered invalid as the same was signed under duress or the peaceful liberation of Tibet becoming a semi-autonomous state. Dalai Lama disputed the agreement stating that it was signed under duress. In 1954, India signed the Panchsheel accord with China, (five principles of peaceful coexistence), and acknowledged the sovereignty of China over Tibet. After the unsuccessful Tibet uprising of 1959, Dalai Lama had to flee Tibet along with most of his ministers. India gave them political asylum till they could return to their homeland. The Tibetan ministry in exile made McLeodganj near Dharamsala in the state of Himachal Pradesh, their headquarter. Sixty-one years have passed; Dalai Lama is appreciated globally as an icon of peace and non-violence for which he was conferred the Nobel Peace prize in 1989. India is also respected worldwide by human rights activists for giving their support to Tibetan people in their struggle.

A few lines about Tibet and Dalai Lama, although nothing to do with the 1962 war, will help the reader understand the issue of Tibet–China–Dalai Lama in the future. The process of identifying the next Dalai Lama is a complex exercise. The Panchen Lama, the second-most important spiritual leader after Dalai Lama, has a major say in choosing the new Dalai Lama. After the death of the tenth Panchen Lama in 1989, the current fourteenth Dalai Lama identified and declared Gedhun Choekyi Nyima, a six-year-old boy, as the incarnation of the eleventh Panchen Lama on 14 May 1995. The search committee appointed by the PRC rejected the 14 May announcement of Dalai Lama and declared Gyaincain Norbu as the eleventh Panchen Lama on 11 November 1995. Gedhun Choekyi Nyima was taken into custody and since then, he has not been seen by anyone. Dalai Lama at such an advanced age knows that after him, the next Dalai Lama, if declared by the eleventh Panchen Lama appointed by the PRC, will work as per the advice and wishes of the political masters of China. Panchen Lama identified by him is not traceable. No one knows if he is alive or dead. So, Dalai Lama has declared that he will be the last Dalai Lama to be appointed by the old custom. The fifteenth Dalai Lama will be elected by the people of Tibet.

Dalai Lama reached India through Tawang in NEFA. Mr Kamakhaya Prasad Tripathi, father of one of my school friends Kamlesh Tripathi, was a minister in the Assam government. He was the person who officially received Dalai Lama on behalf of the Government of India in Tezpur on 18 March 1959.

In the lead-up to the 1962 Sino–Indian War, the Forward Policy by Indian Prime Minister Nehru was a set of tactical strategies and presumptuous theories designed with the ultimate goal to effectively force the Chinese out of territory that the Indian government had claimed. Nehru's Forward Policy was primarily information from intelligence agencies and assessment of the situation by the officers on the ground. Sadly, input from the defence forces was missing or was very minimal. The Forward Policy was pushed with the instruction to occupy the frontier area along the McMahon Line and Aksai Chin. It was presumed that China would not retaliate as they had too many problems of their own to open a new front. Their struggle with the Republic of China was not coming to an end. This presumption proved very costly for India. Some other developments had taken place in the world too. India was leading the Non-Aligned Movement and had kept away from the Cold War. Nehru had the assurance of both the USA and USSR that in case of any future conflict with China, they would support India. Nehru also believed that the mighty Himalayas were a great defence against China forgetting that the Korean war had provided China with good practice in mountain combat.

Zhao Enlai (Chau Enlai) had visited India before also but after the arrival of the Dalai Lama, this was the first visit of the Chinese Premier in 1960 to discuss bilateral issues along with the border-dispute issue. Before 1979, Zhao Enlai was Chau Enlai, Mao Zedong was Mao Tse Tung, Beijing was Peking. The old names were the Anglicized spellings and pronunciations whereas in 1979, after the One China Policy, Chinese identity was asserted and hence the new names and pronunciations, as per the Pinyin method of convey in Mandarin in the Roman alphabet, was adopted.[3] Zhao Enlai offered major plans to ease tension at the border. It was suggested that India should accept Chinese claim over Aksai Chin in the Western Theatre and in return, China would acknowledge Indian sovereignty on NEFA in the Eastern Theatre. It was also proposed that both the countries would withdraw their armies 20 km from the McMahon Line. Both proposals were not acceptable to India. As a result tension and a low-level confrontation prevailed at the border. India deployed the Indian Army in place of Assam Rifles on the NEFA border. China interpreted this move as a grave threat and thought that India wants to either free Tibet or annex it. The liberation of Goa in December 1961 from Portuguese rule by Indian Forces was considered as annexation by China. It made them believe that India was pursuing a policy of expansion.

China started the war on 20 October 1962 and overran NEFA via Tawang in four days and came right up to Tezpur located near the Brahmaputra. The diplomatic machinery of both the countries started working overtime and for three weeks, the fighting was on a very low scale on both the fronts – Aksai Chin and NEFA. The Chinese offered both the parties to withdraw 20 km from the current position. But this was not acceptable as the Chinese were already more than 40 km inside Indian territory. Negotiations failed and Nehru got his birthday gift, on 14 November 1962, fierce fighting resumed especially in the Western Theatre, and on 21 November 1962, China withdrew unilaterally. The battle of Rezang La in Ladakh is remembered for the grit and bravery shown by the Indian Army. One hundred and twenty-three soldiers of the 13 Kumaon regiment led by Major Shaitan Singh had the task of defending the forward area of Chushul Air strip. This battle was fought at the height of 17,000 ft with no proper protective gear suitable for high altitudes. Even the weapons used by Indian forces were vintage as compared to the latest Russian rifles of the Chinese Army. The C Company of 13 Kumaon comprising 3 platoons had 120 Yadav soldiers mainly from Rewari in Haryana and a few from Alwar in Rajasthan. When the Chinese attack came on the morning of 18 November, they fought till the last bullet and it is said that few of the Ahir soldiers who had no ammunitions fought with their bare hands. They killed small structured opponents by crushing with their hands. The entire company gave their lives barring six. Out of these six, five were made prisoners of war and a lone survivor had to leave under the orders of company commander Major Shaitaan Singh to inform the base camp. The dead count of Chinese was about 1,300. The ratio was one Indian for ten Chinese killed. Shaitaan Singh's body was discovered after the war was over and was conferred with the highest battle honour of Param Vir Chakra.

During the 1962 war, it is said that both US and Soviet Russia were sympathetic to India but due to various reasons, none of them came to our rescue. Chinese fought the war with the superior rifles and guns supplied by Soviet Russia, which in times to come became the most trustworthy friend and ally of India. It is a fact that India was caught unaware and the Chinese had planned it well for a couple of months if not years. The timing chosen by the Chinese was perfect. Two superpowers—USA and USSR—got entangled in the Cuban crisis from 16 October to 28 October 1962 and the world came very close to witness a nuclear war between the two. So the intervention from these super powers as expected by India never came. The speed at which the Chinese Army came up to Tezpur can only be accomplished by long and meticulous planning of an attack. In the end, the Chinese withdrew from NEFA but stayed back in Aksai Chin.

In public opinion, three controversial figures were guilty of this military debacle. The central figure in the operations was General B.M. Kaul. He was Chief of General Staff (CGS)—a key operational post in Army Headquarters (AHQ). He was appointed commander of IV Corps for the Northeast. He created a strong trust in Nehru's mind based on the ethnic kinship of being a Kashmiri Brahmin. Commissioned in 1933, he moved to Army Service Corps by 1936. Instead of fighting corps, he preferred to stay in non-combat postings. He was the first recipient of the Param Vishisht Seva Medal and his citation reads: *For successfully completing the project 'Amar' which entailed the construction of 1,450 quarters for troops in Ambala. This was the first project of its kind and was completed through hot weather and the monsoons in the face of numerous problems. Lt General Kaul overcame these difficulties by dint of hard work and initiative of the highest order. He displayed organizing ability, drive, and resourcefulness. It was by his determination, leadership, and personal example that the task was completed by the due date.* This award was given for building houses. During the war, Corps Commander Kaul fell ill and was sent back to Delhi. He joined the war again in November 1962.

General Thimayya was succeeded by his coursemate

General Prem Nath Thapar as Chief of the Army Staff (COAS). He was a good soldier. General Thapar is perceived as the second guilty person responsible for the defeat. Indian media was scathing in the indictment of General Thapar who was also related to Nehru. His wife, Bimla Thapar was the sister of Gautam Sehgal, who was married to Vijay Laxmi Pandit's daughter Nayantara Sehgal. The war ended on 21 November 1962, when China unilaterally withdrew. General Thapar resigned on 19 November and General J.N. Chaudhari took over on 20 November 1962 and remained COAS till 6 June 1966. Due to this resignation, two records were made. General Thapar became the first and the only Chief of Army who resigned and General Chaudhari to date is the only COAS who headed the Indian Army in two wars, 1962 and 1965. General Thapar later served as Indian Ambassador in Afghanistan from 1964 to 1969. General Thapar is the father of veteran journalist Karan Thapar and historian Romila Thapar happens to be his niece.

Rightly or wrongly, the 1962 debacle got ascribed to Defence Minister V.K. Krishna Menon in a big way. He was considered to be the third guilty person. He continues to be held chiefly responsible for India's misadventure with China. In my opinion, he was one of the gifted statesmen who had contributed immensely in the initial years to establish India in the world scenario. On 31 October, V.K. Krishna Menon resigned and Jawahar Lal Nehru took over as defence minister. Menon's resignation was due to immense public pressure right in the middle of the war, proof enough of how unsure we were as a nation. The public fury was so much that it was believed that if Menon did not go, then Nehru himself would have to quit. Nehru took over as Minister of Defence from Menon.

The 1962 China war was a severe blow not only to the

reputation of the country but also to Prime Minister Jawaharlal Nehru. The backstabbing by China was a moral blow and psychologically debilitating. Nehru was deeply hurt and was never able to get over it. The wound was too deep and never healed. Nehru breathed his last on 27 May 1964. There are two specific areas for which the Nehru era will always be remembered. Nehru not only sowed the seeds of democracy but also saw to it that the roots went so deep that India could proudly boast about it for times to come. Nehru respected democratic traditions. The worst of his critics like Dr Lohia, who not only attacked his policy outside the parliament but severely criticized him on the floor of the house, was never heckled. No efforts were made to silence the dissent. It is impossible to imagine today that during the height of the 1962 war the parliament was not only in session but the strong parliamentarians could create so much pressure due to which the defence minister had to resign during the war. Under tremendous public and parliamentarians' pressure, Menon had to submit his resignation to the Cabinet, which Nehru had to accept. India's political environment has changed over the years. It stifles dissent and difference; we can witness a political regress to a lower level of democracy. It is sad that our past hasn't given us a sense of plurality and accommodating differences.

The second achievement of Nehru was to give India a solid public sector base of its core industries – the Steel Authority of India Limited (SAIL), the Bharat Heavy Electricals Limited (BHEL), the Bharat Earth Movers Limited (BEML), the Metals and Minerals Trading Corporation (MMTC), the Shipping Corporation of India Limited (SCIL), the Hindustan Aeronautics Limited (HAL) and many more. One characteristic of Nehru, which in the initial years of Independence became very catchy and attractive, was the secular image which he always tried to exhibit. In contrast, Gandhi always positioned himself as a practising Hindu. Secularism in the later years was used by different political parties as a tool to get votes. Though on the ground there was no friction, a section of politicians' appeasement policy of Muslims to get the votes proved to be counterproductive. For many general elections, a combination of Brahmin–Muslim–SC gave Congress a winning edge. Going by the calculator, Muslims with 14 per cent of the population in a 545-member parliament should have 76 MPs. The maximum number of Muslims in Lok Sabha was 49 in 1980 and 22 in 2014, which is the minimum number. Nehru was very careful of his and the nation's secular image but India after 75 years of independence is facing a huge religious and caste-based divide.

Notes

1. During the decolonization era of the 1950s, the idea of five principles, which were to be the driving force between the two sovereign nations were (i) mutual respect for each other's territory (ii) mutual non-aggression (iii) mutual non-interference in each other's internal matters (iv) equality and mutual benefit (v) peaceful co-existence. These five principles became the core issue of the Panchsheel treaty signed between India and China on 29h April 1954 in Peking, China.
   Vasudhaivakutumbakam has its origin in the Hindu scripture *Hitopadesha* meaning 'the whole world is one family'.
2. Available at: https://thediplomat.com/2018/04/why-did-nehru-want-the-peoples-republic-of-china-in-the-united-nations (accessed on 31 January 2021).
3. Pinyin is the alphabet for the Chinese language; it is how the Chinese words are pronounced.

Chapter-4

Jai Jawan, Jai Kisan

The War of 1965 and Lal Bahadur Shastri's Demise

11 January 1966, Tuesday

Who after Nehru? This was the biggest question the nation faced after Jawaharlal Nehru died on 27 May 1964. One era was passing and another, whose outlines were still undefined, was to follow. There were many claimants for that position but the Congress party was still a collective decision-making forum. The support of K. Kamraj, the Congress president, was essential for anyone who wished to lead the country. Considering the constitutional requirement that the office of the prime minister cannot be vacant, Gulzari Lal Nanda's swearing-in was held within hours of Nehru's death. This was only an interim arrangement. Lal Bahadur Shastri started as a minister in Uttar Pradesh but was a part of the Union Cabinet right from the first general elections. He was minister without portfolio when Nehru died. Those days, ministers without a portfolio used to be powerful. They were responsible for overseeing various important tasks of the government and would excel in crisis management. Lal Bahadur Shastri was the most trusted man of the prime minister. V.K. Menon had also served prime minister Nehru as minister without a portfolio before becoming the defence minister. Four names were in circulation for the post of prime minister – JP (Jayaprakash Narayan), Morarji Desai, Indira Gandhi and Lal Bahadur Shastri. JP was more of a thinker and had left power politics; so, he was ruled out. It must be remembered that Nehru during his lifetime never promoted Indira Gandhi in party or government. To be fair to Indira Gandhi, she had sacrificed and contributed more than many of the Congressmen who enjoyed government posts or party positions after Independence. Indira never staked her claim for the prime ministerial position. One of the reasons—though not written anywhere—can be because she was indebted to Shastri as in 1959, he had proposed her name in the CWC (Congress Working Committee) for the post of Congress president and then it was time to return the favour. Morarji Desai stood his ground and was a serious candidate for the post. One of the major strengths of Shastri that is not much talked about is his strength in managing elections. This strength could be seen clearly when he was the General Secretary of the AICC (All India Congress Committee) and Nehru was the president of Congress in 1952. Shastri was incharge of the selection of candidates and election management. Shastri had an important role in all the three general elections of 1952, 1957 and 1962, and it was a fact that he was also instrumental for the handsome victory of the Congress. Kamraj met the Congress parliamentary party MPs individually so that elections could be avoided and a leader could be elected on a consensus basis. Morarji Desai was not ready to yield but when elections looked imminent, he withdrew knowing it very well that Shastri commanded more respect and better goodwill and was sure to win.

Kamraj, on becoming the president of Congress, came out with the famous Kamraj Plan.[1] He resigned as chief minister of Tamil Nadu and subsequently, six more ministers resigned and were entrusted with the work of the organization of the party. The country and the Congress party were led by a cabal of five also known as the Syndicate.[2] Together they proved to be a formidable force.

Lal Bahadur Shastri became the choice of the party and the nation accepted him as their leader with an open heart. The strength of Shastri was his simplicity and no group affiliation. He was honest to the core. His modest background connected him to the common man of the country. The nation was passing through difficult times, resources were meagre and the China war had inflicted a wound that was not going to heal very soon. The war had resulted in a diversion of money towards defence, food was in short supply, and Nehru, whom the nation looked up to, was no more. The biggest crisis the nation was facing was on the food front. There were too many mouths to feed with too little agricultural productivity. The high birth rate constantly outstripped growth in agricultural production. Shastri gave a call urging the public to sacrifice one meal at least once a week. He got an overwhelming response from countrymen. Not only common men but even the restaurants, big or small abided by his words for the next few weeks. They downed shutters on Monday evenings. The entire nation skipped a meal a week. This was known as the iconic *'Shastri Vrat'* in response to the food crisis in India. It is to be remembered that this was purely a voluntary act. He motivated the country to maximize the cultivation of food grains and in the prime minister's residence, the vacant land was ploughed by Shastri himself and grains were sown.

Shastri's personality was in stark contrast to that of

Nehru. The soft-spoken, demure man was known best for his simplicity and austere lifestyle. Shastri maintained a low profile and he started tentatively as a prime minister as he had to lead senior colleagues and friends. Shastri faced three no-confidence motions against his government. The first no-confidence motion was within three months of his becoming the prime minister. It was moved by an independent MP N.C. Chatterjee and seconded by Umashankar Trivedi of Jansangh. The debate was on several issues and the split of CPI (Communist Party of India) and CPM (Communist Party of India [Marxist]) in July 1964 was witnessed on the floor of the house. While replying to the debate, prime minister Shastri had to mention that the personal attack on him by Hiren Mukherjee of CPI had more to do with his erstwhile comrade A.K. Gopalan of CPM with whom he was upset. The motion was defeated by 307 against and 50 in favour and 13 Swantantra party members abstained from voting.

Pakistan was going through a lot of internal turbulence at the time. The army was calling the shots and the country was breaking due to inherent contradiction since its birth. East Pakistan, other than the name, had nothing in common with West Pakistan. It was a doomed attempt to bind together two disparate sections of Asia separated not only by language, custom, economics, politics, aspirations and tradition but also thousands of miles separating the two areas. The only cement it could rely upon was religion. The leadership of Pakistan was happy with the closeness with the US. It gave them a lot of false security and safety. India was still sulking from the wounds of the 1962 war. The leadership of India was questioned not only by the world but within the country too. There were fierce debates in the parliament which questioned the leadership. Eminent politicians, scholars, intellectuals and poets criticized the government. India was going through the process of becoming not only the largest but one of the strongest democracies in the world. The dissent, criticisms, debates were the essential vitamins for the making of a robust democracy. Strong opposition is an essential check on elite power in a democracy.

The timing of military adventurism of Pakistan though was well calculated but they just missed to read that in a short period of eighteen years, India was a grown-up nation, strong, united and capable of taking up any adversary. India had a decisive, deterrent conventional edge over Pakistan. Pakistan was under a military general who had to legitimize his rule. His strength was not the people of Pakistan but his uniform. Foreign Minister Zulfikar Ali Bhutto believed that they had a superior defence force not only in terms of manpower but in terms of arms and ammunition as well. Pakistan had the latest Jet fighter planes and most modern Patton tanks from America.

Going into the details of the 1965 war, Y.B. Chavan's name along with Shastri's stands out prominently. Y.B. Chavan had replaced V.K. Menon as defence minister of India in 1962 (Nehru held the defence portfolio for a few days after Menon resigned during the Indo–China war of 1962) and remained defence minister in Shastri's cabinet as well. He was the first chief minister of Maharashtra after the state was restructured from Bombay state and was one of the most competent ministers of Congress. After the 1962 war, the revamping of defence was imperative.[3] During the Chinese aggression, the US was more sympathetic towards India than Soviet Russia and it was decided to have a five-year defence plan in consultation with the USA. On an official invitation conveyed through Chester Bowels, American Ambassador in India, a high-level delegation led by defence minister Y. B. Chavan went to America in May 1964 looking for modern fighter and bomber planes. The other members of the delegation were: Defence Secretary P.V.R. Rao, Lt General Moti Sagar of Army, Air Vice Marshal of Air Force, Rear Admiral S.M.S. Nanda of Navy, Director General, Ordnance Factories S.J. Shoney and other senior officials to assist them. Y.B. Chavan went to Washington to meet Robert McNamara, the then defence secretary of the USA, who later became the president of the World Bank. McNamara possessed one of the sharpest and toughest geopolitical minds in President Johnson's team. Y.B. Chavan and McNamara became good friends. This friendship came in handy later when Chavan became the finance minister during Indira Gandhi's regime and had to deal with McNamara as World Bank President. B.K. Nehru was the Indian Ambassador in America. Chavan's meeting with President Johnson was fixed for 28 May and accordingly, the Indian delegation went ahead with its other engagements in the other states of America. R.D. Pradhan, private secretary to Chavan, was in the adjoining room in the hotel. Past midnight, he was woken up from deep sleep by Chavan informing him of the demise of Nehru. In his book *Debacle to Revival,* Pradhan has written details of Chavan's journey from America to India on getting the news of Nehru's death.[4]

The news of Nehru's demise was conveyed to Y.B. Chavan by Talbot, assistant secretary of the USA. At 0430 hrs, the defence minister took off from Peterson Airfield, Colorado Springs in a small aircraft. Chavan was on his way to New York to catch a flight back to New Delhi. The plane was equipped with a teleprinter and Chavan drafted a letter for President Johnson regretting that meeting with him could not take place as he was rushing back to New

Delhi via New York. Before that letter could be sent, he received a message from President Johnson that a Boeing 707 from the presidential fleet was being placed at his disposal. The aircraft was then diverted to Washington. Another request came to Chavan that if not inconvenient, the secretary of state Dean Rusk and Ambassador B.K. Nehru would also accompany him to participate in the last rites of Nehru. Chavan arrived at the air force base in Washington to switch to the presidential plane and found Robert McNamara, Talbot, Chester Bowles, Mrs and Mr John K. Galbraith, American Ambassador during Kennedy's regime, waiting to show their concern and see him off. After refuelling at Tehran, the plane was to go via Mumbai as flying over Pakistan was restricted. It was impossible to reach in time for the funeral which was scheduled at 4 in the evening. Dean Rusk checked with President Ayub of Pakistan and immediately the airspace of Pakistan was opened and Chavan reached before time. The last part of the story is important that on reaching Delhi, Dean Rusk came to Chavan to personally thank him for accommodating the American diplomats on his plane. Such incidents in the diplomatic history of our country raise some questions in our minds: What was the reason for all the courtesy shown by the USA and Pakistan? Was it because of the larger-than-life stature of Nehru or was it the normal routine procedure? Was it due to the importance of India as a country or was it the combination of all three reasons? The signing of the defence deal with America was aborted due to the death of Nehru and subsequent events changed the course of history. India got backing from Soviet Russia in times to come.

Chavan's contribution to building the Indian defence force is immense. He not only modernized the forces but was the key person responsible for recruiting, training and inducting young officers into the forces. Apart from the regular training institutions, two Officers Training Schools (OTS) were established at Chennai and Pune in January 1963 after the 1962 Chinese war. The Pune OTS was subsequently closed in May 1964 and Chennai OTS is still functioning. OTS Chennai was later renamed Officers Training Academy in 1988 making it at par with the Indian Military Academy, Dehradun. Officers through the 12 Emergency Commission (EC) were inducted from January 1963 and the last batch (EC-12) passed out in October 1965. After EC training was over, OTS started courses for SSC (Short Service Commission). It also included the Compulsory Liability Scheme for Class I and II gazetted officers of the central government and public sectors. The scheme ended in 1968 and since then, only officers of defence forces are trained.

The 1965 war was the first war where all the three arms of defence forces actively participated in the war. The bravery and leadership of General J.N. Chaudhary of Army, Air Marshal Arjun Singh of Air Force and Admiral Bhaskar of Navy motivated not only the forces but the Indian masses for a very long time. Though there are stories of General Chaudhary lacking the quality of soldering and he was not considered as good a strategist and leader as his predecessors General Thimayya or General Kariappa. The 1965 war was preceded by the India–Pakistan military confrontation in the Rann of Kutch earlier in the year. Pakistan was building up hostility and started misadventure on 9 April 1965. Pakistan's 51 Infantry Brigade crossed the border in Rann of Kutch and occupied Sardar Post near Kanjarkot. They continued the aggression and on 24 April attacked and occupied four more posts. The entire area of

Kanjarkot came under their control. Why India remained silent instead of replying militarily and why did they prefer to take this up diplomatically is still a question. In June 1965 during the Commonwealth conference in London, British Prime Minister Harold Wilson took a personal initiative and played the role of a negotiator. As a result of the British diplomatic efforts, Shastri and Ayub Khan signed the ceasefire agreement on 30 June 1965. Pakistan agreed to withdraw its forces and restore Indian control over the area and in return, India allowed Pakistan to use their roads in Indian territory. A committee was formed to finalize the demarcation of the international border in Kutch. The meetings continued for years. Finally, 75 sq. miles of land was given to Pakistan many years after Shastri's death.

Operation Gibraltar

An event that made Pakistani rulers believe that they have the support of the common man of Kashmir was the disappearance of the holy relic from the Hazratbal shrine in Srinagar.[5] After the arrest of Sheikh Abdullah in August 1953, his long-time associate and second-in-command Bakshi Ghulam Mohammad not only replaced him as prime minister (Chief Minister of Jammu and Kashmir was called prime minister till 31 March 1965) of Jammu and Kashmir but also became the President of the National Conference. Sheikh Abdullah's followers rallied under the Plebiscite Front.[6] To bring Abdulla to the negotiation table, Nehru suggested that Bakshi should resign. Bakshi made his confidant Khawja Shamsuddin speaker of the legislative assembly as his successor in October 1963. But he kept the reins of administration in his hands. Those days Shamsuddin was referred to as 'Chamchuddin' (stooge) of Bakshi. It was during his administration on 26 December

1963, that the holy relic was stolen from the Hazratbal shrine. On 27 December 1963, news broke out that the holy relic was missing from the shrine. This led to widespread protests not only in Kashmir but all over India. Riots broke out in West Bengal and East Pakistan (Now Bangladesh). The unrest was so severe that the central government also got involved. One section of the society believed that this act was the conspiracy of Pakistan but there was no evidence. The Awami Action Committee (AAC) was formed under the leadership of nineteen-year-old Mirwaiz Maulvi Farooq (His son Mohammad Umar Farooq is the current Mirwaiz of Kashmir and also part of All India Hurriyat Conference). Agitation against theft of the holy relic was spearheaded by the AAC. The protest was so intense that prime minister Nehru not only had to send the IB (Intelligence Bureau of India) B.N. Mullik to Srinagar for investigation but he also had to make a public broadcast on All India Radio to express his grief over the sacrilege and urge for calm. Pakistan was not leaving any opportunity—Bhutto issued a statement and Karachi observed black day. President Ayub in his radio broadcast reiterated the determination of Pakistan to secure the Jammu and Kashmir people's right to choose the country they wished to join. The West Pakistan Assembly adopted a resolution on the issue and on 3 January 1964, after Friday prayers, entire Pakistan was out on the street to protest. In India, Hindus and Sikhs also joined the agitation making it more difficult for the government. Home Secretary V. Vishwanathan was sent to Srinagar to supervise and control the situation personally.

On 4 January, 1964 Shamsuddin informed on Radio Kashmir, Srinagar, 'Today is indeed Eid for us, the holy relic is recovered.'[7] The relic was reinstalled in the shrine.

A public holiday was declared and Kashmir was illuminated. The jubilation was short-lived as people had doubts regarding the genuineness of the relic. There were allegations that the government had substituted, not recovered, the holy relic. The AAC made the identification of the relic an issue. Home Secretary V. Vishwanathan was sent on 3 January to oversee the investigation. As the demand for identification did not die down, Nehru had to send his best man Lal Bahadur Shastri to Srinagar on 3 February 1964 to settle this demand. The parleys went on for days and on 6 February, a settlement was reached. A seventeen-member Action Committee led by Syed Mirak Shah Kashani (the most respected spiritual leader of Kashmir) after a limited *deedaar* gave a verdict that the *Moi-e-Muqqadas*. The Committee praised Shastri for his genuineness, negotiating skills and efforts to sort out the crisis. This was still not the end. Now there was a demand for the revelation of the 'real culprit'. People wanted to know who the culprit was. On 12 February in parliament, home minister Gulzari Lal Nanda and opposition MP Atal Bihari Vajpayee were engaged in a debate on this issue. On 17 February 1964, Indian parliament was informed by the home minister of India that one of the five *mujavir*s (the caretakers of the shrine), one of the Banday brothers Abdul Rahim Banday, was the main suspect. Abdul was arrested with his associates. Though it was widely believed that Abdul was made a scapegoat. The rumour was that one of the old ladies in Bakshi's house wanted to have a look at the holy relic and so it had been removed briefly. But since the family had failed to return the relic in time, it came into the notice of the people. The caretakers who had allegedly facilitated its temporary removal, were unnerved for the fear of getting exposed.

Kashmir was always a sour point for Pakistan as, at the time of Partition, their leadership misjudged the minds of not only the leaders and the King of Kashmir but also the minds of Kashmiri people. Pakistan thought that because of Kashmir being a Muslim majority state and due to its proximity to Pakistan, it would opt to merge with Pakistan. The leadership of Sheikh Abdullah knew the real pulse and intention of Pakistani leadership and chose to be a part of India. He refused to accept any proposal of integration with Pakistan due to the exploitation of Kashmiri fellowmen by them. The dilly-dallying and indecision of Maharaja Hari Singh was aptly handled by Sardar Patel who ultimately signed the document of accession to merge Kashmir with India. The Pakistani game plan took a beating but they managed to occupy the north eastern part of Kashmir and termed it Azad Kashmir.

Sheikh Abdullah, the tallest leader of Kashmir, was released on 8 April 1964 after eleven years in prison. This was done because Nehru wanted a solution to the Jammu and Kashmir problem. Sheikh Abdullah's popularity even after and perhaps because of his long imprisonment was undented. His name was involved in the Kashmir Conspiracy case. All charges against him were dropped. Nehru wanted Sheikh Abdullah to go to Pakistan to try and settle the Kashmir question with Ayub. Talks took place between Sheikh Mohammed Abdullah and President Ayub Khan of Pakistan. The idea of a confederation was discussed by the two leaders at length. It was also decided that Nehru and Ayub would meet in Delhi in the middle of June. But Nehru died in May 1964 and the proposed meeting, scheduled in Delhi in June between Nehru and Ayub, never happened.

The political unrest and movement in the Valley

escalated and Sheikh Abdullah was again arrested in 1965. Pakistan to fish in troubled waters planned Operation Gibraltar (Pakistan specifically chose this name to draw a parallel to the Muslim conquest of Spain that was launched from the port of Gibraltar). It was aimed to take over the Valley and ultimately capture Jammu and Kashmir. It was a plan to provoke uprisings in Jammu and Kashmir by infiltrating teams of military personnel. It was planned that Pakistani soldiers dressed as locals would infiltrate into India, mingle with the crowd in the celebration of the annual festival of Pir Dastagir Sahib on 8 August 1965. It was expected that on that day, people would assemble and protest against the arrest of Sheikh Abdullah. Pakistani planners were convinced that it would be very easy to scale up these anti-arrest protest into an anti-India uprising. They were wrong in assuming that the local people would support Pakistan. The locals informed about the activities of these infiltrators to the police and the army and immediate action was taken. On 8 August, two Pakistani officers were captured and interrogated and the entire plan of the Pakistan army was revealed. No local support was available as expected by the Pakistani think tank; as a result, infiltrators were stalked, engaged and finally liquidated. A large number of arms and ammunition were captured. Few infiltrators were not able to go back and they surrendered. By 12 August 1965, Operation Gibraltar was over.

Operation Grand Slam (started on 1 September 1965)

The political leadership of India with Lal Bahadur Shastri as prime minister and Y.B. Chavan as defence minister showed grit and an aggressive attitude. This moral fibre, the strength of character and courage of the leaders were normally not mentioned in the media. The Indian Army crossed the Ceasefire Line and captured Haji Pir Pass on 28 August 1965. In the next three days, they moved in the Neelam Valley in front of Uri. Muzaffarabad was under threat and Pakistan started Operation Grand Slam. On 1 September 1965, Pakistan forces crossed the Tawi River and Indian border. They came very close to Akhnoor threatening Jammu. The assault was massive, five Pakistani brigades with heavy artillery fire attacked the Chumb sector making the entire area vulnerable as only one Indian brigade was defending the borders in line with the regulation of the United Nations to keep minimum forces on borders. Pakistan put all its might on this sector to make inroads, get hold of the chicken neck and cut off the supply line of Indian defence forces. The Indian Air Force led by Air Force Marshal Arjun Singh did something unbelievable which had no match in air warfare. India had the outdated 1948 jets Vampire and Pakistan was equipped with the latest and most modern fighter jets supplied to them by the USA. On 3 September 1965, Sqn Ldr Trevor Keelor, flying in lightweight Gnat fighter aircraft, became the first Indian pilot to shoot down Sabre Jet F-86F, an American fighter plane considered to be much superior to Gnat. There is a fascinating anecdote regarding the legend Field Marshal Cariappa, which elevated him far above others who could rival his glory. His only son was an Indian Air Force pilot. His plane was shot down and he was taken prisoner of war. President Ayub, who had served with General Cariappa offered to release his son. The offer was turned down with the reply, 'They [POWs] are all my sons, look after them well.' Field Marshal Cariappa is best remembered as the legend who made the Indian Army truly Indian.

Pakistan Air Force shot down an Indian civilian plane

carrying the Chief Minister of Gujarat Balwant Rai Mehta on 19 September 1965. Very few people remember this incident today. Mehta was the President of Servants of People Society. The Servants of People Society was formed in November 1921 by Lala Lajpat Rai in Lahore. It was inaugurated by Mahatma Gandhi. My maternal grandfather Swami Satyanand was the Vice President of the society with Lala Lajpat Rai as President. A civilian Beechcraft plane, piloted by ex-Air Force Jehangir Engineers took off from the airstrip of the Tata Chemical Mithapur plant for Kutch. It was carrying Chief Minister Mehta, his wife, a journalist and three of his staff members. Pakistan Air Force Pilot Qais Hussain intercepted the plane in Indian territory, informed his superiors that it was a civilian aircraft and under instruction shot down the plane killing all on board. In August 2011, Pakistani pilot Hussain wrote to Indian pilot Engineer's daughter apologizing for his mistake – 'civilian plane was mistaken for a reconnaissance aircraft by Pakistani controllers'—and he was ordered to shoot it down.

The Air Force was able to stop the advances of Pakistani forces in the Chamb sector. And then came the masterstroke of Indian defence forces led by Shastri. The war was escalated in the Punjab and Rajasthan sectors, new fronts were opened, which came as a surprise for Pakistan. It was decided to push towards Lahore and Indian forces after a fierce battle captured Barkee on the Pakistan side and as a mark of victory, the Indian flag was hoisted on Barkee Police Station. The Pakistani Army retaliated in the Khem Karan Sector of Punjab. In the famous Battle of Asal Uttar (Fitting Response), Company Quarter Master Havildar Abdul Hamid of 4 Grenadiers with his recoilless gun not only faced the onslaught of Pakistani tanks but also destroyed three tanks. In the course of the battle, he was wounded and died. For this supreme sacrifice, he was given the highest gallantry award, the Param Vir Chakra posthumously. Mentioned as the biggest tank battle in the history of wars, the Battle of Phillora in the Sialkot Sector of Pakistan will always be remembered by Indian defence forces. Pakistani forces were severely hit and in two days (the battle started on 10 September), they had to vacate Phillora. India lost six tanks against Pakistan's loss of sixty-six tanks. Lt Col. Ardeshir Burzorji Tarapore of Poona Horse was given Param Vir Chakra (posthumously). On route to Lahore Dograi, another village was won by the Indian defence forces. When Indian troops crossed the Ichhogil canal capturing Lahore was only a matter of few hours. One must remember that Indian tanks, mainly AMX-13, had smaller guns and no night vision whereas Pakistani Patton tanks could operate at night with many heavy guns.

The Indian Navy also kept its vigil and guarded the western and eastern coasts of the country exceedingly well. During 1965, Pakistan was the only country in the entire subcontinent to have a submarine, Ghazi. Indian Navy acquired its first submarine in 1967. The anti-submarine unit of the Indian Navy did a fantastic job of keeping Ghazi in check and throughout the war period, the vigil made this submarine virtually immobile. On the eve of the ceasefire, Pakistani radio made a false claim that Indian Frigate was sunk by Ghazi. To refute the claim naval attaches of all the countries and press was called for tea on board INS Brahmaputra.

The date on which the 1965 war started is different for different sets of people. One group believes that the war started in April 1965 when Pakistan attacked and crossed the border in Rann of Kutch. One group believes that the war started in August when Pakistan launched Operation Gibraltar. Another date is 1 September 1965 when Operation Grand Slam was launched by Pakistan and they crossed Ceasefire Line (which is now called Line of Control) in Chamb sector. Pakistan celebrates 6 September as its National Defence Day every year with a lot of fanfare. The date of 6 September marks the day in 1965 when Indian troops crossed the international border to launch an attack on Pakistani Punjab and started their march towards Lahore. In official accounts, Pakistan makes 6 September the day of the starting of the war when Indian forces crossed the border. On the other hand, in India, we record 1 September, the day Pakistan crossed the border as the day when the war started. Pakistan has always tried to build up a false narrative for the consumption of its people as well as for the international community that Jammu and Kashmir, and India are two different borders whereas in reality, be it Siachen in Jammu and Kashmir or Rann of Kutch in Gujarat, all are integral parts of India. Pakistan, while addressing their people, give a wrong narrative that the 1965 war was a specific contest for Kashmir. In the 1965 war, one of the miscalculations by Pakistan was that they wanted to decide the place of war whereas Lal Bahadur Shastri's stand was clear that once someone attacks the border of India, then we will decide where and how to counter-attack.

United Nations intervened and passed a resolution for an immediate ceasefire on 22 September 1965. On 23 September when war came to a sudden halt, Indian Forces were overseeing Lahore and it was a matter of few hours to reach there. India occupied 1,920 sq. km of Pakistan's territory and yielded 540 sq. km to Pakistan. India lost 2,862 soldiers and Pakistan lost 5,800 soldiers. Indian prime minister Lal Bahadur Shastri after the ceasefire, said in the famous speech, 'President Ayub had claimed while attacking India, he along with his forces will walk through Delhi so I [Shastri] thought why not I go to Lahore to welcome him?'

Before we finish the story of the 1965 war, we must understand the difference between India, a secular nation, and Pakistan, a theocratic Islamic country. Major General Akhtar Hussain Malik, GOC 12th Division, was the overall commander of Pakistani forces in the 1965 war. He was a brave soldier, an excellent strategist, brilliant in field warfare and a smart tactician. General Malik had planned to have control over complete Jammu and Kashmir by capturing Jammu. As per the plan of General Malik, Pakistani forces crossed river Tawi and the next target was Akhnoor on their way to Jammu. The next day when General Malik was finalizing the assault on Akhnoor, Pakistan Army Chief of Staff flew in with Major General Yahya Khan (later became Head of the State). As per the orders of Field Marshal Ayub, General Malik handed over the charge to General Yahya Khan with immediate effect, and with wrong planning and tactical error of General Yahya Khan capturing Jammu remained a distant dream for Pakistan. The explanation given for changing the guard midway was that General Malik would have been a national hero in Pakistan after capturing Jammu and might have emerged as a threat to President Ayub; so he wanted his close confidant General Yahya to get the credit. But this reason doesn't seem to hold ground. The real reason was completely different. General Malik was Ahmadiyya Muslim and Sunni leadership never allowed these honours to go to Ahmadiyya Muslims. The government of Pakistan under Bhutto brought in the second amendment to their constitution by which Ahmadiyya Muslims were declared non-Muslims. President Zia-ul-Haq also brought an ordinance according to which if Ahmadiyyas called themselves Muslims or posed as Muslims, it would be punishable under law. After these two amendments, the central headquarter of Ahmadiyya Muslims was shifted to London from Pakistan. This is one of the worst persecution and discrimination by the Sunni majority in Pakistan.

The slogan, *'Jai Jawan, Jai Kisan'*, hailing the defence personnel and farmers of the nation was given by Shastri after the war first time in Urvan village about 30 km from Allahabad. It touched the very nerve of every Indian—it had pride and a sense of commitment. The slogan even after more than half a decade is as fresh and motivating as it was in 1965. The relationship of Shastri with two ministers of his Cabinet, T.T. Krishnamachari and Indira Gandhi was not very smooth. T.T. Krishnamachari had to resign as finance minister in 1958 for his involvement in the Haridas Mundhra scandal. After his election in 1962, he was refused the finance portfolio by Nehru. Krishnamachari subsequently became finance minister and resigned on 31 December 1965 hoping that Shastri would request him to withdraw his resignation; but showing firmness, the polite Shastri accepted it. It was decided that Indira Gandhi would move out of Delhi as High Commissioner of India to Britain so that Shastri could run his government without any problems. This was to be implemented after the prime minister returned from Tashkent but history has a cruel habit of taking utterly unpredictable twists and turns. As there was a ceasefire with Pakistan and the war had not formally ended, Premier Kosygin of Soviet Russia proposed to mediate and resolve the issue. This was the only time India had accepted a third-party mediation in resolving bilateral issues between India and Pakistan. Though till then, we had maintained equidistance between the USA and USSR, it was realized that India needed an all-weather friend. Pakistan was already a part of CENTO (Central Treaty Organization) and SEATO (Southeast Asia Treaty Organization) and aligned with the USA in the Cold War. This could also be one of the reasons to go to Tashkent (now Uzbekistan) in Soviet Russia to finalize the terms of the treaty/pact with Pakistan.

Shastri left for Tashkent on 4 January 1966 with a promise that the land occupied at the cost of the lives of our soldiers will not be returned. The talks went on for seven days and under huge pressure from the United Nations, USA and USSR on 10 January 1966 the peace agreement known as the Tashkent Declaration was signed between India and Pakistan. Broadly speaking it was decided that both the nations would return to their positions as it was on 5 August 1965 by 25 February 1966 ending the ceasefire of September 1965. India and Pakistan both returned the land occupied by each other but since we had to return a larger chunk, a general perception was created that the agreement was not in favour of India. So, whatever was gained on the battlefield was lost on the negotiating table. Shastri died on 11 January 1966 at the age of 61 and till today no one has a final answer regarding how he died. There are doubts that he was poisoned. Some say he was not able to bear the shock of signing an agreement due to which India had to return the land won after the sacrifice of so many soldiers. It is also said it was a cardiac arrest. The impact of Shastri's 18 months' rule was tremendous. Though he is always remembered for leading a decisive Indo—Pakistan war, his initiative to make India self-sufficient in food grains had a bigger impact on the future of our country.

The war of 1965 and subsequent Tashkent agreement

apart from settling border issues raised a very pertinent question regarding who won the war. Both countries claim that they won the war. Who won and who lost can be decided by a few basic questions that can explain the ground reality. Who started the war? What was the objective of crossing the border? Was the objective achieved? The answers to all these questions are Pakistan crossed the Indian border to take over Jammu and Kashmir and were pushed back to their side of the border. So it is Pakistan that lost the war. The role of India was to defend its border which they defended successfully and they also busted the general perception regarding the Pakistani army that it is better equipped in terms of arms and ammunition. The Air Force of Pakistan with Sabre jets and F-104 star fighters equipped with missiles was capable of fighting at night. Indian Air Force had to fight with clunky, obsolete and unreliable airplanes/fighters. They had Gnat and antiquated air planes belonging to the Second World War era, no missile capability, no night-flying gadgets. When defence minister Y.B. Chavan visited one of the fighter planes manufacturers in the USA, he was told that the Indian Air Force had been allowed to become a museum of vintage war planes.Though it is a fact that we lost more planes as compared to Pakistan, one must remember that the collateral damage inflicted by our Air Force was much more. The Indian Air Force was in an attacking mode and the Pakistani Air Force was in defending mode. We lost more planes, not in mid-air combat but were hit by the anti-aircraft guns when we attacked inside Pakistani territory. The plucky Indian Air Force employed guts and gumption to send the Pakistan Air Force into defensive mode. The number of casualties on the Pakistan side was more but on the Indian side, the major brunt was taken by the young officers. Though we had only two Param Vir Chakras in the 1965 war, the result would not have been the same if the young freshly commissioned officers in Indian forces had not fought the war with unprecedented valour and vigour.

The 1965 war transformed a seemingly weak and crisis-ridden India after the Chinese debacle just three years before into a stronger nation, whereas Pakistan could never recover from the aftermath of this self-inflicted war. Two nations evolved in diametrically opposite directions from this point onwards. India grew in strength whereas Pakistan went downhill. It is unlikely that both nations will ever look at history from the same perspective though that may be a crucial step towards any intended reconciliation between India and Pakistan.

Notes

1. Congress, led by Nehru, won the third general elections in 1962. Then came the 1962 China war and some hard time for the country. It was felt that the people's representatives, who were sitting in the government, had lost the connect resulting in the erosion of not only the party base but also governance. In 1963, Kamraj the third-time Chief Minister of Madras (now Tamil Nadu) came up with the plan of all the senior ministers at the centre and chief ministers of the state to resign to rejuvenate the party and get the connect reestablish with the common man. Nehru appreciated the merit and gave the go-ahead by offering himself to resign but was persuaded by Kamraj to stay as he was unique as a leader of the Congress and prime minister of the country. Kamraj's plan was rolled out with six senior central ministers including Morarji Desai, Jagjivan Ram and Lal Bahadur Shastri and six chief ministers including Kamraj himself. S. K. Patil and Biju Patnaik resigned and were entrusted with the organizational job of the party. Kamraj himself became one of the most powerful Congress presidents after Independence.

2. It was a group of non-Hindi-speaking heavy weights namely – Nijilingapa, Sanjiva Reddy, S. K. Patil, Atulya Ghosh and of course Kamraj himself. This group controlled the Congress party, which till 1991 gave prime ministers, not only from Uttar Pradesh (UP) but from a specific districts of UP. The Syndicate not only was instrumental in making Shastri and Indira Gandhi prime minister of the country but decided on cabinet formation, selection of candidates during election and all important decisions of the Congress party till Indira Gandhi dumped them.
3. Bombay Presidency was made the Bombay province by the British, and after Independence, the Bombay Presidency became the state of Bombay (now Mumbai).
4. R. D. Pradhan, 1998, *Debacle to Revival: Y. B. Chavan as Defence Minister, 1962–65*, New Delhi: Sangam Books Ltd
5. The holy relic is believed to be a single hair of the Prophet's beard—*Moi-e-Muqqadas* (a strand of holy hair of Prophet Muhammad) attached to a silver pendulum in a glass tube.
6. Note; After the merger of Kashmir with India and Sheikh Abdullah became the Prime Minister of Jammu & Kashmir, under his patronage, his loyal follower Mirza Mohammad Afzal Beg started the movement for plebiscite under UNO supervision. Though Sheikh Abdullah never became a formal member of the Plebiscite Front, he remained the guiding force till he became Chief Minister of Jammu & Kashmir in 1975 after his accord with the union government. The Plebiscite Front merged with National Conference and Afzal Beg became Deputy Chief Minister with Sheikh Abdullah.
7. Available at: https://kashmirlife.net/hanging-by-the-relic-issue18-vol06-61615/ (accessed on 2 February 2021).

Chapter-5

India Trumps Pakistan

1971 War, Birth of Bangladesh and Emergence of 'Durga' Indira Gandhi

16 December 1971, Wednesday

Since Partition and the creation of Pakistan, seeds of conflict between East and West Pakistan were sowed. The population of Pakistan as per the 1951 census was 75 million (7.5 crores). West Pakistan with an area of 796,095 sq.km. had 33 million (3.3 crores) population and East Pakistan (Bangladesh) with an area of 143,998 sq.km. had 42 million (4.2 crores) population.[1] It was surprising that the Constituent Assemblies of India and Pakistan were elected simultaneously but it took almost ten years for Pakistan to frame their constitution.

East Pakistan was carved out from eighteen districts of erstwhile United Bengal of undivided India and the ruling class and decision-makers were mostly from West Pakistan. There was always a sense of discontentment amongst the general citizens of East Pakistan. At the time of Partition, H.S. Suhrawardy, the poster boy of the Muslim League in Bengal had tried for United Bengal when the two-nation theory was in the final stage. Initially, he also got some support from a few Hindu leaders but later, this idea was abandoned. After Partition, Suhrawardy stayed in India and moved to Pakistan only in 1949. He was subsequently removed from the Muslim League and this led to the formation of the Awami Muslim League, which was to later become the Awami League to represent non-Muslims as well. Sheikh Mujibur Rahman started as a close aid of Suhrawardy and a student leader. Suhrawardy retired from politics, went to Beirut and died in 1963. With this, the hold of Sheikh Mujib, not only on the Awami League but on the people of East Pakistan was complete.

Though General Ayub was a military ruler, he came with a constitution in 1962 by which Pakistan switched from a parliamentary system of government to a presidential form of government. In the first election of Pakistani presidentship in 1964, Sheikh Mujib sided with Fatima Jinnah against Ayub. This presidential election was held through an indirect system of voting. The people of Pakistan did not directly elect the president. But the election was through an electoral college of basic democrats. These basic democrats were elected representatives through districts, tehsils, etc. Fatima Jinnah, sister of Jinnah, got about 36 per cent vote and General Ayub was elected with 62 per cent of the votes. After the elections, General Ayub as President of Pakistan tried to bring industrial development to the neglected, underdeveloped East Pakistan. Going by the logic of the majority of the population living in East Pakistan, Dacca was declared the second capital of the country and it was also planned to house the national parliament in Dacca. An architect was appointed to work on the design of the national parliament. Due to internal pressure, General Ayub was replaced as President by General Yahya Khan who abrogated the 1962 constitution. Yahya Khan announced the Legal Framework

Order (LFO) and called for direct election. A new constitution was to be written by the newly elected government after the elections.

Under the leadership of Sheikh Mujib, the struggle of East Pakistan was going on. He was charged with treason and sedition by the government. The western Pakistan ruling class was always suspicious of Sheikh Mujib's actions. He was accused of conspiring with India after the 1962 and 1965 wars. The Indian leadership had consultations and meetings with Sheikh Mujib. The major direct struggle between the Awami League and the Pakistani government started with Sheikh Mujib's Six-Point Programme (SPP) which was propagated in 1966. The SPP wanted greater autonomy for East Pakistan. One factor which worked in favour of Sheikh Mujib was the fact that he was considered to inherit the legacy of Suhrawardy. Another factor that worked in favour of Mujib was the policy of Jinnah where he wanted to push Urdu as a state language of Pakistan, in both West and East Pakistan. The freedom struggle of East Pakistan was based on the issue of language, which is Bangla and culture, which is Bengali. East and West Pakistan were culturally distinct. Mujib capitalized on the resurgent Bengali 'nationalist' sentiment in the East. This finally culminated in the formation of Bangladesh. Religion could not keep the two parts of Pakistan together for long. It is rightly said that the birth of Bangladesh was a triumph of language and culture over religion.

General elections were held in Pakistan on 7 December 1970. They were the first general elections held in Pakistan. The National Assembly of Pakistan was constituted with 313 members – 300 elected and 13 women members to be nominated (7 from East and 6 from West Pakistan). The Provincial Assembly of West Pakistan was divided into four

Provincial Assemblies of Punjab, Sind, Northwest Frontier and Baluchistan. The East Pakistan Provincial Assembly remained as one provincial assembly. So the first general election of Independent Pakistan for the National Assembly and five Provincial Assemblies were held on 7 December 1970. The whole nation was in the grip of election fever as for the first time, the electorate of this nation was going to vote and elect their representatives after twenty-three years of independence. Both India and Pakistan became newly independent nations at the same time but both have undergone differing political trajectories ever since. The right to vote has always been there with the Indian people ever since independence. In fact, by 1970, India had already voted four times and the Fifth General Election was also held in the same year. Politically, India has been progressing on all the parameters of democracy and in contrast, Pakistan has been ruled by the bayonet of the gun. They have extremely *divergent political pathways. India has undoubtedly performed better than Pakistan on most democratic indicators.*

For the general elections held in 1970 in Pakistan, about twenty-four parties participated in the election. The election for the National Assembly was to be held on the 7th of December 1970 but on 3 November, Cyclone Bhola struck East Pakistan. The devastation was big, more than 5,00,000 people perished. The ruling class of West Pakistan had little to offer and the divide between the two areas became wider. Out of 300 National Assembly seats, 162 were in East Pakistan and138 were in West Pakistan. The Awami League led by Sheikh Mujibur Rahman put a total of 170 candidates for the National Assembly. They contested for all 162 seats of East Pakistan and 8 seats in West Pakistan. Zulfikar Ali Bhutto led Pakistan Peoples' Party, which contested for 120 seats (103 seats in Punjab and Sindh Provinces, and 17 in Northwest Frontier Province and Baluchistan) in West Pakistan and none in East Pakistan. The number of voters for the first election in the history of Pakistan was 5,69,41,500. The majority of 3,12,11,220 voters were in East Pakistan and 2,57,30,280 in West Pakistan. People participated in the election wholeheartedly and voter turnout was 63 per cent which was very good for a nation that is still breathing under the rule of uniform. In his book *Diaries of Field Marshal Mohammad Ayub Khan from 1966-1972*, President Ayub had accused Bhutto of declaring himself an Indian citizen in Indian courts till he became a minister in 1958 to get compensation (Rs 1.5 lakh) for the property left by his parents in India.

The results were on expected lines; in East Pakistan, the Awami League bagged 160 seats out of 162 and got an absolute majority in the National Assembly. The PPP with 81 seats was to be the main opposition party. The PPP also got a majority in the Provincial Assemblies of Punjab and Sind. The Marxist National Awami Party won Northwest Frontier and Baluchistan provinces. The Eastern Pakistan Province with 300 seats gave 288 seats to the Awami League. The nation had given the verdict but the ruling elites of Western Pakistan were not ready to be ruled by the East Pakistani leader and his party. Different excuses were given and the duly elected government was not formed after the elections. General Yahya Khan and Bhutto were in no mood to hand over the reins of the country to Sheikh Mujibur Rahman. One of the reasons given by Bhutto was that the Awami League had not won any seat in West Pakistan so they did not qualify to rule Pakistan, blatantly forgetting the fact that the Awami League put up a few candidates in West Pakistan who fought elections and lost but Bhutto's

PPP had not put even one single candidate in East Pakistan. Yet, Bhutto dared to claim that forming a government without him would be like staging Shakespeare's Hamlet without the role of the Prince of Denmark. The irony of the first general elections of Pakistan was that the first session of this elected assembly was called after about more than two-and-a-half years when Bhutto became Prime Minister of Pakistan on 14 August 1973 based on the National Assembly election of 7 December 1970.

The movement in East Pakistan (Bangladesh) started building up when the legitimate claim of the Awami League and Mujibur Rehman was not only denied but the nexus of Yahya Khan and Bhutto planned to suppress Bengalis (Bangladeshi) in East Pakistan. Operation Searchlight was planned in the last week of February 1971. Being aware of the ground reality and unwilling to support the military attack on civilians, Shahzada Yakub Khan, commander of Eastern Command (Bangladesh) opposed the crackdown. He was replaced by General Tikka Khan. General Yahya Khan visited Dhaka in March to hold talks with Mujibur Rahman but no workable solution was arrived at in that meeting. Mujibur Rahman was arrested on 25 March 1971 and Operation Searchlight started by Khadim Hussain Raza, General Commanding Officer of 14 Division. The first target was Dhaka University and about 100 to 300 teachers and students were killed.

On 27 March 1971 at 7.45 pm Major Zia, on behalf of the Awami League and Mujibur Rehman, declared the independence of Bangladesh on radio Chittagong. Mujibur Rehman was shifted to West Pakistan jail. The only way of bridging the distance of 2,000 km between West and East Pakistan (Bangladesh) was by ensuring the rule of equality. But the events did not unfold as the people of East Pakistan had hoped. The West-Pakistani government proved even more discriminatory and their denial of the legitimate claims of the elected representative only widened the gap. The World Media, while reporting the atrocities of the Pakistani military on East Pakistan (Bangladesh) used the word 'genocide' while reporting the event. It is estimated that anywhere between 3 to 30 lakh Bangladeshis were killed, lakhs of women were raped, an estimated 10 million fled to India and another 30 million had to leave their homes. The refugees, after crossing the border, started arriving in the Indian states of Assam, West Bengal, Tripura and Bihar. This posed a colossal burden on India's scarce resources. On humanitarian grounds, refugees were given shelter in the refugee camps and provided with food, clothing and necessities of life. The provisional government of Bangladesh was formed on 17 April 1971 with headquarters at Kolkata. In an apparent sense, it was a government-in-exile, as the activities of the government were conducted from outside of the territory of Bangladesh. So, there were two governments-in-exile operating from India—the Tibetan government-in-exile and the Bangladeshi government-in-exile.

India under the leadership of Indira Gandhi was providing economic, diplomatic and military support to the freedom fighters of Bangladesh, which was a big drain on their meagre resources. It was becoming clear that this state of affairs must have a logical end and the only answer was to provide support to agitating Bangladeshis in their war of independence. On 25 April 1971, Indira Gandhi summoned a cabinet meeting in which an unusual participant was Chief of the Indian Army Field Marshal Sam Manekshaw. Indira enquired with him about India's preparedness for immediate war, and the answer given by

Manekshaw will forever be engraved in Indian history. He said, 'I guarantee you 100 per cent defeat. 'The general needed time not only to reassemble and fortify his forces but he had to keep in mind several other factors, such as the hostile weather, heavy monsoons due to which road transport got blocked and the entire countryside was flooded. He also knew that India would be fighting not only on the eastern front but on the western front as well. He wanted to wait for the arrival of winter and the snow to block the northern passes as that would ensure that China could not react in support of Pakistan. It was decided that the political leadership would ensure that India had trustworthy friends. India wanted to show the true face of Pakistan to the world and wanted to ensure that world opinion and world leadership, if not in favour, should not turn hostile in the event of war. The USA was supporting Pakistan openly and India was looking for a powerful ally who could be a trusted all-weather friend. Kissinger, who was the Secretary of State of the US, visited China in July 1971. This showed an emerging new axis between America–China and Pakistan. Those were the days of the Cold War and the Russians did not want Americans to sit in Pakistan and breathe down their neck. A friendship with Non-Aligned India would also give Soviet Russia the crucial reach to the nations of the Non-Aligned Movement. On 9 August 1971, the external affairs ministers of the two countries A.A. Gromyko and Swaran Singh signed the historical 1971 Indo—Soviet Treaty of Peace, Friendship and Cooperation with twelve articles. The most important clause was guaranteeing security to each other. Swaran Singh was the longest-serving union cabinet minister in the history of India to date (1952–76). He was known as one of the best ministers who understood diplomacy. His speech at the United

Nations in 1971 at the height of the Bangladesh crisis is considered to be a masterpiece befitting reply to USA's Ambassador to the United Nations George H.W. Bush (who later became president of the US) and foreign minister of Pakistan Zulfikar Ali Bhutto (who became prime minister of Pakistan). This Indo–Soviet treaty neutralized the threat of the Seventh Fleet of America during the war.

The Bangladesh Armed forces that comprised mainly of officers and jawans of the Pakistani military, who were leaving and joining hands for the liberation of their country was formalized on 11 July 1971. Colonel M.A.G. Osmani was the commander-in-chief (C-in-C) of the defence force and was given the status of a cabinet minister. Lt Col Abdur Rabb was his chief of staff (COS). Ten training camps were set up on the border to train the Mukti Bahini and the target was to send 20,000 Mukti Bahini soldiers every month from September onwards. Manekshaw made Brigadier Sujan Singh incharge of training and providing suitable ammunition to the Mukti Bahini. The strategy was to engage the West Pakistani troops with the Mukti Bahini and to provide local ground support when India entered the war.

The situation in the middle of 1971 was indicating that India was inching towards a third war in less than ten years. President Nixon of the USA and his Secretary of State Henry Kissinger, who were considered champions of democracy and human rights, were openly advocating and lobbying for Pakistani dictatorship under General Yahya Khan. The US government supplied military equipment worth $3.8 million to Pakistan when genocide was going on, even after telling the Congress that all shipments to the regime had ceased. During one of his numerous visits to China and Pakistan, Kissinger made a stopover in India.

Indira Gandhi invited Kissinger for a private breakfast. General Manekshaw was also invited by Indira for the breakfast meeting with a request to come in full uniform. She did not disclose as to who her other guests were. Manekshaw, not knowing the agenda, reached for the meeting in his uniform, and he met Kissinger there. Indira pleaded with Kissinger to intervene and stop the genocide and rape in Bangladesh and the influx of refugees to India. Kissinger continued to be evasive and did not give any assurance to do something about the situation. Rattled, Indira Gandhi told Kissinger in no uncertain terms that if the world (implying USA) order remained a moot spectator in East Pakistan, then India had a war option as well to settle the issue.

Indira knew that before going to war India needed to reach out to the world leaders. She went on a state visit to Soviet Russia in September 1971 and the dividends of the visit are history. We had one reliable powerful nation not only giving support on the ground but also taking care of the interests of India in the United Nations whenever the USA and China conspired against it. On 24 October 1971, she went for a three-week world tour to appraise Lebanon, Belgium, Austria, United Kingdom, United States, France and West Germany of the influx of refugees from East Pakistan and the genocide of Bengalis. The attempt was to muster support for India in case it was pushed towards war. Indira covered Lebanon, Belgium, Austria, the United Kingdom, the United States of America, France and West Germany. During the visit to America the treatment given to Indira by the US President Nixon and Secretary of State Kissinger was not at all cordial or friendly. The insult made Indira much stronger and iron willed in handling Pakistan Crisis in days to come. All these offensive and abusive conversations of Nixon and Kissinger came into the public domain when the US state department declassified 28 Nixon tapes between July 2019 and May 2020. These tapes reflect the way the US failed to denounce atrocities and turned a blind eye to the genocide, rape, human rights violations and crushing of democracy by the military dictators of West Pakistan in East Pakistan (Bangladesh).

On 3 December 1971, Indira Gandhi travelled in the eastern parts of the country to get a first-hand report of military preparations and refugee management. These refugees from Bangladesh had crossed the mark of 10 million. She was addressing a rally in the brigade ground of Kolkata when news of the Pakistani attack was conveyed to her. She rushed back to Delhi along with Sidharth Shankar Ray, chief minister of West Bengal. Her plane was diverted to avoid the threat of attack from the Pakistani Air Force. She reached Delhi, which was under blackout. To understand the level of war preparedness, Indira called the three heads of defence forces General Sam Manekshaw, Admiral S.M. Nanda, and Air Chief Marshal P.C. Lal. It is said that during the 1965 war, the Navy was given instruction not to cross Indian waters which amounted to some loss inflicted on the Indian navy. When Nanda asked for permission to cross the territory the short reply of Indira was, 'War is a War'. So, Indian defence forces had full authority to make decisions without going back to their political masters. After the briefing with the defence, the Prime Minister chaired the Union Cabinet meeting and it was followed by a meeting with the opposition parties. It was past midnight when the prime minister addressed the nation over All India Radio.

The formal entry of India into the war galvanized the Mukti Bahini. Indian forces with the ground support of the

Mukti Bahini made rapid progress in East Pakistan (Bangladesh). Pakistan opened a front on the western borders of India so that the pressure on eastern borders could be released and Pakistan could get a breather. On 4 December, Brigadier Tariq Mir of Pakistan with his brigade planned an attack on Longewala with an eye on Jaisalmer. The Pakistani plan was to have breakfast at Longewala, lunch at Jaisalmer and dinner at Jodhpur. The Longewala post was defended by Major Kuldip Singh Chandpuri (the character played by Sunny Deol in Hindi film *Border*) of the 23 Punjab Regiment with 83 soldiers. The armoured regiment of the Pakistani army outpaced their infantry, which was a cardinal error in warfare. The Pakistani tanks mistook the barbed wires laid by the Indian army to keep out dogs and animals as a marker for minefield and they held back. They waited for their infantry to catch up which gave much-required time to the Indian Army. Major Chandpuri supported by hunters of the Indian Air Force and artillery support from Sadhewala wrote history. Thirty-four Pakistani tanks were either destroyed or captured. Operation Trident was launched by the Indian Navy. For the first time, the Indian Navy was in an attack mode. Karachi port was destroyed by Navy planes on 5 December where a fire in the petroleum products storage tanks lasted for many days. On the eastern side, the pride of India INS Vikrant played havoc with Kaks Bazar and Chittagong Port. The dreaded submarine Ghazi of Pakistan with 93 men on board capsized near Vishakhapatnam without firing a single shot.

At the height of the war, the USA came openly in favour of Pakistan against its declared stand of containing the war. In the declassified records, it is now revealed that Kissinger personally met the Chinese Ambassador to the UN, Huang

Ha with a request to initiate troop movements against India. Kissinger assured the Chinese that in case Soviet Russia came out to help India, the US would support China. The Chinese, after considering the offer, refused to take the bait. USA threatened India by sending Task Force 74 (TF 74) of the dreaded Seventh Fleet to get engaged in the war. The Seventh Fleet was raised during the Second World War and played an important role during the Korean and Vietnam wars. It comprised 60–70 ships, about 300 aircraft and 40,000 sailors, naval personnel and coast guards. TF 74 comprised nuclear-powered aircraft carrier Enterprise, assault carrier, destroyer, guided-missile escorts ship, a nuclear-powered attack submarine and a supply ship. The fleet entered the Bay of Bengal on 15 December 1971 on its way to Dhaka but had to make a hasty retreat when they found that Soviet Russia had sent the 10th Operative Battle Group of its Pacific Field in support of India.

On 6 December 1971, Indira Gandhi announced in parliament that a new nation Bangladesh was born and India was among the first few nations to give it recognition. As expected, the USA tried to raise the matter in the United Nations Security Council, but the same was vetoed by Soviet Russia. When all this was going on, Indira was aware that the time was running out as the fear was that if this matter was taken up in the UN, then the freedom of Bangladesh would be delayed which would be militarily and economically disastrous for India. General Manekshaw, Lt General Jagjit Singh Arora GOC-in-C (General Officer Commanding-in-Chief) of the Eastern Command in Kolkata and Major General J.F.R. Jacob started putting pressure on Lt General Abdullah Khan Niyazi heading Pakistani forces in Bangladesh. Surrounded by Indian defence forces, the morale of the Pakistani Army was shattered on 14 December when the governor's residence was attacked and bombed by the Indian Air Force. Niyazi sent an offer of a ceasefire and the guns of India were put on hold. On 16 December 1971, Major General Jacob landed in Dhaka and met Niazi with the offer of surrender and in return, he ensured the safety of his family and treatment of POW (Prisoners of War) with dignity in line with the Geneva Convention. Niyazi tried to make it ceasefire instead of surrender but Jacob was resolute in his offer of surrender. Niyazi was given a stark choice: Surrender unconditionally and publicly, and receive the protection of the Indian Army or face an Indian military onslaught. The guns of the Indian forces that were silent would start firing again if the surrender document was not signed. In four hours, Jacob made Niyazi and his 93,000 men surrender to the Indian forces. Lt. General Jagjit Singh Arora with his team reached Dhaka in five MQ helicopters to formally complete the process of surrender which had started at 1430 hrs. On 16 December 1971, at 1631 hours in the race course ground in Dhaka, Lt General A.K. Niyazi signed the papers, removed his stars and handed over his pistol to Lt. General Jagjit Singh Arora, GOC-in-C of Indian and Bangladesh forces. Bangladesh Mukti Bahini was represented by the chief of staff Captain Khonkar. General Manekshaw before Independence had sold his motorcycle to his colleague General Yahya Khan for Rs1,000, Yahya Khan had promised to pay the amount later. In between, Partitioned happened and he went to Pakistan without paying the price of the old motorbike. After the fall of East Pakistan, Manekshaw used to joke, 'Yahya never paid me the Rs 1,000 for my motorbike, but now he has paid with half his country.'

Indira, in her address to the nation on 16 December, told the world, 'Dhaka is now a free capital of a free country.' India unilaterally declared a ceasefire on the western front. Within fourteen days, India changed the history and geography of West Pakistan. Pakistan lost half of its territory with the birth of Bangladesh. One question which remains unanswered is, What was primarily Indira's intention? Was it to create Bangladesh or divide Pakistan? General Agha Muhammad Yahya Khan, the third President of Pakistan resigned on 20 December 1971 and Zulfikar Ali Bhutto became the fourth President of Pakistan. Bhutto was in America when East Pakistan had fallen. As the deputy prime minister and foreign minister of Pakistan, he was trying hard in the United Nations to intervene and stop the war. Bhutto was introduced to the world of politics in America, while pursuing his honours in Political Science at the University of California, Berkley. In 1950, he was a member of the campaign group for the Congressional candidate Helen Gahagan Douglas, who lost to Richard Nixon (who later became President of USA).

Indira Gandhi had fought and won a costly war with Pakistan which was in danger of slipping away unless Bangladesh got its leader Mujibur Rehman back. The only major task now was to get Mujibur Rehman released from the Pakistani jail. After arresting Mujibur in March 1971 in Bangladesh, he was brought to West Pakistan and tried for treason in the military court. He was sentenced to death. A grave was dug in his prison cell with a rope attached to the ceiling to constantly remind him that he could be hung any time.

Bhutto returned from his Washington trip. His speech on 15 December not only reflects his anger but also indicates his desperation of losing half of Pakistan. In the Security Council, Soviet Russia vetoed all the attempts of the USA and China to stop the war midway without Bangladesh becoming a reality. Bhutto was also angry with the United Kingdom and France who preferred to abstain. For Indira Gandhi, it was important to read the mind of Bhutto regarding Sheikh Mujibur so that the next course of action could be decided. Imagine the fate of not only Bangladesh but India as well if Pakistani decision-makers had decided to carry out the verdict of the military court and executed Mujib. The important breakthrough came from D.P. Dhar, a close confidante of Indira. As an Indian ambassador in Soviet Russia, he was also the architect of the Indo–Soviet Friendship Treaty. Muzzafar Hussain, Chief Secretary of East Pakistan was also part of POW and was lodged in D.P. Dhar's official residence in Delhi.

Hussain's wife Laila had gone to London and was unable to return when war broke out on 3 December. Laila was very intimate with Bhutto and both were good friends. It was decided that Laila would meet Bhutto at Heathrow Airport in London when his plane stopped for refuelling on the pretext of getting her husband released and in the course of the conversation, she would try to gauge Bhutto's plans for Mujibur Rahman. Sashanka S. Banerjee, a diplomat in the Indian High Commission was assigned the job of arranging the meeting of Bhutto and Laila in the VIP lounge of the airport.

Laila, as decided, pleaded for the release of her husband but Bhutto was sharp enough to know the real purpose of the meeting and, as described by Banerjee told Laila, 'Laila, I know what you want. I can imagine you are carrying a request from Mrs Indira Gandhi. Do please pass a message to her that after I take charge of office back home, I will shortly thereafter release Mujibur Rehman, allowing him to return home. What I want in return, I will let Mrs Indira Gandhi know through another channel. You may now go.' The secret message did reach Mrs Gandhi, a verbal commitment of returning POW in exchange for letting Sheikh Mujibur go alive.

Yahya Khan while handing over the reins of Pakistan to Bhutto on 20 December 1971 also gave him an envelope having an undated death warrant of Sheikh Mujibur Rehman. He said it was a mistake not to carry out the death sentence awarded to Mujibur Rehman and in the interest of Pakistan, Bhutto must put a date and execute the death warrant. Mujib was confined in cell no. 73 of the Mianwali Jail. He was transferred to the residence of jailor Habib Khan on 26 December and on 1 January 1972 was shifted to Shahulla, a village close to Rawalpindi. Bhutto tried to convince Sheikh Mujibur to maintain links with Pakistan in the form of a loose confederation or associati0on and not to break away completely. The persuasion went on for a week but Sheikh Mujibur, even in that hostile environment, held his ground that he could promise nothing without being free and without consulting his people in Bangladesh. On 8 January 1972, Bhutto went to the airport to see off Sheikh Mujibur who was sent to London in PIA Boeing. On 10 January 1972, a Royal Air force Plane took off with Sheikh Mujibur for Bangladesh from London Comet. He stopped at Delhi to pay his gratitude to Mrs Gandhi and the Indian people. The plane reached Delhi at 8 am and Mrs Gandhi along with all the top leaders of India and ambassadors of twenty countries was at the airport to receive Banga bandhu Sheikh Mujibur Rehman. Till then, only India and Bhutan had recognized Bangladesh. The diplomats of Soviet Russia were in full attendance. The only country absent was the USA. Sheikh Mujib said, 'The people of India stood by us in our darkest hour and we will never forget it. 'This was for the first time Sheikh

Mujibur met Indira Gandhi. Sheikh Mujib reached Dhaka at 3 pm the same day to an unprecedented welcome. The twenty-one-gun salute given to him at the airport was not audible as the air was filled with full-throated cheering and slogans of '*Joi Bangla, Joi Bangabandhu*'.

Indira Gandhi turned her attention to how to end the ceasefire status with Pakistan. On 23 April 1972, terms of discussion were finalized between the two countries and it was decided to have bilateral talks in June at Barnes Court (Raj Bhavan) in Shimla. In six years from 1965, India had emerged as a force to reckon with. There was no need for either a third-party intervention or a neutral venue. India was holding negotiations in its territory. In June 1972, Bhutto arrived with his daughter Benazir Bhutto (who later became the prime minister of Pakistan). The formal negotiations went on between the foreign ministers of the two countries and the agreement was signed on 2 July 1972 (technically it was signed at 00:40 hrs on the night of 2–3 July). Though the agreement says drafted on 26 June 1972 but it was the sixth draft that was finalized. It was termed as a peace treaty and was signed by the Prime Minister of India, Indira Gandhi and the President of Pakistan, Zulfikar Ali Bhutto. It had to be ratified by the parliament of both the countries and was effective from 4 August 1972. Besides English, the agreement was also in Hindi and Urdu. It was decided that henceforth the Shimla Agreement and not the UN Security Council Resolution of 1949 would be the reference point between the two countries for settlement of bilateral issues including disputes. The Shimla Agreement of 1972 supersedes the earlier UN resolution.

According to the agreement, the Ceasefire line was to be called the Line of Control (LOC). India agreed to return 93,000 prisoners of war and about 5,000 square miles of land occupied during the war. In return, Bhutto gave a verbal assurance to Indira Gandhi that after returning to Pakistan, he would make the Line of Control into an international boundary. It had appeared during negotiations that the demand of India to settle the Jammu and Kashmir issue once for all by converting the LOC into an international border had been resisted by Bhutto. Indira met the Pakistani media a day before and cleared the stand of India. Bhutto went to meet Indira Gandhi all alone past midnight on 2 July and pleaded that if he returned empty-handed, the army would take over and it would be the end of democracy in Pakistan – India will have a military-ruled state as a neighbour. Bhutto was trying to bolster his domestic stature. Though it cannot be verified by any document now since it was a one-on-one meeting but it is said Indira agreed to return the Pakistani POWs when Bhutto reminded her of her promise of returning them when he released Sheikh Mujibur. The detractors of the Shimla Agreement accuse Indira Gandhi of failing to settle the Kashmir issue, and also not mentioning about the release of 54 POWs of India languishing in the Pakistani jail. Gandhi's aggressive and bellicose critics complained that she had gone soft on Pakistan.

In the euphoria over the war victory, no one knew about these POWs then. It was many years after the war that the news about our POW still in Pakistani jail started trickling in. To make matters more complicated, before the Shimla Agreement, there was no note/document by any ministry about these POWs. The absence of documentation was responsible for their continued detention. If this was a slip, then it was very grave indeed and the entire system has to share the blame. And as the onus ultimately rests with the prime minister, one may accuse Indira of this gross negligence.

The handing over of Pakistani Prisoners of War lasted for about three years. The last POW to be handed over was Lt. General Niyazi on 30 April 1975. On his return, he was tried by the war commission. He was found guilty and was stripped of his rank, decorations, medals and awards. In the eyes of an average Pakistani, General Niazi was a soldier, who by surrendering had brought humiliation to the nation. People never realize that fighting a war is not easy. His surrender saved the lives of thousands of soldiers who were doomed to perish in Bangladesh. The Prisoners of War on their return never got the respect of their countrymen.

All the three principal figures of the 1971 war, who were the state heads of their country had a tragic end. Sheikh Mujib[2] was murdered in 1975, Bhutto was hanged in 1979 and Indira Gandhi was shot dead in 1984.

Notes

1. Available at: https://www.pbs.gov.pk/content/population-census (accessed on 30 January).
2. Sheikh Mujib-Ur-Rehman is popularly known as 'Sheikh Mujib'.

Chapter-6

Aao Mardo . . . Namard Bano

Dark Days of Emergency, Civil Liberties Suspended

25 June 1975, Wednesday

Indira Gandhi had won the 1967 (fourth Lok Sabha) elections but called for elections one year in advance in 1971 and won the 1971 (fifth Lok Sabha) elections as well. She also has a dubious record of extending the term of the fifth Lok Sabha for one year during an emergency. For the first time, the nation witnessed an assault on the freedom and democracy of our country, impinging upon the rights of the citizens. It marks the darkest moment of Indian democracy when elections were stalled by Mrs Gandhi. The turning point in the career of Indira Gandhi was the presidential election of 1969 when the official Congress candidate Neelam Sanjiva Reddy lost the elections to V.V. Giri who was backed by Indira Gandhi. The election was so close that the results were declared after counting of the second preference votes. V.V. Giri had polled 50.9 per cent and Sanjiva Reddy 49.1 per cent votes. Former Finance Minister C.D. Deshmukh was the official candidate for the two conservative parties—Jana Sangh and Swatantra party. Congress President Nijalingappa was so desperate that he sought second preference votes from the Jana Sangh and Swatantra party. These two parties were ideologically poles apart from the established and declared Congress ideology. Jana Sangh was a right-wing Hindu party and the Swatantra party favoured the capitalists.

In the parliamentary board meeting, to decide the presidential candidate of the Congress party, Indira Gandhi had proposed the name of Jagjivan Ram, which was voted out by the Syndicate. Sanjiva Reddy had more supporters in the parliamentary board and so he became the official candidate of the Congress. Therefore, Indira was one of the proposers for the nomination papers of Sanjiva Reddy for the presidential election. V.V. Giri was the opposition candidate and to show her authority, Indira decided to back V.V. Giri. The appeal of Nijalingappa to get the support of right-wing parties gave Indira the justifiable opportunity to ask the Congressmen to vote as per their conscience, keeping in mind the ideals of secularism and socialism. It was the night before the elections when she called on her party to 'vote according to conscience'. V.V. Giri got more votes from the opposition party than from the Congress party. From the Congress, only a minority group voted for V.V. Giri. The fifth presidential poll stands out as the reference point when political individualism surfaced in India's political process. The 1969 presidential election is considered a milestone for Indian politics primarily on account of the ramifications it had for the entire nation in the years to come.

The split in Congress was a foregone conclusion after the presidential election of 1969. Indira dropped four junior ministers from her cabinet and as retaliation, the Congress president decided not to include three of her loyalists in the CWC (Congress Working Committee). These three loyalists were C. Subramaniam (who was conferred the Bharat Ratna in 1988), Fakhruddin Ali Ahmed and S.D. Sharma (both of them became president of India). Indira Gandhi was expelled from Congress on 12 November 1969 and same day, the Indian National Congress (Requisitionists) was formed with C. Subramaniam as interim president. The original Congress Party was called the Indian National Congress (Organisation). Congress (R) got the symbol of a cow with suckling calf, which later symbolized Indira as the cow and Sanjay Gandhi as suckling calf. The Congress had 429 Members of Parliament (both Lok Sabha and Rajya Sabha) and it was claimed that Indira enjoyed the support of 310 to 330 members. The parliament session started on 16 November 1969 and Indira no longer enjoyed the majority support in the Lok Sabha based on only Congress(R) MPs. The split had rendered Mrs Gandhi's government to minority status. Thus started the period of coalition in the centre, purely for keeping the power. Indira Gandhi was supported by the Communist Party of India (CPI), the S.M. Joshi faction of the Samyukta Socialist Party (SSP), the S.N. Dwivedi faction of the Praja Socialist Party (PSP) and the Dravida Munnetra Kazhagam (DMK); the Madhu Limaye–Raj Narain group of SSP, the H.V. Kamath group of PSP and the Communist Party of India (Marxist) (CPM) were more guarded in providing their support. The Swatantra party and Jana Sangh supported Congress (O) giving the leverage to Indira Gandhi that her policies were closer to socialism and communism and oriented towards the poor.

This was the beginning of coalition politics in the centre and also the end of collective leadership in the Congress. In the past, the leadership had seen challenges but all of them were due to ideological commitments. But now, Congress was split due to the clash of individuals rather than ideologies. This split and events after that are evidence of the diminishing power of the organizational wing of the Congress party. The ministers were more important than the office-bearers of the party. The regional parties, like the Dravida Munnetra Kazhagam (DMK), the Akali Dal and the Bhartiya Kranti Dal (BKD) took a decisive role in national politics. Indira was under the routine pressure and pulls of running a government with outside support and decided to call for an early election, fourteen months in advance. This was her first test to prove that she had understood the mood and nerve of the people. In a campaign spanning forty-three days, Indira did more than 300 election meetings. Her slogan was—'*Garibihatao*' (Remove Poverty) in reply to the opposition call of '*Indira hatao*' (Remove Indira). Indira Gandhi's Congress (R) had an absolute majority with 352 seats. In 1972, riding the wave of popular sentiment in her support after the creation of Bangladesh, the performance of Congress (R) in the state elections of Madhya Pradesh, Rajasthan, Maharashtra, Karnataka, Gujarat, Bihar, Punjab and Haryana was spectacular. Barring Tamil Nadu, Nagaland, Meghalaya and Manipur, all the states then had a Congress government. In Kerala, the Congress as the largest party (with thirty MLAs) gave support to the United Front Government headed by C. Achutha Menon of CPI. E. Namboodripaad of CPM was the leader of the opposition with twenty-nine MLAs.

With virtually entire India under her control and with

a well-cemented position in the parliament, Indira Gandhi started taking decisions that led to the imposition of Emergency.[1] On 5 November 1971, the Constitution (24th Amendment) Act was passed, which empowered the parliament to amend any provision of the Constitution including the power to dilute the Fundamental Rights. In April 1972, Indira brought the 25th Amendment of the Constitution changing the verdict of the Supreme Court regarding the nationalization of banks. Also, regarding the privy purse case, the payment of compensation was to be determined by the parliament and not by the courts. The 25th Amendment was followed up by many other amendments during the Emergency, the most important being 38th, 39th and 42nd Amendments, which brought sweeping changes in the Constitution. All these amendments tried to clip the powers of the judiciary and gave more authority to the Legislature (parliament) changing the balance between the two as decided by the Constituent Assembly. All these powers were strengthening the position of the prime minister. The 24th and 25th Amendments were challenged in Court and it is popularly known as the Keshvanand Bharti Case. A thirteen-judges bench was constituted and judgement was delivered on 24 April 1973. In the history of the Supreme Court, to date, this is the largest ever constitutional bench. The verdict was split and by a wafer-thin majority of 7–6, it was decided that the parliament is not empowered to change the basic structure of the Constitution. This incident made Indira Gandhi meddle in the appointment of judges, justifying the need for a 'committed judiciary'. Judicial appointments became a surrogate way to control the judiciary and finally the Constitution of India. The Chief Justice of India Justice Sikri retired the next day after the Keshvanand Bharti verdict was given, and against established norms, Justice A.N. Ray superseded three judges and became the Chief Justice of India. The three judges resigned in protest—Justice Shelat and Justice Hegde resigned in April 1973 and Justice Grover resigned a month later. Justice A.N. Ray had given a dissenting note in the Keshvanand Bharti case and had also given judgements favouring the government in the past. Not only did the bar protest against the appointment but Jai Prakash Narain (JP) also wrote an open letter to all the MPs stressing the need to curb the unlimited powers of the prime minister in the appointment of the Chief Justice of India. This was needed to keep the balance between legislature and judiciary as envisaged by the Constitution. The letter was not taken by Indira very kindly and she felt threatened by JP. This was the beginning of the tussle between JP and Indira that culminated in the imposition of Emergency and the arrest of JP. One of the last leaders of the Gandhian era, JP used to hold a meeting every year on 12th February in his village Sitabdiara in memory of Gandhi. This was as per the Hindu tradition of *Tehravi* (13th day of death) as Gandhi died on 30 January.

After the war, the whole country was reeling under the rising prices of food grains and other essential commodities. The Congress had done exceedingly well in the 1972 state elections of Gujarat winning 140 seats out of a total of 168 seats. Chimanbhai Patel replaced Ghanshyam Oza as Chief Minister of Gujarat in July 1973. The corruption and the price-rise during his regime became the reason for a lot of unrest. On 20 December 1973, students demanded rollback of the 20 per cent increased mess bill. The spark lit by students of L.D. Engineering College, Ahmedabad, started the massive Nav Nirman Andolan (New Construction Movement) in 1974 due to which an elected government had to resign in independent India. The protests on the issue of food and education coupled with corruption charges on Chimanbhai Patel became viral in education institutions and subsequently led to the participation of the common man. The call for a state-wide *bandh* on 25 January 1974 led to the use of force by the government which resulted in more than 100 deaths and 8,000 arrests besides many injuries. This was a leaderless protest and students, lawyers and teachers formed committees called Nav Nirman Yuvak Samitis to guide the agitation. Curfew was imposed and the army was called to contain the protest and bring back normalcy. Chimanbhai resigned on 9 February 1974 and President's Rule was imposed.[2] Indira had thought that with the resignation of the chief minister, status quo would be established soon after. The politicians saw their chance and Morarji Desai started his fast with the demand for dissolution of the assembly. The Congress with a majority of more than 80 per cent seats in the state Vidhan Sabha was pressurized for fresh elections. JP also gave it ethical sanction with the call of the citizen's right to recall before the elected term is over. Ninety-five out of 168 MLAs resigned from their membership and on 16 March 1974, the assembly was dissolved.

Taking a cue from Gujarat, Bihar, one of the most politically vibrant states of the country, became the place where the movement against the Congress and Indira Gandhi started. Laloo Yadav became the General Secretary of Patna University in 1970. Next year, he contested for the post of the president and lost to Dr Ram Jatan Sinha. In 1973, he was elected president of the Patna University Student Union and Sushil Modi of Vidyarthi Parishad (student wing of Janasangh) was elected General Secretary of Patna University Students' Union. Like Gujarat, Bihar also saw a change of leadership. Kedar Pandey was replaced by Abdul Ghafoor as Chief Minister in July 1973. The students–police clash in Patna on 18 March 1974, gave impetus to the movement. Students felt that a regular political leader would try to pursue his political agenda, therefore students and youth leaders of Bihar approached JP to lead their movement. He agreed on one condition that the movement had to be completely non-violent, even the standard stone-pelting during student agitations was to be shunned. JP taking up the leadership role was not liked by Indira and on April Fool's Day (which is also Orissa Day) in 1974, Indira did a foolish mistake in a public rally in Bhubaneshwar. She attacked JP verbally, 'How can such persons who continue to seek favours from the moneyed people ... dare speak of corruption?' For Indira Gandhi, Bhubaneshwar had been a place that gave her grief and sorrow. In 1967, her nose had been broken by a stone hurled by someone during her election campaign; in 1974, her speech referring to the Sarvodaya leader widened the gap between the two leaders, and in 1984, this was the city where she delivered her last public speech before being gunned down by her bodyguards. JP and Jawaharlal and their wives Prabhawati Devi and Kamla Nehru were very close. For JP, Indira was like a daughter and he used to address her as Indu. JP used to often write on government policies and other national issues. At times, this was not liked by Indira but still, a workable, cordial relationship existed. After JP took over the leadership of the students, the relation kept on deteriorating and when on 1 November 1974, they met to work out a compromise formula, the meeting failed. JP handed over a bunch of letters to Indira. These letters had been written by Kamla Nehru to

Prabhawati (Prabhawati had died in 1973).

To coordinate the movement against the misrule and corruption of the Congress government, the Bihar Chhatra Sangharsh Samiti was constituted with representatives of all the opposition parties' student frontal organizations – the Samajwadi Yuvjan Sabha (SYS) of socialists, the Akhil Bhartiya Vidyarthi Parishad (ABVP) of Jana Sangh, the All India Students Federation (AISF) of CPI, the Tarun Shanti Sena, etc. JP led the Mook (silent) Rally on 8 April 1974 in Patna. In April 1974, JP formed the Citizen for Democracy along with V.M. Tarkunde in Delhi. He was the president of this body and they called for free and fair elections to defend democracy. There was another unrest simmering among the railway employees for a very long time. The All India Railwaymen's Federation (AIRF) was the first union of Indian Railways founded in 1925. After independence, JP was the president and Jyoti Basu was the vice president of AIRF. In 1973, the firebrand leader George Fernandes became its president. Many long pending issues were not resolved. The most important issue since the time of Britishers and private railways was the long working hours. George led this strike from 8 May to 27 May 1974 in which an estimated 1.7 million people (17 lakhs) participated, making a world record. More than 50,000 railwaymen were arrested, thousands were thrown out of their houses. Indira Gandhi's inept handling converted an industrial dispute into a mini civil war.

On 5 June 1974, in the historical Gandhi Maidan in Patna, JP gave the call of 'Sampurna Kranti' (Total Revolution). The revolution that started with the students' agitation acquired a larger dimension and brought all opposition political parties barring the CPI under the leadership of JP. This was the time when JP became

'Loknayak'. As already stated, a meeting was arranged between JP and Indira on 1 November 1974 in Delhi. JP wanted to meet her alone with no one present from both the sides, but Indira preferred to keep Jagjivan Ram and Y.B. Chavan with her. JP presented nine demands of the movement, which included the dissolution of the Bihar government led by Abdul Ghafoor; he also called for fresh elections. Instead of bridging the differences, this meeting widened the gap between the two leaders. On the same day, in a public rally in the Ram Lila Ground, Indira announced her decision not to sack Abdul Ghafoor. In a protest rally on 4 November 1974 in Patna, the Bihar police lathi-charged, and even JP was not spared. JP started travelling to different parts of the country to address the people and make them aware of the Total Revolution movement. Slowly, the movement started gaining momentum. In the meantime, elections were announced in Gujarat after Morarji Desai went on an indefinite fast. The election results of the Gujarat Assembly were announced on 12 June 1975 and for the first time, a non-Congress government was formed in the state. The Janata Morcha—a front of Jana Sangh, Congress (O), the Samyukta Socialist Party (SSP) and Bharti Lokdal formed the government with the help of Chimanbhai Patel, the erstwhile Congress chief minister. Ironically, Chimanbhai was the person against whom Janata Morcha led an agitation due to corruption charges and he had to resign. But later, they had no hesitation in taking support from the same person. There is a proverbial saying—'Politics makes strange bedfellows'. Though Chimanbhai lost, his party Kisan Mazdoor Lok Paksha (KLP) with eleven MLAs supported the first opposition government of Gujarat. The same Janata Morcha was converted into the Janata Party on 18 January 1977.

Indira had won the 1971 elections from Rae Bareli getting 1,83,309 votes, defeating Raj Narain a veteran socialist by more than 1,10,000 votes (Raj Narain polled 71,499 votes). An election petition challenging her election was filed by Raj Narain in Allahabad High Court. Shanti Bhushan (who later became Union Minister of Law) appeared on behalf of Raj Narain. At the beginning of 1975, after the usual delay in court, petition number 5 was in the final stages of hearing in the court of an upright judge Justice Jagmohan Lal Sinha. On 18 March 1975, for the first time in the history of India, the prime minister in office Indira Gandhi had to personally appear in High Court to get her statement recorded. Indira was cross-examined for five hours in the court. Prashant Bhushan (son of Shanti Bhushan) has given a first-hand account of the case in his book, *The Case That Shook India*.[3] The arguments closed on 23 May 1975 and the judgement was reserved. The High Court was also closed on account of summer vacation. Justice Sinha took a promise from his secretary Manna Lal that he would not share anything about the judgement, even with his wife. The Chief Justice of Allahabad High Court Justice D. S. Mathur met Justice Sinha. Dr K.P. Mathur, personal physician of the prime minister and local MP of Allahabad, and numerous other people met or tried to influence Justice Sinha. He was told that he would be elevated to the Supreme Court. Besides this, various other direct and indirect offers were also made. To avoid these pressures, Justice Sinha bolted himself inside his house and all visitors calling on him were told that he was out of station. From 28 May to 7 June, no one met him. Even phone calls were not received. On 7 June 1975, the Chief Justice Mathur called him from Dehradun to convey the message of Additional Secretary, Home Affairs P. P. Nair to postpone the judgement till July. To avoid further requests from different quarters, he went to High Court the same day, called the registrar to inform the parties that judgement would be delivered on 12 June. Since no one was able to tell what the judgement was going to be, Indira could sense that something was wrong. Late in the evening on 11 June 1975, a CID team landed at Manna Lal's house, and since he remained silent despite a lot of probing, he was also threatened. Manna Lal was so scared that after shifting his wife to some safe place, he went to the house of Justice Sinha late at night and stayed there. The next morning when he went back to his house to get ready, the CID team returned and asked him to personally tell the judgement to Indira Gandhi on the hotline. The CID team kept on harassing Manna Lal even after the verdict to know about Justice Sinha's visitors and details of his lifestyle. Even Shanti Bhushan was lured by the Attorney General, hinting that a post of Additional Attorney General could be created for him. On 12th June 1975, Justice Sinha read out the operative order –'In view of my findings on Issue No. 3 and Issue No. 1 read with additional issue No. 1, additional issue No. 2, and additional issue No. 3, the petition is allowed and the election of Smt. Indira Nehru Gandhi, respondent No. 1, to the Lok Sabha is declared void.' The judgement ran into 258 pages. Indira's election was set aside. She was barred from fighting elections for six years. But the judgement stayed for twenty days which is a standard clause in any judgement. This would give her time to appeal to a higher court if she wanted. This judgement invoked extreme reactions. Supporters of Indira were crestfallen and for the JP movement, it was the biggest impetus. The world media hailed it as proof of a healthy and strong democracy. The day of 12th June brought more bad news for Indira—her confidante and advisor D.P. Dhar died.

Though the charges of use of government staff (Yashpal Kapoor) and use of government vehicle for the electoral campaign were trivial, it constituted an abuse of position and being the prime minister, she had to be more judicious in such matters. According to the *London Times*, it was equivalent to – 'removing a prime minister from office over a traffic fine'.[4] The political heavyweights of her party – Sidharth Shankar Ray, Chief Minister of West Bengal and also a leading lawyer, the Union Law Minister H. R. Gokhale, Umashankar Dikshit, Jagjivan Ram, the Congress Party President Dev Kanta Barooah and many others reached her residence. It was decided that an appeal against the High Court order would be made in the Supreme Court and as an interim arrangement, Indira would resign and swap position with Barooah. So Barooah would be the next prime minister and Indira would become the Congress President. On getting the news of the court verdict, Sanjay Gandhi, the younger son of Indira Gandhi who was busy in his Maruti factory, rushed home. He took Indira by her arm, away from the meeting and insisted and convinced her not to resign. Her twenty-eight-year-old son Sanjay Gandhi in less than twenty-eight minutes decided not only the fate of the country but inflicted a black spot on the charismatic leadership of Indira, which to date overshadows her bold decisions like the 1971 war, making India *atmanirbhar* (self-reliant) in food security, the inclusion of Sikkim in India, the SAARC (South Asian Association for Regional Cooperation) leadership, etc. One must consider that a duly elected Gujarat government was terminated under public pressure by Indira and fresh elections were called just because till then, she showed respect for democratic traditions. Sanjay Gandhi's immediate concern was his Maruti project, which was certain to come under probe and enquiry if his mother was not at the helm of affairs.

A Special Leave Petition (SLP) was filed against the High Court order in Supreme Court, which was closed due to vacation. Justice V.R. Krishna Ayer presiding as vacation judge passed an order on 24 June 1975 which stated– Indira Gandhi will not have any voting right, no emoluments as prime minister or MP but can continue as prime minister. On 25 June 1975, JP with all the opposition leaders, held a huge rally in Delhi's Ramlila ground. He gave a call for an all-India agitation and decided to sit in protest outside the prime minister's residence. JP also urged the police and army not to obey unethical orders of the government. Indira considered this call by JP as a provocation for men in uniform and made it the grounds for the imposition of Emergency. Indira met President Fakhruddin Ali Ahmad for twenty minutes to fulfil the constitutional requirements. President Fakhruddin agreed with the prime minister's proposal of imposition of emergency. At 11.40 pm, R. K. Dhawan took the letter of Proclamation of Emergency to Rashtrapati Bhavan and which was immediately signed by the president. Extra-constitutional authority surfaced at the prime minister's house. Sanjay Gandhi started calling the shots and taking decisions on behalf of his mother. Under his direction, a list was prepared which had the names of the opposition leaders who had to be arrested. This list was prepared in consultation with the Minister of State for Home Affairs—Om Mehta, Lt Governor of Delhi Krishan Chand and the chief minister of Haryana Bansi Lal. At 2.30 am on 26 June, JP was arrested from the Gandhi Peace Foundation in Delhi and brought to Parliament Street Police station. He was then transferred to Sohna Guest House in Haryana under Section 107 of the Indian Penal Code (IPC). The arrest of the opposition leaders started all over India and this continued for months. It is estimated that more than one lakh people were arrested without any information, reason or trial. The meeting of the union cabinet which was supposed to be held before the imposition of Emergency was called on 26 June at 6 am. No one dared to utter a word against it. During the day, Indira Gandhi addressed the nation and informed the people about the implementation of an Emergency and also the reasons for implementing it.

Sanjay Gandhi decided that no newspaper should come out in Delhi on the 26th morning. Accordingly, the power supply of Bahadur Shah Zafar Marg, the newspaper hub was switched off. Most of the papers had their offices there. Sanjay Gandhi directly instructed I. K. Gujral, the information and broadcasting (I & B) minister, to send all the press releases and press notes for his approval. Gujral claims that he declined to do that and as a result, the prime minister issued instructions that every day, all releases should be brought to her residence for clearance by an officer of the information ministry. Press censorship was in place and Gujaral was replaced by Vidya Charan Shukla, who was always eager to oblige Sanjay Gandhi. It was Vidya Charan who banned Kishore Kumar songs on All India Radio and Delhi Doordarshan (DD) when he refused to sing for the Youth Congress rally and was not ready to promote the twenty-point programme of the government. Film star Dev Anand publicly spoke out against the Emergency with his brothers Chetan and Vijay Anand. He even formed a political party called the National Party at that time to take on the government. Manoj Kumar not only refused to directa pro-Emergency and a pro-government documentary written by Amrita Pritam but also telephoned her to convey his displeasure. It is said that Amrita Pritam was so ashamed that she asked Manoj Kumar to burn the script. Just before the theatrical release of Manoj Kumar's movie *Shor*, Vidya Charan got it telecast on DD. As a result, the film flopped at the box office as no one went to the theatres to buy a ticket to watch the film. Satyajit Ray, Mrinal Sen, Gulzaar, Hrishikesh Mukherjee, V. Shantaram, Rajkumar, Uttam Kumar, Sandhya Roy, Pran, Shatrughan Sinha, Vinod Khanna, Danny Denzongpa, and National Award winner south Indian actress Snehalatha Reddy opposed and spoke against the Emergency. Reddy was jailed and tortured under MISA (Maintenance of Internal Security Act) in Bangalore for eight months and was released when her health deteriorated. She died within four to five days after her release.

Vinoba Bhave sanctioned the Emergency and described it as *Anushasan Parv* (festival of discipline). Bal Thackeray, M.G. Ramachandran, Mother Teresa were few people who supported the Emergency. Khushwant Singh not only supported the Emergency but was also one of the advisors and admirers of Sanjay Gandhi. Most of the chief ministers of the Congress-ruled states were more than keen to please Sanjay Gandhi who held no portfolio in the government or the Congress party. Indira Gandhi's helplessness in front of Sanjay Gandhi can be illustrated by a story in Washington post written by Pulitzer Prize-winning journalist Lewis M. Simons who was posted in India when the Emergency was declared. The story goes that before the imposition of Emergency, at a dinner party in Delhi, Sanjay Gandhi slapped Prime Minister Indira Gandhi in full public view. Simons was deported from India when he wrote a story on the views of the Indian defence forces on the Emergency. The journalist was posted back to India after the Emergency, and he met Indira, Rajiv Gandhi and Sonia Gandhi subsequently. Indira never made mention of the story. However, at a dinner party, Simons was introduced to Rajiv as the writer who had written the slapping story, to which Rajiv only smiled without saying a word. Simon writes that though Sonia remained silent, her looks were furious.[5]

The prime minister's twenty-point programme was introduced to give a fillip to industrial and agriculture growth. Many measures were taken to improve public service. Initially, the government servants, notorious for coming late to office, started coming on time. Routine bribery was stopped or was at a very minuscule level, trains started running on time. So, a section of the population saw it as a welcome relief from years of lethargy and indifferent attitude of government employees. In 1974, Sanjay Gandhi got married to Maneka, who was ten years younger than him. So, not only the Congress politicians' future but the destiny of the country was in the hands of a twenty-eight-year-old Sanjay and eighteen-year-old Maneka who was not even eligible to vote at that point of time, the voting age was twenty-one years. Sanjay Gandhi with no locus standi introduced the five-point programme to focus on literacy, tree planting, removal of casteism, end of dowry and family planning. Out of these programmes, the family planning programme was implemented most vigorously. Targets were given to each state. At the district level, all the government employees were given a quota to get a minimum number of cases of vasectomy or tubectomy. They were not given their salary until they had met their quota of sterilization. This whole sterilization programme of Sanjay Gandhi for birth control was called *nasbandi*. Under the guise of government reforms for birth control, the programme of 'sterilization' did not spare old men over seventy or unmarried boys of less than eighteen years. It is estimated that in the very first year, more than 60 lakh (6 million) people were sterilized. The figure of 4 lakh sterilizations done by Hitler pales in comparison. The anger against this forced move started simmering. In Muzaffarnagar, about thirty people died in police firing in a protest against it. Atal Behari Vajpayee wrote a poem that aptly reflected the state of affairs– *Aao Mardo Namard Bano* (Come and become unproductive due to sterilization and let us become cowards and remain silent against the atrocities).[6] Sanjay Gandhi's cynical way of administration got encouragement from chief ministers like Narain Dutt Tewari who publicly carried his shoes and the vice chairman of Delhi Development Authority (DDA) Jagmohan, who in the name of beautification bulldozed *jhuggis*(hutments) near Turkman Gate in Delhi. The protest by these temporary labourers was crushed by police firing in which more than 150 people died.

Indira Gandhi, in the absence of any opposition in the parliament, kept on changing the Constitution. Three people were primarily responsible for the imposition of Emergency—JP who gave ideological direction and leadership, George Fernandes who led the Rail Strike in which 17 lakh (1.7 million) workers directly participated and shook the Indira government and Raj Narain, the man who pursued the election petition which debarred her election. These three had one thing in common and that was they were die-hard socialists. Finally, on 18 January 1977 after about nineteen months, political prisoners were freed, restriction on rallies withdrawn and elections were called. The Emergency was withdrawn on 21 March 1977 and democracy was restored.

Notes

1. On 25 June 1975, President Fakhruddin Ali Ahmad, on the advice of Prime Minister Indira Gandhi signed the document of proclamation of Emergency. As per Article 352 of the Constitution, Emergency can be imposed due to internal disturbance in the country investing the government with unlimited powers and curbing civil rights.
2. Under Article 356 of the Constitution, if a state government is unable to function, the central (union) government takes direct control of the administration till a popular government is formed. The executive functions are done through the governor appointed by the centre.
3. Prashant Bhushan, 2017, *The Case That Shook India: The Verdict That Led to the Emergency*. India: Penguin Random House. The 336-page book is termed a legal and historical document.
4. Available at: https://www.theleaflet.in/the-judge-who-unseated-a-prime-minister/# (accessed on 15 January 2021).
5. 'First person: The story behind how Sanjay Gandhi slapped Indira six times at a dinner party'. Available at: https://scroll.in/article/736845/first-person-the-story-behind-how-sanjay-gandhi-slapped-indira-six-times-at-a-dinner-party (accessed on 28 January 2021).
6. Jeeta Jagta Purush. 2019, *Meri Ekyavan Kavitay*. New Delhi: Kitabghar.

CHAPTER-7

Sampoorna Kranti

The Collapse of the Janata Parivar, Idealist JP Betrayed

23 January 1977, Sunday

Historically one incident which brought the end of thirty years of Congress rule at the centre and which led to Indian democracy entering the era of multi-party governance was no doubt the Emergency of 1975. The Emergency was declared by President Fakhruddin Ali Ahmed under Article 352 (1) of the Constitution on the advice of Prime Minister Indira Gandhi on 25 June 1975, just a few minutes before the clock struck midnight. It lasted twenty-one long months beginning 25 June 1975 and going on until 21 March 1977. All the top opposition leadership at the national, state and district levels were put in jail. They were put behind bars on some frivolous charges and were treated as political prisoners. Jail gave them time to exchange views and develop camaraderie. Emergency excesses gave them the reason to unite against Indira Gandhi and against her party led by her, which was Congress (R). Letter R stood for 'Requisition'.

Indira wanted to free herself from the old Congress guards and wanted absolute control over the party. Indira ruthlessly outmanoeuvred her rivals, forcing the party to split in 1969—into the Congress (O) comprising the old guard led by Kamraj and her Congress (R). Indira's Congress (R) was of a different breed from the old Congress, which had been a robust institution with traditions of internal democracy. In Congress (R), on the other hand, the progress of the members within the ranks depended solely on their loyalty to Indira Gandhi. The ostentatious display of sycophancy was routine. Indira's influence was so strong that she could install hand-picked loyalists as chief ministers of states, rather than their being elected by the Congress legislative party. Later in the 1970s, the name Congress (R) evolved to Congress (I) where 'I' stood for Indira and gradually Congress (I) became the Indian National Congress.

Indira Gandhi declared on 18 January 1977 that general elections for the sixth Lok Sabha would be held. Leaders started coming out of jail. Jai Prakash Narain (popularly known as JP) presided over the meeting of leaders from different parties and the Janata Party was formed on 23 January 1977. The opposition experiment of Janata Morcha (People's Front) which won the Gujarat state assembly election just before the imposition of Emergency was the cornerstone of the Janata institution. During the Emergency, the leaders and activists of the Janata Morcha were imprisoned. A united front of all opposition political parties—the Bharatiya Lok Dal, the Swantantra party, the Socialist Party, the Bharatiya Jana Sangh, the Congress (O) merged into a common identity to be named as Janata Party. Chandrashekhar was made the president of the party for the rest of his life. He was commonly addressed as *Adyakshji* (President). Ram Krishna Hegde became the General Secretary. The *haldhar*or farmer with a plough symbol that belonged to Charan Singh's Bharatiya Lok Dal (BLD) became the election symbol for the Janata Party. It is again interesting to note that the two most powerful office-bearers of the Janata Party, which were going to fight Congress (R), had come out of Congress itself and both were from upper castes—Chandrashekhar was Rajput and Hegde was a Brahmin. The politics in the post-Janata era saw the emergence of backward class regional leadership, which dominated the entire political spectrum. The Janata Party still has its presence even after four decades and manifests itself in its various offshoots. In 2020,we can see that the Bharatiya Janata Party (BJP), Biju Janata Dal (BJD), Janata Dal (U), Janata Dal (S), Rashtriya Janata Dal (RJD)—all having Janata in their names are the offshoots of the Janata Party. They all have something common to draw from the 1977 Janata Party.

Things were happening at a rapid pace. A post-Emergency breakaway group from Congress (R) led by Jagjivan Ram, Hemvati Nandan Bahuguna, Nandani Sathpathy, etc. formed Congress for Democracy (CFD) on 2 February 1977. The condition of CFD to keep its identity and not formally merge or join the Janata Party was accepted. Perhaps, this shows that even the leadership of the Janata Party was not sure of its victory. Some sort of behind-the-scene arrangement was at work with old Congress buddies. The CPM (Communist Party of India [Marxist]) had declared that they would not put up a candidate against the Janata Party. The manifesto of the Janata Party was released on 10 February 1977.

Out of about 32 crores voters, 62 per cent participated in the elections. The campaigning was fierce. The Janata Dal with a galaxy of star campaigners was covering every nook and corner of the country. For the first time, a religious head came on the election platform of a political party urging to vote for the opposition. It is interesting to note that Shahi Imam of Jama Masjid, Delhi was roped in by the secularist Hemvati Nandan Bahuguna to campaign for Congress for Democracy (CFD) and the Janata Party. Bahuguna tried to create his vote bank and was therefore not genuine in his secularism. In the 1980s, Lal Krishna Advani coined the term *'pseudo-secularism'* to describe what he believed was tokenism towards members of India's minority communities. As per the Election Commission's directives, appealing for votes from any religious place such as a temple, gurudwara, church, masjid, etc. or using them for the election campaign is a violation of the Model Code of Conduct.

Results came out on 23 March 1977. The Bharatiya Lok Dal (BLD) won 295 seats out of 405 it fought. Technically, the election symbol used by the Janata Party was of BLD and in the Election Commission archives, it is reflected as BLD and not as the Janataparty's symbol. Congress with 154 seats and 34.5 per cent votes emerged as the main opposition party. One of the most shocking outcomes of the election was the defeat of Indira Gandhi from her constituency of Rae Bareilly, which she lost to her opponent Raj Narain by a margin of 55,200 votes. George Fernandes, still in jail, won with record votes from Muzaffarpur in Bihar. The Janata Party alliance won 345 seats with 51.89 per cent votes. The results showed a North–South divide. The majority of Janata Party seats came from the Hindi heartland of Uttar Pradesh—85/85, Bihar—52/54, Rajasthan—24/25, Madhya Pradesh—37/40, Haryana—10/10. The Janata Party got only 6 seats from four southern states and was not able to open its account in Kerala.

JP and Acharya J.B. Kripalani administered the oath to

newly elected MPs at Rajghat on 24th March. They pledged to walk on the path shown by Gandhi. The most difficult and challenging task was choosing a leader to become India's new prime minister. The main contenders for the post of prime minister were Morarji Desai, Charan Singh and Jagjivan Ram. All three were former Congressmen. It was ironic that the people responsible for choosing the prime ministerial candidate had been anti-Congress all their lives. Since independence, parties like Socialist, Communist and Jana Sangh, and their leaders had worked against Congress philosophy and rule. Since no consensus was achieved, to avoid a potentially divisive contest, Janata leaders asked JP and Kripalani to select the prime ministerial candidate, agreeing to abide by their choice. Ironically, these two leaders, who were entrusted to choose one of the former congressmen to lead the group, were also the champions of anti-Congress policies. This group had nothing in common besides their opposition to Indira Gandhi and the Congress. After a lot of deliberation, JP and Kripalani chose Morarji Desai as the prime minister. The Congress tradition of choosing the parliamentary party leader by the high command (in this case JP and Kripalani) and not through election was also maintained. To please everyone, both Charan Singh and Jagjivan Ram were given the title of Deputy Prime Minister. They were also given additional portfolios. Charan Singh became the Minister of Home Affairs, the second-most important position in the Council of Ministers, while Jagjivan Ram took charge of the Ministry of Defence. The hope was kept alive that someday they will reach the prime ministerial position for which party principles, etc. could be compromised.

One example can be given to illustrate the morality and personal honesty of leadership in India. After three decades of getting independence, when Indira Gandhi lost her seat from Rae Bareli, neither she nor her family had any accommodation. She was not entitled to any government bungalow. The plot on the outskirts of Delhi, originally purchased by her estranged husband Feroze Gandhi, was the only property that this dictator, architect of Emergency and the murderer of democracy had. The move by some Janata Party leaders to throw her out of her Akbar Road residence was stoutly opposed by JP. She moved to the 12, Willingdon Crescent bungalow of Mohd Yunus and was charged the market rate as rent. She remained president of the party which headed for another split. She was expelled from the party and Congress (I) was born. One of the reasons to contest and return to parliament was to get a roof above her head. The political reasons to fight the elections were many but being an elected member of parliament would not only give her a voice inside the parliament but would entitle her to meet a lot of foreign dignitaries. It also gave her protection against lots of cases, enquiries and commissions instituted by the Janata government. Congress had won 26 out of 28 seats in Karnataka. D.B. Chandra Gowda who was in the Praja Socialist Party, later joined Congress and became MP from Chikmagalur, vacated his seat to allow Indira Gandhi to contest and win the election from there. Indira defeated Virendra Patil by 77,000 votes in 1978 and entered parliament. Raj Kumar the south Indian film icon was approached to contest elections against Indira Gandhi. When he refused, Virendra Patil became the Janata Party candidate. The campaign of Patil was spearheaded by Hegde and the son of the soil George Fernandes. Regarding D.B. Chandra Gowda, he later left Congress (I) and joined Congress (U). In 1986, he was elected as Member of Parliament in Rajya Sabha, representing the Janata Dal. He finally became MP on a BJP ticket in the 2009 Lok Sabha elections. It reflects the classic example of defection in Indian polity to gain power. The huge floor-crossing which was done by the members of the political parties sometimes gives them the epithet *'Aaya Ram, Gaya Ram'*. The politics of defection exposes the most immoral and unethical character of our politicians making a mockery of our democracy.

N. Sanjeeva Reddy, who was the official presidential candidate of congress in 1969, lost to V.V. Giri an independent, backed by Indira Gandhi, who appealed to her party voters to vote as per their conscience. After the defeat, Reddy took retirement from active politics (politicians taking retirement is a rare phenomenon). However, on the call of JP, he entered active politics again. He was the only non-Congressman to win a seat from Andhra Pradesh, in 1977 when Congress won all the remaining Lok Sabha seats. He became the speaker of the Lok Sabha for the shortest period of three months and seventeen days. After the death of the President, Fakhruddin Ali Ahmed, he was elected unopposed President of India in July 1977. This is another record to his name to win the election unopposed.

One act of imposition of Emergency had put Indira Gandhi in the category of leaders who had no respect for the law of the land and for endangering all the democratic institutions. Elected governments formed by Congress (R) in various states were not allowed to complete their term and elections were called by the Janata Party who were considered as the new custodian of democracy. The justification given was that since Congress (R) had lost parliament elections, so they had lost the moral right to continue for the rest of the term in the states as well. Elections were held in ten states. The Janata Party formed a government in Uttar Pradesh, Bihar, Orissa, Haryana, Madhya Pradesh, Rajasthan, Himachal Pradesh and Delhi. Shiromani Akali Dal (SAD) in coalition with the Janata Party formed a government in Punjab. Sheikh Abdullah returned to power in Jammu and Kashmir. Though the parties had merged, they maintained their loyalty with the bosses of their pre-merger original parties. The new chief ministers in the four states—Kailash Joshi in Madhya Pradesh, Bhairon Singh Shekhawat in Rajasthan, Shanta Kumar in Himachal Pradesh and Kedar Nath Sahni in Delhi—were all RSS (Rashtriya Swayamsevak Sangh) veterans. In these four states, the erstwhile Bharatiya Jana Sangh was numerically in a commanding position.

Devilal in Haryana and Nilamani Routray in Orissa were known as Charan Singh (BLD) loyalists and were made chief ministers. The stakes in Uttar Pradesh (Uttarakhand was a part of UP) and Bihar (Jharkhand was part of Bihar) were high as in these two states 138 MPs out of 140 were elected on Janata Party tickets. In Bihar, Karpoori Thakur backed by Charan Singh and the Socialist Party was pitted against Satyendra Narain Singh of Congress (O). The election of the state legislature party was held on 21 June 1977 to elect their leader and the legislature belonging to the erstwhile Bharatiya Jana Sangh voted for Karpoori Thakur. The following day on 22 June, the State Legislature party of Uttar Pradesh was to elect their leader. It was a sequel of Bihar in which Ram Naresh Yadav was backed by Charan Singh and Ram Dhan was backed by C.B. Gupta (Cong. O). Again, legislature having allegiance to Bharatiya Jana Sangh threw their weight behind Ram Naresh Yadav. Morarji Desai was the prime minister but Charan Singh with four chief ministers under his command was in no mood to play second fiddle to Morarji Bhai.

The seeds of the end of the Janata Parivaar experiment started the day Morarji Desai took the oath of office. Charan Singh who was a grassroots leader from Uttar Pradesh, the state which had the privilege of giving the maximum number of prime ministers always maintained that his claim for prime ministership was ignored. He considered himself as worthy of being the prime minister as Desai. He had agreed to be number two on one condition that the CBI should come under the direct control of the Ministry of Home Affairs. Till then, the CBI was under the administrative control of the prime minister.

The cabinet took some important decisions like it withdrew the Baroda Dynamite case and reinstated the suspended rail strike workers of 1974. Some other major decisions taken by the Janata Party government were setting up various commissions, committees and inquiries against Indira Gandhi on charges of corruption, favouritism, human rights violations, etc. An inquiry was set up on the working of Maruti Udyog Limited. Though publicly, Janata Party had taken a stand that no vindictive politics for wrong doings of Emergency would be done, Charan Singh started his plan of putting Indira Gandhi behind bars. An FIR was lodged by CBI in August but at the last minute, Morarji Bhai put his foot down and the same was postponed. In the meantime, the Shah Commission started its hearing of many old Indira loyalists deposed before the commission blaming Indira and Sanjay.

Indira Gandhi had an uncanny sense of timing. She knew the pulse of the people and had no match in Indian politics regarding her expertise in seizing a political opportunity. On 27 May 1977, eight Harijans and three Sunars (goldsmiths) were burnt alive by Kurmis in a tiny, nondescript village called Belchi. This village was in Bihar

Sharif under the Nalanda district in Bihar. It was a stronghold of Kurmis. In the post Mandal era, Nitish Kumar had strong control over this area. This is the constituency from where Nitish Kumar was elected MP and also got George Fernandes elected before denying a party ticket to him in Muzzafarpur. The leader of opposition, Y.B. Chavan had announced his plan to visit Belchi but somehow this visit was not materializing. Indira's political acumen sensed the opportunity. She reached Patna by air on 13 August 1977 and started her journey by road. Due to the rainy season, roads were in bad shape; so, she dumped the car and started the journey by a tractor. The tractor got stuck and it seemed the journey had ended. The consensus was to abandon the trip, go back to Patna and come back after the downpour stopped. But Indira was made of different stuff. She started her march on foot. She had walked a few kilometres without showing any signs of tiredness and fatigue when Moti, the elephant, came to her rescue. Riding on Moti, Indira had started her journey back to regain the lost prime minister's chair. The welcome response from the local population and media gave Indira the confidence and fillip needed to fight her adversaries. The Belchi visit at once changed the perception about the Gandhi family and the Congress. After Belchi, Indira Gandhi just marched from one place to another, emerging a 'saviour' of the oppressed class.

On 3 October 1977, CBI knocked at 12,Willingdon Crescent at 4.55 in the evening to arrest the former prime minister of India. All the family members did their bit to maximize the advantage of this arrest. Maneka called the *Surya* office, the magazine she edited. Her assistant editor Raghu started mobilizing media, especially foreign correspondents. Sanjay was super active and stepped out to organize the sloganeering. They were apprehending this situation and the counter measures planned well in advance for such an eventuality were set in motion. On receiving the call, Jagdish Tytler came with a couple of vans loaded with young people. All the big wigs and politicians close to Indira Gandhi gathered. Indira was taking her time to maximize the political benefit from the arrest. As per the report of magazine *India Today*, two people were visibly upset. Bansi Lal's reason for dismay was because the policeman outside failed to recognize him as he had lost a lot of weight and Rajiv Gandhi walked up and down with a screwdriver and plier in hand for reasons unknown. Indira insisted to be handcuffed when she walked out of her house to give the desired filmy effect. The crowd had gathered and at 7.30, she decided to come out. Indira Gandhi marked her time well. The magazine reports that the slogans were not yet loud enough. As if she was giving an encore, she went in and out of her bedroom door three times so that the volume and the pitch of sloganeering were raised. She finally came out, waved from the car and the cavalcade moved with Sanjay and Rajiv driving separate Matador vans. These Matador vans were patronized by Sanjay during the Emergency period. It was the dream car of every aspiring Youth Congress leader. In recent times, Toyota Fortuner has occupied that slot in the Hindi heartland. Anyone, who wants to leave the impression that he is something in politics, must ride a Fortuner.

Charan Singh who as the home minister was keeping a close tab on her arrest reached the cabinet meeting fifteen minutes late. By that time, the proposal of Jagjivaan Ram that CBI should not take her on police remand was accepted. Indira was freed the next day and this proved to be a turning point not only for her comeback but also the beginning of the end of the Janata Party experiment. Indira, who had survived many divisions in Congress, used this arrest and inquiries in a way that she was portrayed as the victim or oppressed and Janata leaders as her oppressors. Observers compare the 3 October arrest of Indira Gandhi to make a point that though India and Pakistan embarked on their journey of democracy together the Indian democracy had grown deep roots in thirty years despite an-eighteen-month Emergency. Zulfikar Ali Bhutto, ten years younger than Indira Gandhi, was arrested about three months before her on 5 July 1977 and subsequently hanged.

India was moving ahead under the leadership of new leaders who were not led by a strong prime minister. One of the decisions of Morarji Bhai which was remembered for a very long time was to introduce prohibition from 1 April 1977. Going by his track record of putting Gujarat state under prohibition, his proposal was not taken lightly. Though years after Tamil Nadu and Bihar enforced prohibition in different forms, IBM and Coca Cola were shown the door by the Industry minister George Fernandes when they refused to follow the FERA (Foreign Exchange Regulation Act) norms.

On the international front, the victory of the Janata Party was hailed both by Pakistan and China. Pakistan jubilation was understandable as they held Indira responsible for their 1971 crushing defeat and for creating Bangladesh. India, in all these years, had moved closer to the Soviet Union making China uncomfortable. Atal Bihari Bajpayee, who was the Foreign Affairs minister in 1979, was the first to visit China after 1962 and resumed ties with our north-eastern neighbour. Bang Bandhu Sheikh Mujibur Rahman, the founding father of Bangladesh, was treated in India as a half-brother. After the assassination of Mujib in 1975, the relations between the countries were not very congenial. The Janata Party government ended the support extended to guerrillas loyal to Mujib. The visit of the American President is always important for any country. In the past, two presidents of the US Eisenhower and Nixon had visited India but it was part of the tour package of India and Pakistan. In 1978, Jimmy Carter came for an exclusive three-day visit to India.

The difference between Charan Singh and Morarji Bhai grew and in April 1978, Charan Singh resigned from the executive committee of the Janata Party. The race for the chair was becoming murkier with each passing day and the sons of Morarji Bhai and Jagjivan Ram were targeted. Questions were asked about alleged business dealings conducted by Kantibhai from the prime minister's residence. Questions were raised when the prime minister's plane while coming back from the Soviet Union made an unscheduled stopover at Tehran to drop Kantibhai. Deputy Prime Minister and Home Minister Chaudhary Charan Singh with CBI directly under his ministry was becoming difficult for Prime Minister Morarji Desai. The other contender Jagjivan Ram was in a hot spot when *Surya* magazine, edited by Maneka, printed semi-nude pictures of his son Suresh Kumar. The photographs were delivered to Khushwant Singh from an unknown source.

Indira Gandhi was back in parliament, which gave her a lot of privilege. She was using the opportunity more outside the parliament than participating in any serious debate in the parliament. A unique thing happened in December 1978. The Janata government, to tame Indira, decided to play the masterstroke. The masterstroke designed and executed by the Chanakyas of the Janata Party was executed on 19 December 1978. In an unprecedented move, she was expelled from parliament for the alleged breach of privilege and contempt of the fifth Lok Sabha and sentenced to jail till the prorogation of the session. The motion was passed by 279 votes in favour and 138 against, while 37 preferred to abstain. She again grabbed the opportunity with open arms and never even challenged the expulsion. Indira was able to change the attitude of voters. She was successful in presenting herself as a victim and oppressed.

Backroom negotiations were on. After a long negotiation, Charan Singh was back as the finance minister but Raj Narain, a socialist and the former health minister who was also shown the door with Charan Singh, was not rehabilitated. It was wrongly presumed that Charan Singh was so busy in planning to dislodge Morarji Desai, had forgotten Raj Narain. The next move by the camp against Charan Singh was to dislodge his chief ministers. Another undercurrent in the party was going on, which Madhu Limaye, one of the best political analysts of his time, was able to read. Bharatiya Jana Sangh, the most disciplined party in the history of Indian democracy even after thirty years of independence, was slowly working towards the goal of capturing the organization of the Janata Party. The different groups of the Janata Party had only one goal in common and that was to oust Indira Gandhi. The socialists, who were the champions of the anti-Congress crusade, had no problems being led by a Congressman either within the party or in the government. Jana Sangh remained the most cohesive group in the Janata Party at both the centre and state levels. Being guided by the Rashtriya Swyamsevak Sangh (RSS), they were guided by people outside the party. Madhu Limay objected to the organization election knowing fully well that no one stood a chance with the discipline and bargaining power that Jan Sangh enjoyed.

The question of dual membership was raised. It was argued that Janata Party members of different parties, who had merged their political outfits must give up their membership of other organizations. By this logic, Jana Sangh members who continued to be members of RSS must leave their RSS affiliation. The issue of dual membership had simmered for two years as the Jana Sangh was seen rapidly consolidating its base while socialists and other disorganized splinter groups faced political erasure.

Now, new alignment and regrouping started within the party. Friends started becoming foes. Morarji Bhai now had new friends in form of Jana Sangh who had to fall back on him after Ram Naresh Yadav sacked a few Jana Sangh ministers due to religious clashes in the state. This Uttar Pradesh chief minister was a known Charan Singh loyalist. Socialists were no longer friends of the Jana Sanghis. Jagjivan Ram, who was also a contender for the prime minister's post, and party president Chandrashekhar were comfortable with Morarji Desai. The first surgery was performed in Uttar Pradesh. Ram Naresh Yadav had to vacate his seat and old Congress (O) veteran Banarsi Das became the chief minister in February 1979. Satyendra Narain Singh whowas defeated by Karpoori Thakur in the state legislature party election in 1977 now backed Ram Sundar Das. As a result, Charan Singh loyalist Karpoori Thakur was ousted by Ram Sundar Das who became the Chief Minister of Bihar in April 1979. The surgery was complete on the Charan Singh camp when Devi Lal lost chief ministership to Bhajan Lal in June 1979. When the rival camp was busy in fixing Charan Singh, the wily Raj Narain was engineering a coup against Morarji Bhai's government. He was in contact with Sanjay Gandhi.

Another record was being set in the sixth Lok Sabha. Y.B. Chavan became the leader of the opposition on 1st July 1977 after the Janata Party came to power and remained in position till 11 April 1978. After the split in Congress and a majority of MPs throwing their weight behind Indira Gandhi, C.M. Stephen became the leader of the opposition from 12 April 1978 to 9 July 1979. Once again, a breakaway group of some Janata Party MPs became part of the Chavan Congress and going by the number game, he replaced C.M. Stephen of Congress (I) on 10 July 1979 as leader of the opposition. Chavan remained in that position for nineteen days up to 28 July 1979. The story continued further and Jagjivan Ram, a serious contender for the prime minister's post became the leader of the opposition from 29 July to 22 August 1979. The sixth Lok Sabha had the distinction of having four leaders of the opposition, a record not easy to be broken.

The monsoon session of Lok Sabha started on 9 July 1979 and Y.B. Chavan moved a no-confidence motion which came up for discussion on 11 July. Raj Narain, the chief architect of making Charan Singh the prime minister met President Sanjeeva Reddy with a list of forty Janata Party MPs who had lost trust in the Morarji Desai government. The debate continued for four days; Charan Singh refused to defend the government. On 14 July, George Fernandes, one of the best speakers of free India, was at his best in defending the Morarji Desai government. 15th July being Sunday, the vote on the confidence motion was put on for 16 July 1979. Morarji knew he had lost the numbers. He resigned on 15 July. Charan Singh resigned from the Janata Party on 16 July to form a new party Janata Party (S). Indian parliament had never witnessed such a sale purchase of torchbearers of democracy. Both the Janata

Party and Janata Party (S) submitted a list to the President claiming majority.

The formal list of Charan Singh along with letters and a list of the supporting parties was submitted to the President on 23 and 25 July to stake claim to form the government. It was proposed to form a coalition government of the Janata Party (S) and Congress (U). The coalition got support from outside by Congress (I). Though Janata Party remained the single largest party, Charan Singh got support from 77 MPs of Janata Party (S), 14 Independents, 75 Congress, 72 Congress (I), 22 CPM and 18 ADMK making it 278 to cross the halfway mark of 273. The President was satisfied and Charan Singh was called to form the government. The letter of support of Congress (I) mentioned that they are supporting the coalition to keep Jana Sangh out of government. Charan Singh with eight cabinet ministers took oath on 28th July 1979. Y.B. Chavan in the bargain was made Deputy Prime Minister with an additional portfolio of the home ministry. The frontline socialist Madhu Limay, George Fernandes and Raj Narain kept themselves away from the government to strengthen the party and organization. The bigwigs of Congress like Brahamanand Reddy, Karan Singh, K.C. Pant, T.A. Pai, etc. had to wait as Indira was not ready to include their names. They were part of the Indira cabinet during the emergency and had given statements against her in various inquiry commissions. Once again, behind-the-scene operators worked overtime and six Congress ministers took oath on 30 July. The Indian voter felt cheated. They had voted for Janata Party on the promise of changing the system, they had voted to end the misrule of Congress and Indira, but now they had a government where it was difficult to decide who fought against whom.

Morarji Desai resigned as leader of the parliamentary party and Jagjivan Ram was elected the new leader. Indira played her cards well. Charan Singh was asked to withdraw the cases instituted against her immediately and without giving further time, withdrew support. Charan Singh resigned after twenty-three days in office without facing the parliament. The claim of Jagjivan Ram was not entertained and fresh elections were announced by the President. Despite a strong start, the Janata government withered due to ideological and political differences. Its tenure in office was tumultuous and not very successful. The myopic personal ambitions of its leadership, Morarji Desai, Charan Singh and Jagjivan Ram, caused political turmoil in New Delhi. In less than thirty-four months, Indira Gandhi, who was supposed to have been 'consigned to the dustbin of history', was back in power. Jayaprakash Narayan, the man who dreamt total revolution and worked so hard towards it, saw the end of all his dreams and values buried by his men before he breathed his last on 8 October 1979.

Chapter-8

Kapil da Jawab Nahin

From Under Dogs to World Champion

25 June 1983, Saturday

The year 1983 was one of the most happening years. The country was engaged in handling the Punjab problem but it also proved to be the year, which changed the way sports were to be seen in the country. On 25 June 1983, India won the coveted third edition of the World Cup, then known as the Prudential Cup. India defeated the mighty West Indies in the finals at the iconic Lord's ground in England. It will be interesting to glance at the achievement of Indian sports after Independence. A nation came into existence where all the citizens were stakeholders in writing the destiny of the country from day one. The largest democracy in the world made decisions for the overall growth of the country. A country plundered of its economic wealth for centuries is not only able to provide for a large population but is now a global power. Sports has never been the priority area—neither at the time of Independence nor today and whatever is achieved in this field is just because of the passion of individuals.

At the time of Independence, hockey was no doubt the pride of India. The journey started in 1928 at the Amsterdam

Olympics. India was the first non-European nation to compete and win a gold medal. This was no mean achievement. This was followed up in 1932 at Los Angeles and then in 1936 at Berlin Olympics. It was in Berlin, where the famous conversation between Dhyanchand and Hitler took place. An Indian group of twenty-four players went to Berlin. Out of these twenty-four players, sixteen were hockey players. They participated as a separate contingent. Technically they were representing colonial India. In 1931, the International Olympic Committee awarded the 1936 Summer Olympics to Berlin, when Germany was not under Nazi rule. Subsequently, the Nazis were in power when the 1936 Olympic was held in Berlin; with Hitler in command, tension was inevitable. Since the Olympic salute was very similar to the Nazi salute, many countries did not want to salute Hitler during the march past. There were fifty-one participating nations and many of them, including Great Britain and the USA, as a grand gesture of defiance refused to do the traditional Olympic salute. Instead, they did the military-style eyes right salute while passing the post where Hitler was standing. The German contingent consisted of 348 sportsmen and they were closely watched by Hitler.

On arriving in Germany, India played a warm-up hockey match with host Germany which they lost by one goal to four. Dhyanchand was the captain and centre-forward of the team. Ali Iqtedar Shah, popularly known as Dara, used to play inside-right and was denied leave to participate in the Berlin Olympics. The shocking defeat was an eye-opener and rang alarm bells in the Indian camp. A meeting was held and Dara was summoned on an urgent basis to reach Berlin. Ali Iqtidar Shah Dara later represented Pakistan as their team captain in the 1948 Olympics following the Partition. India was in a different group than Germany and won all three group matches. They beat Hungary 4-0, USA 7-0 and Japan 9-0. Dara reached a day before the semi-finals with France in which India won 10-0. Now the final was to be played with Germany. The German team was upbeat as Adolf Hitler was scheduled to watch the final along with more than 40,000 Germans. In the first half of the match, India scored just one goal. The second half started and the crowd was dumbfounded to see that Dhyanchand, the captain of the Indian Hockey team, had discarded his spiked shoes and stockings and was playing with simple rubber sole shoes. Team India was in a different mood. After conceding three more goals, the Germans started playing very rough and Dhyanchand was targeted. The deliberate push inside D by the German goalkeeper was so hard that Dhyanchand lost his teeth. Dhyanchand came back on the field and the 40,000-strong crowd saw the artistry and magic of not only Dhyanchand but the entire Indian team. The final score was 8-1 in favour of India.

Though a soldier, Hitler lacked sportsman spirit and he left the ground before the end of the match. Perhaps, he wanted to avoid giving the gold with his own hands to the winning Indian team. Dhyanchand was summoned later by Hitler. An apprehensive Dhyanchand during the conversation told him that he was a lance naik in the Indian Army. Hitler then offered him to join the German army and told him that he would be made the field marshal. Recalling the moment, Dhyanchand said that he was not able to understand whether it was a command or request from Hitler. But his answer to the most powerful man on the earth then was that he was fine serving his country India.

After Independence, India won three straight gold medals in Hockey—in 1948, 1952 and 1956 Olympics. In the finals of the 1960 Rome Olympics, Pakistan won gold after defeating India 1-0. By this time, India had made a record of thirty straight wins in the Olympics without a single loss. India won back gold in the 1964 Tokyo Olympics and had to satisfy herself with bronze (third place) in the 1968 and 1972 Olympics. In the 1976 Montreal Olympics, for the first time, field hockey was played on astroturfinstead of grass and we were without a medal that year. In 1980, sixty-five nations boycotted the Moscow Olympics to protest against the invasion of Afghanistan by the USSR. Big names like West Germany, Holland, Australia, New Zealand and Pakistan were absent in hockey. Six teams that participated were Poland, Spain, Russia, Cuba and Tanzania besides India. We defeated Tanzania 18-0, Cuba 13-0, Russia 4-2 and struggled with Poland and Spain for a draw. In the finals, we defeated Spain 4-3 and won the gold.

The only time we won the Hockey World Cup was in 1975 in Malaysia. It was the third edition and we defeated Pakistan, winner of the first world cup by 2-1. Since the 1980 Olympics and 1975 World Cup till 2019, the Indian hockey team had not reached even up to the semi-finals in these two events. It is no more the national sports of the country.

Another game in which India earned reputation was tennis. India has been participating in the Davis Cup, the international team event held every year since 1921. It is organized by the International Tennis Federation (ITF). India in the last hundred years reached the finals of the Davis Cup thrice—in 1966, 1974 and 1987. In independent India, Ramanathan Krishnan in 1962 was fourth seed at

Wimbledon and also the most famous of the trio of the sixties which took Indian tennis to new heights. Jaideep Mukherjee and Premjit Lal along with Krishnan earned a lot of respect for India in world tennis. The seventies belonged to Vijay Amritraj and Anand Amritraj who took the Indian team to the finals of the Davis Cup. In 1974, India was to play against South Africa in the finals. But due to the apartheid policy of the South African government, India boycotted to play against them as a mark of protest. In 1974, the Amritraj brothers were in such good form that it was widely believed that the Davis Cup title was in their pocket.

Another British legacy that we inherited is billiards and snooker. Billiards is played with three balls—red, white and yellow. The striker or cue balls of the two opponents are white and yellow. Snooker is played with twenty-two balls—fifteen red, six coloured and one white, which is the striker ball. William Jones, an Anglo Indian, won the World Amateur Billiards Championship (WABC) twice in 1958 and 1964. Michel Ferreira is another legend who had three WABC titles against his name in 1977, 1981 and 1983. Geet Sethi won WABC three times in 1985, 1987 and 2001. He won the World Professional Billiards Championship (WPBC) five times in 1992, 1993, 1995, 1998 and 2006. Pankaj Advani, the youngest of the lot, is also an illustrious billiards and snooker player who has made his mark not only in India but in the world. He had twenty-three world championships till 2019 under his belt. He has five hat-tricks of billiards to his credit. In the years 2005, 2008, 2012, 2017 and 2019, he was the World Champion, Asian Champion and National Champion.

Out of many sports icons of independent India, we will briefly try to touch on the achievements of a few of them. The tallest in the track and field is Milkha Singh, a refugee from Pakistan, who broke the world record but missed the medal in 400 meters in the 1960 Rome Olympics. The same year, while participating in Pakistan, he was called the 'Flying Singh' by General Ayub, the President of Pakistan. This title remained with him throughout his life. 'Payyoli Express' P.T. Usha broke the national record of the 400-metre hurdles at the 1984 Los Angeles Olympic but missed the medal. Her record is still to be broken. Both these athletes won many medals in different international meets but in the Olympics, they had to satisfy themselves by the fourth position.

Badminton is another sport where we can boast of producing world champions. Prakash Padukone was ranked world no. 1 in 1980. Padukone and P. Gopichand won the All England Open in 1980 and 2001 respectively. Srikanth Kidambi was ranked world no. 1 for one week in 2018. In women's badminton, we can boast of many good players. Saina Nehwal a former world no.1 has more than twenty-four international titles to her credit. Though P. V. Sindhu became the first Indian to become the Badminton World Champion, her best ranking is as world no. 2. Jwala Gutta, born of a Chinese mother and Tamil father, is the only Indian player who was in the top-10 world ranking in both mixed (sixth in 2010) as well as women's doubles (tenth in 2015). She has more than 300 match wins in both the disciplines which is the highest by any Indian. Gutta is the only doubles players (out of the top ten) to use a forehand service, unlike other doubles players who use backhand serve.

The journey of cricket started in India when the Calcutta Club (CC) was formed by the Britishers in 1792. It is the second-oldest cricket club in the world after MCC (1787). The present BCCI (Board of Control of Cricket in India) was formed in December 1928 with British businessman Grant Govan as the first president and Anthony De Mello as the first secretary. BCCI is a private body registered as a society under the Tamil Nadu Societies Registration Act. For many years, BCCI worked as a non-profit body and escaped from the Income Tax Act, but in the recent past, they have been under the net of the Income Tax Act and are paying taxes. In 2017, the Supreme Court of India formed a four-member committee of administrators to streamline the affairs of the BCCI.

Limited-overs cricket was popular in England but other test-playing nations were reluctant to adopt this format. Cricket was a 'gentleman's game' played in a standard white dress and a red ball. England and Australia ruled the world of cricket. The International Cricket Council (ICC) was based in England giving them some advantage to run the game their way. Australia with its all-time great Don Bradman in their fold had their specific outlook towards the game. Australia even had an eight-ball over instead of six-ball over. In 1970 in Australia, Karry Packer started the World Series Cricket (WSC) in competition with the International Cricket Council (ICC). It completely changed the way of playing conventional cricket then. It was a revolutionary concept. Coloured dress instead of the traditional white, white ball with black sight screen instead of the red ball with a white screen, matches played in floodlight at night instead of daylight, television multiple cameras, microphones, etc. were all revolutionary innovations that grabbed people's interest. It was the limited-over version that became known as the 'pyjama game'. The ICC responded by organizing limited-overs – sixty overs in the first World Cup held in England in 1975. The tournament had eight participating countries. Six test-playing nations of the time, that is Australia, England, India, New Zealand, Pakistan, the West Indies and the two leading associate nations Sri Lanka and East Africa. Sri Lanka got the test playing status in 1982 as the eighth nation. Though a test playing nation, South Africa was banned from playing cricket from 1970 to 1991 due to apartheid policy.

In 1975, 1979 and 1983, the World Cup was hosted by England. West Indies won the championship in 1975 and 1979, beating Australia and England respectively. A total of eight teams in two groups played each other twice. India, Australia, West Indies and Zimbabwe were in Group B. The top two teams from both the groups qualified for the semi-finals. The biggest upset of the tournament happened on the inaugural day on 9 June in Group B. Zimbabwe, a debutant team of 1983 World Cup, won against Australia, runners-up of the 1975 World Cup. India was pitted against West Indies, who were two times champion of the 1975 and 1979 World Cup. India batted first and scored 260 for 8 and in reply, West Indies were all out for 228 in 54.1 overs. The Indian bowlers put up a brilliant show. Roger Binny took 3 wickets for 48 runs and Ravi Shastri took 3 wickets for 26 runs. They were responsible for sending the entire West Indies team back to the pavilion. This was the first loss for West Indies in the eight-year history of the World Cup. Yashpal Sharma was adjudged Man of the Match for his knock of eighty-nine runs. This was the turning point of the tournament when underdogs India under the legendary captaincy of Kapil Dev became serious about themselves. India won against Zimbabwe and lost to Australia in the first round. In the second round, West Indies defeated India and on 18 June 1983, India played their most sensational match against Zimbabwe. Indian openers Gavaskar and Srikanth were out without scoring. India was

5 down at the score of 17 and then 7 for 78 runs. India would have been out of the tournament if this crucial match was lost. Madan Lal was the eighth man out at the score of 148 with Kapil Dev on the crease. The tenth man to walk in was Syed Kirmani who was the wicket-keeper of India. He was not known for his batting skills but he proved to be the sheet anchor. India's score was 266 at the end of 60 overs without any more wickets falling. Syed Kirmani was 24 not out and Kapil Dev played the innings of his life – 175 not out, strike rate 126.81 unheard of in those days.

The India team got their rhythm and defeated Australia in the last group match. In the semi-final, India won against the home team England and marched ahead to play against the West Indies in the finals. West Indies won the semi-finals against Pakistan. History was to be made on 25 June 1983. India was all out for 183 runs. West Indies had an impressive batting line—up of Greenidge, Haynes, Richards, Llyods and Gomes. They had only one defeat in the three world cups till then. Mohinder Amarnath and Madan Lal took 3 wickets each and sent the West Indies back to the pavilion with 140 all out. India was the new World Champion.

The journey of cricket from a strictly amateur game into a multi billion-dollar industry brought with it the problems and pitfalls of any business. India, which had the oldest tradition of gambling where King Yudhishtira not only lost his kingdom but also his brother and wife, is covered by the Public Gambling Act (1867), which makes all kinds of gambling illegal. The only exception to this is betting on horse racing at the trackside. Betting which is legal in many cricket-playing countries is banned in India. The scale of the game and the money in cricket was phenomenal. BCCI under the leadership of Jagmohan Dalmia and Lalit Modi reached its pinnacle and the match-fixing scandal in 1999–2000 shook not only the entire nation but also the world.

The story starts from Leeds in July 1981, where the third test of the Ashes series between Australia and England was being played. England was one down in the series and Australia batting first made 401 for 9 declared. In reply, England made 174 in the first inning and got the follow-on. In the second inning, with a score of 7 wickets down for 135 runs, the defeat of England was a forgone conclusion. Lillie and Marsh placed a bet on England win which was 500-1, the highest in the history of cricket. England made 356 and set a target of 130 for Australia to win. Australia in the first inning had lost their second wicket at the score of 149. But in the second inning, Australia was all out for 111 and England won the series. Lillie and Marsh won ..7,500. Another incident was in 1994 when Mark Waugh and Shane Warne received payments of 4,000 and 5,000 respectively for sharing pitch and weather information during the Sri Lanka tour. Cricket Australia came to know about this in 1995 and fined the duo but withheld the information from the public till 1998.

It is alleged that in the Indian subcontinent, the seeds of match-fixing were sown when Sharjah started hosting one-day matches during the 1980s and 1990s. Betting was prevalent and match-fixing started under the protection of the criminal syndicate supervision where the result of the match was pre-determined and known to a set of people who were driving the market through bookmakers. So spot-fixing followed match-fixing. Apart from the result of the match, bets were placed on the toss, overs, the number of balls, wide balls, run-outs, etc. and it took test cricket as well as one-day matches in its grip. Slowly this match-fixing—betting coalition spread its wing throughout the world. Singapore, China and India developed as its capital cities.

The Delhi police intercepted the conversation between Hansie Cronje, South African captain and the bookie. The South African government intervened and refused to give their consent for investigation by the Indian agency. In South Africa, before the court of inquiry, Cronje accepted the charges. Three captains were banned for life –Hansie Cronje of South Africa, Salim Malik of Pakistan and Mohd Azharuddin of India. The country was shocked as Azharuddin, Ajay Sharma, Jadeja and Manoj Prabhakar were banned from playing cricket from five years to lifetime. This ban was lifted subsequently. It was very difficult to prove someone guilty. Now the beans were spilt and it was evident that match-fixing was the order of the day. With the massive influx of money and the sheer increase in the number of matches played, cricket has become a big business.

Chapter-9

When a Big Tree Falls, the Earth Shakes

Operation Blue Star, the Cause of Indira Gandhi's Assassination

31 October 1984, Wednesday

On Baisakhi, 13 April 1978, a Sant Nirankari Convention was organized in Amritsar to celebrate the birth of Khalsa. Permission was sought from the Akali government. As per tradition, Guru Gobind Singhji, the tenth guru, finally passed on the 'guruship' to the holy Sikh scripture Guru Granth Sahib, which is now considered the living guru by the followers of the Sikh faith. Nirankari is a sect of Sikhism, which started in the nineteenth century. They follow a living guru instead of Guru Granth Sahib. Later, Sant Nirankari, a breakaway faction of this tradition, also came into existence. The traditional Sikhs always clashed with this sect. The Damdami Taksal and Akhand Kirtani Jatha had a regular clash with them.

The Damdami Taksal started by Guru Govind Singh in 1706 is the educational organization of the Sikhs. It is located in Mehta Chowk about 40 km from Amritsar. In 1978, Jarnail Singh Bhindranwale was heading the Damdami Taksal and was against the Sant Nirankari Sect. He fortified the gurudwara and started keeping arms at Damdami

Taksal. Akhand Kirtani Jatha (the non-stop kirtan group) are the fundamentalist followers of Sikhism. They believe that the words of the Guru Granth are the words of the guru.

Damdami Taksal led by Bhindranwale along with Fauja Singh and the followers of Akhand Kirtani Jatha decided to stop Sant Nirankaris from holding their celebration. The duo, along with their followers, attacked the convention. Fauja Singh, with his sword, attempted to behead Baba Gurubachan Singh who was the third chief of the Nirankaris. But Fauja Singh was shot dead by his bodyguard and in the tussle, Bhindranwale managed to escape. Eleven members of the Akhand Kiratani Jatha, two followers of Bhinderwale from Damdami Taksal and three members of the Sant Nirankari sect lost their lives. A case was registered and all the sixty or seventy accused from the Sant Nirankari group were acquitted by the court on the ground that people were killed in self-defence.

The Shiromani Akali Dal (SAD) got a drubbing in the 1971 general elections by the Congress party led by Indira Gandhi. Subsequently, in the 1972 state assembly elections, Giani Zail Singh from the Congress party was made the chief minister of Punjab. Shiromani Akali Dal won only one seat out of thirteen seats for the Indian parliament from Punjab. They won only 24 seats out of 117 in the state legislature. To get hold of the political power which had slipped out of the hands of the Shiromani Akali Dal, a high-powered committee was formed to work for the aspirations of the Sikhs. The committee had to work out a plan to bring the Shiromani Akali Dal back to power. Over the next several years, the Shiromani Akali Dal attempted to rebuild and re-establish itself as the sole representative of the Sikh community. Several meetings of the committee took place and a draft emerged from their deliberations. This document was adopted unanimously by the working committee of the Shiromani Akali Dal at a meeting held at Anandpur Sahib on 16–17 October 1973 and came to be known as the Anandpur Sahib Resolution. The main reason for the Anandpur Sahib Resolution passed in 1973 was to get back the lost political ground by Akali Dal. After five years at the 18th All India Akali Conference of the Shiromani Akali Dal at Ludhiana on 28–29 October 1978, the same resolution was endorsed.

It demanded greater autonomy for Punjab, transfer of Chandigarh to Punjab, distribution of the Ravi—Beas river water, demand for the socio-economic development of Punjab and protection of the Sikh community in other parts of the country. The rise of Jarnail Singh Bhindranwale is attributed to the Congress. He became the head of Damdami Taksal at a very young age of thirty-one years. The Shiromani Akali Dal had sided with the opposition parties in opposing the 1975 Emergency imposed by Indira Gandhi. In 1977, when Congress led by Indira was ousted at the centre and also in Punjab, the Shiromani Akali Dal was a part of the Janata Parivar in Delhi and formed the government in Punjab. It is widely known and reported in the media that Sanjay Gandhi, along with Giani Zail Singh, was instrumental in giving strength and support to Bhindranwale during and after the Emergency to counter the growing influence of Shiromani Akali Dal. Giani Zail Singh was happy to toe the line of Sanjay. During the Emergency, Sanjay Gandhi had complete control and influence over Indira and the Congress. It is said that even in the 1972 Punjab assembly elections, the Congress used Bhindranwale to put up candidates to split the votes of the Shiromani Akali Dal. But the major backing of Congress to

Bhindranwale came in 1978 for the Sri Gurudwara Prabhandak Committee (SGPC) elections. Out of a total of 140 seats, Bhindranwale candidates fought for forty seats and in spite of help from the Congress were able to win only four seats. As a quid pro quo, Bhindranwale campaigned for the Congress in the 1980 general elections when Indira Gandhi returned to power. Bhindranwale had understood that the game of electoral politics was not his game, he had to position himself as a religious leader and control politics and politicians through this route.

The tension and clashes between the Nirankaris and the Damdami Taksal, Akhand Kirtani Jatha continued without any respite. The Jathedar of Akala Takht also issued a *hukumnama* to socially boycott the Nirankaris. On the evening of 24 April 1980, the Nirankari chief Gurubachan Singh was shot dead in Delhi by Ranjit Singh of Akhand Kirtan Jatha, who later became the Jathedar of Akal Takht. Bhindranwale associates were named in the FIR. He took refuge in Harmindar Sahib and was not arrested.

The influence of Jarnail Singh Bhindranwale kept on increasing. On 9 September 1981, Lala Jagat Narain, owner and editor of *Punjab Kesari*, was murdered. Bhindranwale was the main suspect. He surrendered on 20 September and was released on 15 October as no evidence was found against him. No one was ready to give testimony against Bhindranwale who by now was a force to reckon with in Punjab. The drama of his arrest was duly reported by veteran journalist Kuldip Nayyar. It was reported that when the Punjab Police raided a village in Haryana to arrest Bhindranwale, the chief minister of Haryana Bhajan Lal, on behest of the home minister of India Giani Zail Singh, managed to flee Bhindranwale in his private bus. Violence broke out in Chando Kala village of Haryana from where

Bhindranwale had fled. Two buses of Damdami Taksal were burnt. They were carrying written sermons of Bhindranwale. This is said to be the breaking point of ties between Bhindranwale and the Congress. Punjab witnessed violence in almost all parts of the state and many daylight murders by the supporters of Bhindranwale were witnessed. A train was derailed, an Indian Airlines plane was hijacked and taken to Lahore. Giani Zail Singh, home minister of the country, stated on the floor of the house that there was no evidence of involvement of Bhindranwale in the assassination of Lala Jagat Narain.

The Shiromani Akali Dal and Bhindranwale joined hands to launch the 'Dharam Yudh Morcha' in 1982 to implement the Anandpur Sahib Resolution. Bhindranwale wanted this to be implemented failing which he threatened to create a homeland for Sikhs by establishing a sovereign state called 'Khalistan'. The idea of Khalistan first moved by Jagjit Singh Chohan appeared in America in 1971. Khalistan, as seen by these protagonists, included Punjab of India and Pakistan, Haryana, Himachal, parts of Jammu and Kashmir, Rajasthan in India, and parts of Sindh, Baluchistan, Khyber and Pakhtunkhwa in Pakistan. The Khalistani sympathizers also tried to divide the population of Punjab on linguistic lines, making Hindi a language of outsiders. Indira Gandhi refused to consider this resolution as she saw it as secessionist. She assessed that Jarnail Singh Bhindranwale was backed by ISI and China.

19 July 1982—Bhindranwale along with 200 armed followers took shelter in Guru Nanak Niwas (Guest House) of Golden Temple on the invitation of Harchand Singh Longowal, president of Shiromani Akali Dal, to avoid arrest. Bhindranwale made Golden Temple his headquarter. Militants were taking shelter and openly staying in

gurudwaras throughout Punjab. But the Congress government in Punjab shied away from taking any action as it was felt that any action in gurudwaras would lead to a backlash in Punjab. 25 April 1983—DIG A.S. Atwal was shot dead in Golden Temple by the followers of Bhindranwale when he came out from the temple after finishing his prayers. His assailants came from inside the temple and after murdering him went back inside the temple. His dead body was lying on the streets for more than two hours and no one, including the Punjab Police, dared to remove the corpse. It was only after the chief minister of Punjab Darbara Singh requested Bhindranwale over the telephone to allow the Punjab Police to take away the body of DIG Atwal that they removed the corpse. In retrospect, it is felt that the best time to storm into the Golden Temple and flush out the militants was immediately after this gory killing of DIG Atwal.

The situation in Punjab deteriorated from bad to worse. The rule of the gun was gripping the state. Hindus or anyone, not falling in line with the dictates of the militants, were murdered. It was now evident that Bhindranwale was instigating Hindu–Sikh clashes and he was getting open support from ISI and other agencies who wanted to destabilize India. Six Hindu passengers travelling by bus were killed on 10 October 1983 and President's Rule was imposed in Punjab. This was an unprecedent situation when the same party was in power both at the centre and the state. Darbara Singh, the Congress chief minister of Punjab, was by no means a defiant state head but the centre still felt that the state government had failed and was not competent to handle the law and order situation in Punjab. Darbara Singh was one of the few leaders of Congress who was tough and was not toeing the line of Bhindranwale like Zail Singh. It can be seen as one of the rarest examples when the centre wanted absolute control in governing the state.

The Akali Dal, under the presidentship of Harchand Singh Longowal and the Shiromani Gurudwara Parbhandak Committee (SGPC) chief Gurucharan Singh Tohra, had aligned with Bhindranwale but slowly started to distance themselves when it was becoming clear that he was not ready to listen to anyone and his followers with brute force bulldozed anyone who they felt was a hindrance in the path of Bhindranwale. Giani Zail Singh, another politician who was a key player in the making of Bhindranwale, became President of India on 25 July 1982. Zail Singh's stature can be judged by the famous words he said after his election, 'If my leader had said I should pick up a broom and be a sweeper, I would have done that. She chose me to be President.' Though the importance given by Indira Gandhi to Zail Singh as president can be assessed by the fact that during the customary weekly briefing to the president by the prime minister on 31 May, a day before the Operation Blue Star, nothing was discussed or informed.

The tension was building up every passing day from February 1984. Another development during the period was that all the sympathizers of Bhindranwale slowly began to leave him because of his non-negotiable, stubborn attitude. All the agencies working against India seized the opportunity by supporting and providing material—moral support to Bhindranwale. They tried to convince him that the formation of Khalistan was just around the corner and he needed to intensify his fight with the Indian government. The guns of the followers of Bhindranwale instilled fear in the minds of Hindus living in Punjab.

The Vatican of the Sikhs, the Golden Temple, was totally

under the control of Bhindranwale by December 1983. On 15 December, Bhindranwale moved from Guru Nanak Niwas to Akal Takht in the Golden Temple. The head of the Golden Temple Kripal Singh opposed Bhindranwale's occupation of Akal Takht. The government was avoiding to enter another gurudwara though a known criminal was hiding inside. This gave confidence to Bhindranwale and his followers that come what, the force would not enter Golden Temple. Bhindranwale used to have meetings at Manji Saheb, the darbar hall of Golden Temple every day where apart from giving fiery speeches, he also used to announce the names of the people who opposed his diktat, and they were pronounced guilty. There was uneasiness in the air and the Hindu devotees visiting Golden Temple reduced significantly, people were avoiding visiting the Temple.

Another important thing happening was the collection of arms inside the Golden Temple. Police and security forces failed to stop the inflow of arms. The temple was becoming an armoury. The arms were smuggled into the Golden Temple by the vehicles carrying milk and grocery. The followers of Bhindranwale were increasing day by day. Unemployed youth, criminals trying to get protection from police and deserters from police/paramilitary forces were enrolling themselves in Bhindranwale's forces supporting Khalistan. Anok Singh, one of the key figures of this outfit, was arrested on 6 June 1984. He was convicted of murdering his sarpanch.

Harminder Singh Sandhu, General Secretary of the All-India Sikh Students Federation (AISSF), was one of the key associates of Bhindranwale. He lost his wife during Operation Blue Star. Harminder Singh was gunned down in 1990 as some people thought he was a mole of the government. Major General Shahbeg Singh, a veteran of the 1971 war, was the most important person of Bhindranwale. He served as a military adviser to Bhindranwale. He trained the Khalistan movement's paramilitary forces in the use of weapons, developed strategies and planned for an armed confrontation which seemed inevitable. During the 1971 war, General Shahbeg was a brigadier. He trained the Mukti Bahini, the liberation army of Bangladesh, as Beg Ali. General Shahbeg, a brilliant officer, was dismissed from the army without a court-martial a day before his retirement. He pleaded his case before ministers and all the political leaders. But everyone showed helplessness. So, on the advice of some senior leaders, he approached Bhindranwale.He had found a new soldierly cause with Bhindranwale.He gifted his personal weapon to Bhindranwale. General Shahbeg moved inside Golden Temple with his wife to supervise and train the followers of Bhindranwale. His wife moved out of Golden Temple on 3 June 1984.

Multiple meetings were conducted between the government and the Akali from February 1984 to May 1984. Harchand Singh Longowal nominated four people to carry out negotiations—Prakash Singh Badal, Gurcharan Singh Tohra, Surjeet Singh Barnala and Narsimha Rao who was the foreign minister of India at that time. Narasimha Rao was leading the negotiations from the government side. The patience of the government was on the test as Punjab was made hostage. Everyday, news of someone killed by the militants was a regular feature. On 26 May, the last meeting was held which turned out to be without any results. The Akali Dal announced a morcha (demonstration against the government) from 3 June 1984, the martyrdom day of Guru Arjundevji. The Akali Dal chief Longowal announced that the transportation of wheat from Punjab to other parts of the country would be stopped. Bhindranwale's idea of Punjab was that all the Hindus living in Punjab should leave and all the Sikhs living outside Punjab should come to Punjab. A migration based on religion which the country had witnessed at the time of partition between Hindus and Muslims was now to be held between Hindus and Sikhs.

Inside the Golden Temple, six armed groups were active. Babar Khalsa International, led by Jathedar Sukhdev Singh was the best-trained and best-funded militant group with the objective of the formation of Khalistan. This was the same group that had killed 329 civilians aboard Air India Flight AI182 when it took off from Montreal to Delhi via London on 23rd June 1985. The second group was Dal Khalsa, involved in the hijacking of the Indian Airlines plane in 1981 when Bhindranwale was arrested. They were banned in 1982 for anti-national activities. Bhindranwale publicly never acknowledged them but it was common knowledge that they worked in close coordination with him. The third armed group inside the Golden Temple, was Akhand Kirtani Jatha led by Bibi Amarjeet Kaur, wife of Fauja Singh. The fourth armed group was the youth wing AISSF led by Harminder Singh Sandhu. Akal Federation was the fifth armed group inside the Golden Temple. There were about 25 persons ready to give their lives for the cause of Khalistan and Bhindranwale. The most dreaded of the group of about 250 armed men was led by Bhindranwale himself. He initially located himself in room number 49 of Guru Nanak Niwas and when things started heating up, he transferred himself to Akal Takht.

On 1 June 1984, Golden Temple was handed over to the army. Indira Gandhi addressed the nation on Doordarshan on the night of 2 June 1984. This was her last effort to convince the supporters of Khalistan and Bhindranwale to negotiate their demands through dialogue. On 3 June, the media was put into buses and left outside Punjab borders in Haryana and complete media censorship was imposed. All the telephone lines and other means of communications including public transport were suspended. A thirty-six-hour curfew was imposed. Even the electricity supply was interrupted, creating a total blackout throughout the state. Pakistan's border was sealed. Lt Gen K. S. Brar, was in charge of this operation, General A. S. Vaidya, Army Chief, and Lt General K. Sunderji, Vice-Chief supervised the whole operation. By a twist of events, General Brar, a Jat Sikh, was trained by Gen. Shahbeg at the Indian Military Academy. He was now going to fight for his nation against his guru. Another proud moment for the Indian army was when Gen. Brar, just before the operation, addressed his forces. Knowing the delicate and sensitive nature of Operation Blue Star, he told them that due to religious sentiments attached, those who wanted could optout of the operation, and the same would not be held against them. None of the soldiers of the Indian army opted out of this operation, the nation was supreme for them.

Third June being the Guru Parv of Guru Arjan Devji, curfew was relaxed. It is estimated that a large number of criminals took advantage of this and fled from the Golden Temple during this period. Bhindranwale held his last press conference on 3 June. On 4 June, SGPC chief Tohra made a last-minute effort to convince Bhindranwale to surrender but the effort was futile. Announcements were made over loudspeakers asking pilgrims to leave the Temple. But till 5th June, only about 125–150 people came out. Bhindranwale and his followers were dissuading and threatening the devotees to go out of the Temple as they were their shield against the inevitable attack. A large number of people were trapped inside the Golden Temple.

The full operation was started on 5 June at 7 in the evening. The army was taken aback by the firepower displayed by the militants. Some say that the intelligence agencies failed to give a correct report on the strength of the militants but some believe that due to the paucity of time, the Army was not able to process the entire lot information given to them. It was clear on the night of 5th and 6th June that without the use of tanks, it would be difficult to overcome militants. The tanks were brought in to counter the Chinese-made rocket launchers, machine guns, anti-tank guns. This whole exercise resulted in a lot of collateral damage. The library was burnt and part of the sacred Akal Takht was damaged. Later, the proposal to rebuild the Takht by the government was turned down and the same was built by the Sikhs themselves without any government help. The dead bodies of Bhindranwale and Shahbeg Singh were recovered on 6 June. One of the saddest operations where no one was a winner and all the stakeholders lost something came to an end on 7 June 1984. For the next three days, the search operation was on to get hold of the militants still hiding. President Giani Zail Singh visited the Golden Temple on 8 June and a bullet was fired on him inside the temple. As per General Brar, 83 army personnel along with 4 officers gave their lives, and 248 were injured; 252 militants and civilians were killed.

Punjab had to face militancy for a very long period and it took almost a decade for normalcy to return to the state. The feelings of Sikhs were hurt all over the world and a group of Sikhs held Indira Gandhi responsible for the events. There was outrage among Sikhs at the desecration of their shrine. The sacred sanctity of the place was desecrated most brutally with death and destruction. The Akal Takht, the symbolic seat of supreme Sikh temporal authority, was reduced to rubble. Gurdwara Darbar Sahib was damaged with bullets. The Sikh Reference Library with precious hand-written manuscripts of the gurus got burned. The temple treasury *toshakhana* with priceless historical artefacts of Maharaja Ranjit Singh also got badly damaged.

The intelligence, seeing the threat perception, removed Sikhs from the personal bodyguard duties of Indira Gandhi. But since Indira Gandhi was a peoples' leader she thought that the removal of Sikhs from her security duty would send wrong signals and reinforce her anti-Sikh image among the public. Therefore, she ordered the Special Protection Group to reinstate Sub-Inspectors Beant Singh and Satwant Singh. Beant Singh was with her for almost ten years and Satwant joined her security group just five months before.

Indira Gandhi returned from Orissa on 30 October 1984 where the speech delivered by her proved to be prophetic – 'I am alive today, I may not be there tomorrow...I shall continue to serve until my last breath and when I die, I can say, that every drop of my blood will invigorate India and strengthen it. ... Even if I died in the service of the nation, I would be proud of it. Every drop of my blood... will contribute to the growth of this nation and make it strong and dynamic.' Peter Ustinov, the British actor, writer and director who had a Russian origin was scheduled to shoot her documentary. He was making this documentary for Irish Television. On 31 morning, Peter was ready for filming the documentary, and Indira was informed. She came accompanied by R.K. Dhawan and Rameshwar Dayal, her personal assistants. Around 9.25 am, she came out of the official prime minister residence, 1 Safdarjung road for the last time, and started walking towards the adjacent bungalow, 1 Akbar Road which was used as the camp office of the prime minister.

It was 9.29 am on 31 October 1984 when on reaching the wicket gate of the bungalow she was greeted by her bodyguard by words and bullets. Beant Singh after shooting thrice with his .38 calibre revolver threw the firearm on the ground. In the meantime, Satwant pumped in 30 rounds from his Sten submachine gun. Beant was killed on the spot by ITBP officers and Satwant was handed over to the police. The main conspirator Kehar Singh, who was the uncle of Beant Singh, was arrested later. He was a clerk in the Directorate General of Supply and Disposal. Satwant Singh and Kehar Singh were found guilty by the court and hanged to death on 6th January 1989.

The bullet-ridden body of the Prime Minister of India was lying on the ground. Just when it was most needed, the security machinery's carefully planned emergency drill went to pieces. It was a practice of more than thirty-seven years to keep an ambulance in readiness for such an eventuality at the back of the house; it could not be taken out, because the driver could not be instantly located. He had gone out to have tea. She was rushed to All India Institute of Medical Sciences in an official white ambassador car in the lap of Sonia Gandhi. The All India Institute of Medical Sciences (AIIMS) was informed that some VIP was coming, but the babus running the country failed to tell them that it was the prime minister of the largest democracy with bullet injuries who was being brought. Doctors took no time and were on the job. Sixty bottles of blood were arranged out of which by afternoon more than 40 bottles were used. Rajiv Gandhi was in West Bengal campaigning for the party along with Pranab Mukherjee. They were brought to Kolkata (that time Calcutta) by helicopter and then to Delhi by charter plane. In the ten-seater plane, Rajiv Gandhi was accompanied by Pranab Mukherjee, Balram Jakhar—speaker of the house, Uma Shankar Dixit, Governor of West Bengal, his daughter-in-law Sheila Dixit, Subhash Kashyap—Secretary-General of the Lok Sabha. The BBC announced the death of Indira Gandhi at 1 pm and Rajiv Gandhi came to know about it with literally no ground under him as he was in the air. Apart from a political void, a lot of uncertainties, too, had been created by this assassination. It was decided that Rajiv Gandhi should be elevated as the next prime minister without wasting any time. It was also felt that there should be no disruption in the governance of the country. All the passengers on board decided that Rajiv Gandhi should be requested to take over as the full-fledged prime minister to meet the challenge posed by this extraordinary situation. But Rajiv was a bit apprehensive and asked them to discuss this matter of succession with each other and with the governor. Sheila Dixit was carrying a copy of the Constitution which she had brought from Raj Bhavan. This copy of the Constitution was also referred to for technicalities.

Subhash Kashyap recalls that he told Rajiv Gandhi to take over as the prime minister immediately and not even think of a caretaker prime minister. The other leaders on board were told that the only requirement was the nomination of Rajiv by his party as the leader to take over the prime-ministerial position. It was also discussed who would administer the oath of office since then-president Giani Zail Singh was not in the country and also he might be reluctant to swear him in as prime minister due to his annoyance after Operation Blue Star. Subhash Kashyap recalls that the provision of the Vice-Presidents swearing him as the prime minister was also discussed. The fate of the country was decided in the air keeping in view the avoidance of any civil-war-like situation. When Rajiv arrived in New Delhi, it had been more or less decided that he was going to take over. P.C. Alexander, Principal Secretary to the Prime Minister, met Rajiv Gandhi in the bathroom of AIIMS on the eighth floor to discuss the details. A hurried meeting of the Congress parliamentary party was convened where he was elected leader of the party. Giani Zail Singh, who had returned from Yemen, administered the oath of office to Rajiv Gandhi at 6.30 pm. Salma Sultan, at the 8 pm news on Doordarshan, announced the death of Indira Gandhi. India had two prime ministers from 6.30 pm to 8 pm till the time her death was announced.

By that time the violence against Sikhs spread across the country and Delhi especially was badly affected. Rajiv Gandhi addressed the nation.[1] It took three days to stop the violence and more than ten years to bring Sikhs back into the mainstream of nation-building. After Mahatma Gandhi, Indira was the first victim of communal violence. Her last rites were done on 3 November near Rajghat at Shakti Sthal.

In retrospect, we can say that Sanjay Gandhi and Zail Singh created 'Sant' Jarnail Singh Bhindranwale as 'Frankenstein's monster' and unleashed the forces that precipitated the assassination of Indira Gandhi. The childish handling of matters of political importance by Sanjay Gandhi costed the nation at least twenty years of unrest and mayhem. His strongly authoritarian personality and disdain for parliamentary governance and procedures created huge problems within the country. Had Congress maturely handled the problem, there would have been no terrorism in Punjab and no need for military action in the

Golden Temple. Operation Blue Star is an event for which politicians at the centre and the state need to take collective responsibility.

Indeed, the events leading up to Blue Star are a stark reminder of how even a shrewd experienced leader like Indira Gandhi could be influenced so strongly by her son and needed his counsel in executing her role as prime minister. She was surrounded by cronies who misled her. They lead her to the path of destruction. In a democracy, leaders need to be answerable to the people of the country. Had there been no Operation Blue Star, Indira would not have been assassinated and there would have been no riots in 1984. Perhaps India would have been different today. There is a lesson here which leaders must learn—they should not keep undesirable elements around them who can mislead them. The governments need to learn some lessons to ensure that no community is allowed to feel alienated and isolated. Every person living in the country is indispensable and inseparable from the mainstream. All political parties must rise above partisan politics to avoid such catastrophic disasters in the future. No leader should forget that there is a moral dimension to leadership too.

Notes

1. Rajiv Gandhi made a speech in Delhi on the occasion of a prayer meeting after Indira Gandhi's assassination and the Sikh riots in 1984.

Chapter-10

Campaign against Corruption

Bofors Claims Rajiv Gandhi, V.P. Singh's Rise and Fall

30 November 1989, Thursday

The Bofors Scandal will remain in Indian minds as the mother of all scams.[1] The scandal was considered to be the main reason the Congress party was voted out of power in the 1989 general elections and led to the rise of V. P. Singh. 'Mr Clean' Rajiv Gandhi was replaced by another 'Mr Clean' V.P. Singh. It was a landmark moment as never before in the history of Indian democracy was any government voted out of power on corruption charges. On 24 March 1986, the Rs 1,437 crore deal for the supply of 410 guns named 155mm Howitzer field guns was signed. The deal was signed between India and Swedish gun manufacturer Bofors. Indian journalist Chitra Subramaniam, who was working for *The Hindu* newspaper, happened to be in Sweden when she picked up the story broadcasted for the first time by Swedish radio that bribe was paid by Bofors to secure the deal. She met a couple of leads and was able to reach Sten Lindstrom, the head of the Swedish police team investigating the gun deal. N Ram, the editor of *The Hindu* subsequently met Sten along with

Chitra. In the year 2012, on the 25th anniversary of the revelations into the scandal, Sten Lindstrom gave a long interview and explained the reasons for handing over more than 350 pages of the document on this bribery case. He also gave the reasons as to why he became a whistleblower.

In April 1987, the allegation of paying a bribe to the Indian politicians and defence personnel came to the limelight for the first time. This was strongly refuted by Rajiv Gandhi in the parliament. In August 1987, a Joint Parliamentary Committee (JPC) was formed by the Congress government; it submitted its report in July 1989 just before the general elections giving the government a clean chit. In the history of the Indian parliament, the first Joint Parliamentary Committee (JPC) was formed on Bofors in 1987under the chairmanship of B. Shankaranand, a seasoned Congress Dalit politician from Karnataka. The second JPC was formed by the parliament in 1992 under the chairmanship of R.N. Mirdha to look into the Harshad Mehta share-market scam. The irony is that the Chairman of the first JPC, B. Shankranand was probed by the second JPC. The report submitted to the parliament found that Shankranand had manipulated the tender norms in his capacity as the petroleum minister and chairman of the Oil Industry Development Board (OIDB). This manipulation led to a huge loss for the government which was not less than Rs130 crores. The ultimate beneficiaries were two private firms—Fairgrowth and Essar. However, regarding the Bofors scam, the fact remained that 319.4 million Swedish kronor (Rs 64 crores) were paid to three different companies to swing the deal in the final stages from the French gun, Sofma to the Swedish gun, Bofors. No one knows conclusively what services these three companies rendered to Bofors to receive this payment.

Initially, the story about the Bofors scandal appeared in *The Hindu* but subsequently, under government pressure, they stopped pursuing this scandal. Chitra Subramaniam moved out from *The Hindu* to *The Statesman* and *The Indian Express* and kept on publishing the Bofors Scam. The main character of the whole scandal was Ottavio Quattrocchi, an Italian businessman close to the Gandhi family. He represented a petrochemical firm Snamprogetti and was a known middleman in the Delhi wheeler-dealer circle. During the run-up to the 1989 elections, the opposition, besides raising the issue of the kickback, also put a big question mark on the capability of the guns. Thus, there was a perception that the security of the nation was compromised. The Swedish company was blacklisted and the ban was lifted during the Kargil war when the need for spare parts for the gun became an issue. During the Kargil encounter, the gun showed its superiority. It had a definite edge over the medium artillery guns available with the Pakistani army. This was a fact that was confirmed by the battlefield artillery officers. This gun emerged as the real hero of the Kargil war in 1999.

The Congress lost the election in 1989 and V.P. Singh became the prime minister. He was the leader of the Janata Dal coalition. In January 1990, CBI registered FIRs against Ardbo, who was the President of Bofors, and against alleged middlemen Win Chadda and the Hinduja brothers. Quattrocchi left India in July 1993 and never came back. In the meantime, there was a legal battle going on in Indian and foreign courts. On 22 October 1999, after the National Democratic Alliance (NDA) government led by the BJP came to power, CBI filed the first chargesheet after more than twelve years against Quattrocchi, Win Chadda, the then Defence Secretary S.K.Bhatnagar, Rajiv Gandhi (died in 1991) and others. Win Chadda and S.K. Bhatnagar also died in 2001. The change of the government decided the course of the case. After Congress came to power in 2004, the Additional Solicitor General of India in December 2005, on behalf of the Government of India and CBI, requested the British government to unfreeze two London bank accounts of Quattrocchi. Though the Supreme Court directed CBI on 16 January 2006 to ensure that Quattrocchi did not withdraw money but on 23 January, the CBI admitted that Rs 21 crores ($4.6 million) had already been withdrawn from the two accounts.

Quattrocchi was detained in Argentina in February 2006 but the Congress-led UPA (United Progressive Alliance) government failed to bring him to India as there was no extradition treaty with Argentina. He died on 12 July 2013. Even after 30-40 years, the Bofors case remains to be adjudicated. This speaks volumes about not only the judicial system of the country but also the political will and character of different ruling parties. The former CBI director A.P. Mukherjee has written in his book that Rajiv Gandhi wanted this commission to be used for the Congress party and it was discussed with him by Rajiv Gandhi. Lindstrom, the Swedish Chief of Investigation, maintains that though Rajiv Gandhi had not taken any bribe, he was guilty of knowing about the kickbacks and still not taking any action. The Swedish police head Sten Lindstrom rightly said that Rajiv Gandhi 'watched the massive cover-up in India and did nothing'.

Another story that widely circulated in the national press about the Bofors deal those days was that it was the last genuine effort to free Indian politics from the clutches of businessman and industrialists. Rajiv Gandhi, after assuming office, genuinely wanted to clean politics by putting an end to the influence of money power. After giving money to the party, the Shylocks always demanded favours in return. These favours could be in various forms, such as, they would want the authorities to ignore their tax violation, FERA (Foreign Exchange Regulation Act) violation, exempt their taxes and grant licences without competition and many such things that created problems. In the process, too many people would get involved who would not only share information regarding favours but would also want a share in the funds collected. The two Aruns—Nehru and Singh, both ministers in the Rajiv Gandhi cabinet—gave a solution to this problem of election funding. They suggested getting money from the kickbacks of defence purchases, instead of depending on the traditional route of raising money from corporate India.

Arun Singh, Rajkumar of the princely state of Kapurthala had worked with Metal Box and Reckitt and Coleman. Rajiv Gandhi was his classmate in Cambridge. On his invitation, Arun Singh joined politics in 1982. Rajiv Gandhi replaced P.V. Narasimha Rao on 25 September 1985 as the defence minister. He also brought Arun Singh as his deputy. A circular was issued by the defence ministry that no agent would operate on behalf of any defence supplier and the department or ministry would directly interact with the supplier. It was calculated that the agents of foreign defence supply pocketed hundreds of crores as commission every year. With the removal of agents, the defence supplier would pass on this commission to the Congress party under the table. This arrangement had three advantages. Firstly, one had to deal only with two or three suppliers. Secondly, whosoever got the contract would directly be paying. The agent's role was removed and they could not influence the contract, so India would get a better and more competitive deal. Thirdly, defence purchases are not repetitive so one would never face or deal with the same supplier again.

The scriptwriter of the saga of Bofors was no doubt V.P. Singh. He was the son of Raja Bahadur of Daiya zamindari and was adopted by Raja of Manda Gopal Singh. V.P. Singh became Raja at the age of ten years in 1941. He studied law at Allahabad University where he was elected the Vice President of the Students' Union. He also did BSc in Physics from Fergusson College, Pune. He joined the Congress and won from the Soron seat of Uttar Pradesh Vidhan Sabha in 1969 and was made the chief whip of the party in the Assembly. V.P. Singh became Member of Parliament in 1971 and Mrs Gandhi made him the Deputy Minister of Commerce in her cabinet. During Emergency, he served as the Minister of Commerce from 1976 to 1977.

Indira Gandhi stormed back in 1980, both at the centre and in Uttar Pradesh. The control of the biggest state of the country with 330 MLAs was given to V.P. Singh. The Raja of Manda was the chief minister of Uttar Pradesh from 1980 to 1982. One of the major reasons for choosing V.P. Singh was his clean image and because he had no political clout of his own. His cabinet had forty-nine members but barring five or six, none were under his command. He shuffled his pack of ministers a record nine times. His choice for the chief secretary was overruled and R.P. Khosla, additional secretary at the centre superseded fourteen IAS (Indian Administrative Service) officers to become the chief secretary. Another candidate not of his choice was R.C. Takru. He was a state civil services officer who was promoted to the IAS cadre in 1975. He was made home secretary, though he was pegged at 326th position in the civil services seniority list. The law and order was his priority and he started an unprecedented drive against the dacoits.

Over 1,500 dacoits were killed and policemen also paid a heavy price with the loss of 133 lives. Mayhem continued during his regime. To name a few, the Radhey—Santosh gang killed twenty-four people of Jatav caste in Dehuli of Mainpuri district.[2] Phoolan Devi, Mallah by caste, gunned down twenty-one Thakurs in Behmai village of Kanpur district.[3] She was gunned down by a Thakur in Delhi in 2001. He lost his elder brother, C.S.P. Singh, a judge of Allahabad High Court, along with his nephew in March 1982. Both were gunned down by the dacoits. V.P. Singh termed the killing as the price his brother paid for his office (as chief minister).

The action of V.P. Singh to send his resignation letter directly to the governor without consulting anyone was neither liked by Indira Gandhi nor by the other powerful leaders of the party. In September 1980, when communal violence broke in Moradabad and Aligarh, he sent his resignation to Indira Gandhi, which was turned down. In November 1981, he had announced his resignation when Radhey–Santosh slaughtered villagers but the police nabbed the duo and killed more than fifty dacoits. His public acceptance that he was not able to contain the law and order situation of Uttar Pradesh was an indirect comment on many non-performing chief ministers, central ministers, etc. V.P. Singh was a leader with a unique style of politics. Though he did not have a mass base, still he won seven Congress bye-elections out of nine during his chief-ministership.

In 1983, V.P. Singh became commerce minister in the cabinet of Indira Gandhi. After the death of Indira Gandhi, Rajiv Gandhi won a landslide victory in the 1984 general elections. In these elections, the Congress won 414 seats. For the record, this was the election when BJP started its parliamentary journey with two seats. V.P. Singh was the new finance minister of the country with Bhure Lal, a no-nonsense IAS officer by his side. The Enforcement Directorate (ED) of the finance ministry started doing its job for the first time in letter and spirit. The business–politics nexus under went a complete change. The industrialists, who had supported Congress for years, were made to adjust to the new regime. But there was an upcoming, new player on the horizon who was not in the habit of answering questions posed by the bureaucracy. This new player was Dhirubhai Ambani who had succeeded in cultivating politicians. Very few politicians had the acumen and the gumption to oppose Dhirubhai Ambani. The ED's investigation of Reliance owned by Dhirubhai Ambani and the uncomfortable questions posed to Amitabh Bachchan sealed V.P. Singh's fate as finance minister in Rajiv Gandhi's cabinet. It was hardly a coincidence that soon after V.P. Singh fell out with Rajiv Gandhi.

Now the issue was where to adjust the ṢṢṢemerging Mr Clean V.P. Singh, who was threatening the image of Rajiv Gandhi, who also had the image of Mr Clean. He had vowed to strike down opportunism and corruption which had the Congress in its grip. He carried no past baggage of a Congressman. Prime Minister Rajiv Gandhi was defence minister of the country when the Bofors deal was signed. He decided to swap the ministry with V.P. Singh. In January 1987, Rajiv Gandhi became the finance minister and V.P. Singh moved to the ministry of defence. He was defence minister for only seventy-eight days. His immediate provocation for resignation on 12 April 1987 was an HDW (Howaldtswerke-Deutsche Werftsubmarine) submarine deal and not the Bofors deal as it is widely believed. On receiving information that an amount of Rs 32.55 crores, which was about 7 per cent of the deal price, was paid as a commission, he instituted an inquiry. In a closed-door meeting of Congress heavyweights led by Arjun Singh and N. D. Tiwari, they tried to convince Rajiv Gandhi that V.P. Singh's holier-than-thou attitude was farcical and he was projecting himself as another Mr Clean to emerge as an alternative to Rajiv Gandhi. V.P. Singh was trying to become a symbol of integrity and an upholder of public norms. Rajiv Gandhi reluctantly agreed to ask for his resignation.

A group of congressmen, MPs, and ministers were not happy with the party. This group consisting of Mufti Mohammad Sayeed, Vidya Charan Shukla, Ram Dhan, Arif Mohammed Khan, Satyapal Malik, Arun Nehru, etc. led by V.P. Singh came out of Congress and formed a party named Jan Morcha. This new outfit fashioned itself on the lines of Jayaprakash Sampurn Kranti, struggle against corruption in high places. V.P. Singh was termed '*Raja nahi fakir hai, Desh ki taqdeer hai*'. The first opportunity to test the waters was given by Amitabh Bachchan, the superstar of the Hindi cinema when he resigned as a member of the parliament.

After the death of Indira Gandhi, Amitabh Bachchan, an established star of Indian cinema joined politics at the request of Rajiv Gandhi. They were family friends and Sonia stayed with the Bachchans when she visited India before her marriage with Rajiv Gandhi. Amitabh Bachchan fought elections from Allahabad in Uttar Pradesh in 1984 and won by a record margin of 1,87,795 votes, getting 68.21 per cent of votes polled. He defeated the former chief minister Hemvati Nandan Bahuguna who was one of the heavy weights of UP politics. The record of margin created by Amitabh Bachchan is still not broken, though doyens of Indian politics like Lal Bahadur Shastri, V.P. Singh, Murli

Manohar Joshi have represented Allahabad. In 2019, riding the Modi wave, Rita Bahuguna Joshi, daughter of Hemvati Nandan Bahuguna, was elected with 4,94,454 votes polled but the record of Bachchan still stands.

Amitabh gave different reasons subsequently for his resignation. He said he was torn between his fan followers whom he had wooed in his twenty-five years of film career and party loyalty. His fans could have been the supporters of the opposition party. He was now telling them to love his party as well which he felt was not correct. He felt that politics was the wrong field for an actor. But the general perception was that he resigned as his name was involved in the Bofors scam. As a minister of Rajiv Gandhi's cabinet, V.P. Singh gave a speech in Allahabad which had perfect timing. In his speech, he said that no one, who had stacked money in foreign countries, would be spared; around the same time Ajitabh Bachchan, brother of Amitabh, got non-resident status in Switzerland.

The Allahabad by-elections held on 16 June 1988 proved to be a turning point in Indian political history. V.P. Singh was the opposition candidate and Congress put Sunil Shastri, son of Lal Bahadur Shastri to contest elections against him. Leaders from all over India and all the heavyweights of the Congress party descended in Allahabad. The campaign was fierce. Devi Lal wearing a turban, with a fleet of 200 motorcycles attracted a lot of media attention. They were termed as the green brigade. V.P. Singh's victory cost Bir Bahadur Singh his chief ministership. He was replaced by N.D. Tewari.

The Jan Morcha, Janata Party, Lok Dal, Congress (S) merged to form Janata Dal on 11 October 1988, which also happened to be Jayaprakash Narayan's birthday. It was a message that the new party under the presidentship of V.P.

Singh was to fight against corruption. The second step was the creation of the National Front—the Janata Dal, DMK (Dravida Munnetra Kazhagam), Telugu Desam and Assam Gana Parishad became part of it. V.P. Singh was the convenor of the front, N.T. Rama Rao was the president and P. Upendra became the General Secretary. Riding on the Bofors scam, the new outfit fought the 1989 general elections. They had an electoral understanding with BJP, CPI and CPM.

For the 1989 general elections, no single party got the winning majority. In alliance, Janata Dal got 143 seats (17.79 per cent votes); BJP riding the V.P. Singh wave increased its tally from 2 to 85 seats (11.36 per cent votes), and CPM with 33 seats (6.55 per cent votes) and CPI with 12 seats (2.57 percent votes), reached the halfway mark of 273 seats in the 545-member Lok Sabha. These parties polled 38.27 per cent of votes to win 273 seats. The BJP undoubtedly took the electoral arithmetic of Indian democracy in a new direction in 2014. It got 31.34 per cent votes and still won an absolute majority by getting 282 seats. The strange way how poll arithmetic works is visible in the 1989 election results when Congress got 39.53 per cent votes and became the single largest party with 197 seats, and had to sit in the opposition. Statistics of seats and percentage of votes polled can sometimes give a misleading perspective of popular sentiment.

The Janata Dal parliamentary party met on 1 December 1989. A day before, in the high-powered meeting, Chandrashekhar was adamant on V.P. Singh not becoming the prime minister. V.P. Singh had also on many occasions mentioned that he was not interested in becoming the prime minister. He had a clean image of a crusader against corruption, as someone trying to change the social structure to abolish inequality. Masses sympathized with him. He wanted to follow the path of Jayaprakash Narayan and Gandhi. A compromise was reached on the name of Devi Lal. But Devi Lal somersaulted and changed the course of history when in his address he stressed the need of V.P. Singh to become the prime minister since the mandate given to the Janata Dal was in his name. Chandrashekhar was visibly annoyed and left the meeting. On 2 December, V.P. Singh took an oath of office with Devi Lal as his Deputy Prime Minister. He became the first Prime Minister of India who headed a minority government that enjoyed majority support from outside.

The Janata Dal formed government in five states – Haryana, Gujarat, Uttar Pradesh, Bihar, and Orissa. The National Front government was formed in Andhra Pradesh and Assam. They shared power in Kerala with E.K. Nayanar as chief minister and gave outside support to the BJP government led by Bhairon Singh Shekhawat in the state of Rajasthan. This was for the first time that BJP had formed a government in any Indian state on its own. An important feature of democracy is to elect the leader of the legislature party as the chief minister, instead of the high command nominating the chief minister. This was displayed for the last time in UP and Bihar. In UP, Mulayam Singh Yadav had to contest with Ajit Singh to become the leader of the Janata dal legislature party and subsequently become the chief minister. In this contest, V.P. Singh backed Ajit Singh and Devi Lal backed Mulayam Singh. In Bihar, too Janata Dal legislature leader election was keenly contested. Ram Saran Das from the Dalit background was backed by V.P. Singh and was sure to win. Since Mulayam became the chief minister of UP, Laloo's claim for chief ministership in the neighbouring state of Bihar became weak as he was also a Yadav. Devi Lal along with Sharad Yadav backed Laloo. Sharad Yadav was keen to mentor the backward, especially the Yadavs. Since V.P. Singh was backing Ram Saran Das, help for Laloo was sought from Chandrashekhar. He was more than willing to oblige as he was not happy with V.P. Singh becoming the prime minister. It was Chandrasekhar who made Raghu Nath Jha contest as the third candidate, to capture upper-caste votes. The upper castes were going to vote against Laloo in favour of Ram Saran Das. They now voted for Jha. Thus, Jha secured thirteen votes and Laloo won by three votes. And as they say, the rest is history.

V.P. Singh was in a hurry to undo all that he perceived as the wrongdoings of the previous Congress regime. He started taking decisions that had a long-term impact on the future of India. We will discuss three major decisions of V.P. Singh, which changed the course of history other than the Mandal commission. Firstly, the Indian Peace Keeping Force (IPKF) was hurriedly called back from Sri Lanka. The objective of sending them to Sri Lanka was not fulfilled and ultimately the LTTE (Liberation Tigers of Tamil Eelam) succeeded in killing Rajiv Gandhi. The second decision was regarding the handling of Punjab. V.P. Singh, to please the Sikh community, visited the Golden Temple for forgiveness. Sidharth Shankar Ray was the Governor of Punjab. He was tough, competent and had the experience of running the state of West Bengal as the chief minister. He was replaced by N.K. Mukherjee, a retired IAS officer (Indian Civil Service). The Punjab unrest took more than a decade to calm down and come back on the path of progress once again. The third decision was regarding George Fernandes, one of the most competent leaders of the post-Emergency era. He was made the minister-in-charge of Kashmir affairs. George was the main accused of the Baroda Dynamite case.

He was the trade union leader on whose call the Indian Railways came to a standstill in 1974. He fought with Bala Saheb and Sharad Pawar on Maharashtra politics but could also walk through any ones' home without informing. His home was the centre for those who were involved in Tibetan as well as Myanmar struggle. The Myanmar activists were working from his home for the freedom of their leader Aung Suu Kyi. George started visiting Kashmir but his unorthodox way of opening dialogues with one and all, including the militants, was not liked by many. He used to visit alone to meet the leaders of different groups. He wanted to understand the situation and build a bridge through dialogues. BJP, which was supporting the government from outside, managed to replace George with a BJP candidate, Jagmohan Malhotra. He was appointed Governor of Jammu and Kashmir. The exit of George was unceremonious without taking him in confidence. His Kashmir charge was taken away by V.P. Singh when he was visiting Bhubaneshwar. For the record, the exodus of Kashmiri Pandits happened during Jagmohan's tenure which remains an open wound even after three decades.

Before moving on to the biggest decision of implementing the Mandal Commission, one must understand V.P. Singh, the Machiavelli of Indian politics. He was never a grassroots leader, nor a leader with statesmanship. He is best described as a person with no friends but many allies. All the major turning points in the life of V.P. Singh were having a shade of grey. He was introduced to Indira Gandhi by his elder brother Sant Bux Singh who was MP from Fatehpur for two terms, in 1967 and 1971. Sant Bux Singh was educated in Oxford and would advise Indira on matters of International affairs. It is alleged that V. P. Singh played a role when Sant Bux Singh was denied a ticket in 1980. V.P.

Singh twice represented his brother's constituency, in 1989 and 1991. His eagerness to keep his self-interest and his image above others is attributed to Rajiv Gandhi losing the 1989 elections. None of his Janmorcha colleagues had a mass base. Their area of influence was restricted to their constituencies. When the new party came into existence the stalwarts of opposition were a part of Janata Dal. To keep the balance of power in his favour, he gave seats to BJP which was a party with just two MPs in 1984. These seats were given at the cost of old Janata Dal loyalists. The BJP had made its intentions very clear from the beginning when it refused to give unconditional support to the Janata Dal government. Advani declared his intention of acting both as the 'brake and the accelerator' of the government. It was thus due to sheer selfish interests that V.P. Singh gave so much importance to BJP. The meteoric rise of the all-powerful BJP that we see now started during V.P. Singh's tenure and in 1989 it had 85 MPs. V.P. Singh's prime-ministership proved to be the *sanjivani* (which can reverse death) for BJP. In an interview given to *India Today*, V.P. Singh had said: 'Left to myself I would like to play the role of Balram in Mahabharat.' It is therefore still a mystery as to what transpired on 30 November night that made him accept the position of the prime minister after denying it initially.

Notes

1. Ignoring French Gun, India signed an agreement with Swedish Firm AB Bofors in 1986 to supply 155 mm Howitzer Guns. It was alleged that a kickback was given by Bofors to get this contract.
2. Sixteen armed men led by Radhey and Santosh of Thakur caste.
3. Phoolan Devi, popularly known as Bandit Queen, surrendered in 1983 and subsequently twice became Member of Parliament.

Chapter-11

India Unshackled

Narasimha Rao and the Stock Market Scam

21 May 1991, Tuesday

The Narasimha Rao government will be remembered for a few good, few bad and few ugly things. Soon after the assassination of Prime Minister Indira Gandhi in 1984, the elections for the 8th Lok Sabha for 541 seats were held. They were held in two phases. Five hundred and fourteen Lok Sabha seats went for a poll in the first phase and twenty-seven seats of Assam and Punjab went for a poll in the second phase. The sympathy wave of the 1984 elections gave Rajiv Gandhi unprecedented unmatched victory. Congress with 49.10 per cent of votes won 414 seats, a record—which in my view—will remain unbeatable in times to come. The second-largest party was Telgu Desam with thirty seats and 4.31 per cent votes. The Bharatiya Janata Party won only two seats—Dr A. K. Patel won from Mehsana in Gujarat and Chandupatla J. Reddy won from Hanamkonda in Andhra Pradesh defeating sitting MP P.V. Narasimha Rao of Congress despite the sympathy wave after the death of Indira Gandhi. In the next election of 1989, the same MP Chandupatla J. Reddy fought as an alliance candidate of Telugu Desam and Janata Dal lost to

Congress candidate Kamaluddin Ahmad. Elections in a democracy give results which are beyond human comprehension and logic. In the 1984 elections, BJP got two seats and in terms of vote share (7.74 per cent) was the second-largest party after Congress. Ironically, the vote share of three parties which also got two seats each was – the All India Forward Bloc (00.45 per cent), the Indian Union Muslim League (00.28 per cent) and the Kerala Congress (Joseph) (00.25 per cent).

At the beginning of the 10th Lok Sabha election in 1991, the fight was triangular. The Congress was the main opposition party in the dissolved parliament, the Bhartiya Janata Party pitching for the Hindu votes after Advani's Rath Yatra and Janata Dal, led by V.P. Singh consolidating backward votes after implementation of the Mandal Commission. Elections in 19 seats of Punjab and Jammu & Kashmir were postponed so only 524 seats were going for the poll. The magic figure was 263. A day after the first round of polling took place for 211 seats, Rajiv Gandhi, the former prime minister, was killed. Elections for the second and third phases were postponed for 12 and 15 June 1991. Congress riding on the sympathy wave of Rajiv Gandhi's assassination won 232 seats just short of 31 seats to form a government. Communists provided the required support. The BJP with Ram Janambhoomi as the main agenda, won 120 seats and became the main opposition party. The original Janata Dal broke into many factions. The outfit, still called Janata Dal under the leadership of V.P. Singh, won 69 seats. Subsequently, in January 1992, the Congress won 12 out of 13 seats in Punjab making its tally 244 seats.

During the election for the 10th Lok Sabha, P.V. Narsimha Rao started packing his bags to shift back to Andhra Pradesh and lead a retired life. The death of Rajiv

Gandhi made him the president of the party as an interim arrangement. Leaders knew that Indian voters would vote for Rajiv Gandhi both as tribute and sympathy. No one from the Gandhi family by the remotest possibility was going to join politics at that juncture. Three serious contenders were Sharad Pawar, Arjun Singh and N.D. Tewari for the prime minister's post. Though Maharashtra had the largest number of MPs in the Congress parliamentary party, Sharad Pawar withdrew himself from the race for the top position. Arjun Singh agreed to become Congress president once this position was vacated by Rao after becoming prime minister. It is another matter that Rao never moved out as Congress president during his Prime Ministership. N.D. Tewari (NDT) had all the requisite qualifications for the top job. He had the administrative experience of a chief minister of the largest state and an image of a competent central cabinet minister. He came from the Hindi heartland of Uttar Pradesh and belonged to the Brahmin caste, though this qualification was never openly spoken about. NDT coming from Uttrakhand decided to fight from the Nainital Lok Sabha constituency. Now fate started playing its role. Voting in Nainital was held on 20 May 1991 and Rajiv Gandhi was killed on 21 May. So, N.D. Tiwari could not get the advantage of a sympathy wave. A young 30-year-old BJP leader Balraj Pasi trounced NDT by 11,429 votes. During that era, someone losing the Lok Sabha election was not even considered for a ministerial berth, leave aside prime ministership. The Congress stalwart's prime ministerial aspirations crashed when P. V. Narasimha Rao, the senior-most leader of Congress who had not even fought the general elections, was made the leader of the party and took an oath of the office of the prime minister on 21 June 1991. He later contested from Nandyal, Andhra Pradesh as sitting prime minister and won by a record margin. The seat of Nandyal was vacated by Gangula Prathapa Reddy. It is interesting to note that Balraj Pasi, who defeated NDT, and G. P. Reddy, who vacated his seat for the prime minister, never again returned to parliament.

During his five-year term, P.V. Narasimha Rao faced three no-confidence motions and survived all of them because of different reasons. Just after the Harshad Mehta Stock Market scam broke out, Rao survived his first no-confidence motion in July 1992 by managing 267 votes against and 215 in favour. The second was soon after the Babri Masjid demolition in December. It was not very difficult as all non-BJP parties wanted to be seen as against BJP and Rao survived it by a margin of 334 versus 106 votes. The real test was the third no-confidence motion moved by Ajay Mukhopadhyay of CPM (the Communist Party of India [Marxist]) in July 1993 brought on the charges of corruption. The debate started on 20 July 1993 and lasted till 28 July 1993. The arithmetic of outside support and chemistry within the party—both were against Rao. A powerful lobby led by Arjun Singh wanted Rao to be replaced. Unlike previous no-confidence motions, which Rao had easily survived, the motion before parliament this time was supported both by left-wing parties and by the Hindu revivalist BJP, the largest opposition party. BJP was supporting the motion on the issue of corruption. It wanted to leave the Hindu and Ram Mandir rhetoric on the back burner, to be seen with the opposition on the moral and principled stand of removing a corrupt government. It was an alliance of usually bitter enemies. There was very little hope that the government would survive; Rao was conspicuous by not being present in the house during the debate. Speaking before the vote, his speech lacked conviction and purpose. To everyone's surprise, the no-confidence motion got 251 votes in favour and 265 against and Rao survived the most crucial and last motion against his government. The statement of CPM Prakash Karat was most apt—'The problem created by the suitcase has been solved by the suitcase.' The role of four MPs of Jharkhand Mukti Morcha (JMM) and seven MPs who had defected from Ajit Singh's faction of Janata Dal will always be questioned. They all voted for Rao. The case was investigated by CBI and Rao became the first prime minister to be convicted in a corruption case by the lower court. Later he was acquitted by the higher court. The Supreme Court also took a view that jurisdiction of the court is barred under Article 105 (2) of the Constitution for any action of MPs inside the parliament. It relates to the privilege and immunities of the house of parliament.

The story of the Harshad Mehta Stock market scam will always be remembered whenever someone will talk of Narasimha Rao. Before reading about the scam, it is important to know a brief background of the stock market in India. We had about two dozen stock exchanges in India. But after the Securities and Exchange Board of India (SEBI) which is a market regulator came into existence, we only have two operative stock exchanges – the Bombay Stock Exchange (BSE) and National Stock Exchange (NSE). The pulse of the stock market or market indicator is called S&P Bombay Stock Exchange Sensex or BSE Sensex or commonly referred to as Sensex. BSE and consulting firm Standard and Poor's entered into a formal tie-up on 19 February 2013 and since then it is called S & P Bombay Stock Exchange. The term Sensex was coined by stock market analyst Deepak Mohani in 1989 by merging two words Sensitive and Index as Sensex. It is a basket of 30 top shares of the stock exchange (decided by defined different parameters) with a base value of the then value of these 30 stocks as of 1 April 1979 as 100. The Sensex is published since 1 January 1986. It is important to have a small but relevant technical understanding regarding Full Market Capitalization and Free Float Market Capitalization. The Sensex takes into consideration the free-float market capitalization. This means all the shareholding of the company available in the market is to be traded (less director shareholding which is not available for trading. If director shareholding is considered then it becomes Full Market Capitalization).

The journey of the Sensex started in 1979 with 100 points reaching 1,000 after 11 years on 25 July 1990. The Sensex reached 2,000 on 15 January 1992, 3,000 on 29 February 1992 and 4,000 on 30 March 1992. The Sensex doubled from 1,000 to 2,000 in 18 months and doubled from 2,000 to 4,000 in 75 days. The journey of the Sensex from 2,000 to 4,000 is the story of Harshad Mehta, the big bull. Harshad Mehta was born on 29 July 1954 in Rajkot. Mehta stayed in Kandivali, Mumbai, and completed his schooling in Raipur, Madhya Pradesh (now Chhattisgarh). A typical lower-middle-class career was awaiting when after doing B Com from Lajpat Rai College, Mumbai, he started doing odd jobs, all of them related to marketing. Harshad Mehta had other plans after learning the trick of the trade as a jobber under the guidance of Prasann Pranjivandas, a broker in the Bombay Stock Exchange. Harshad Mehta got membership of the Bombay Stock Exchange in 1984. He established his company Growmore Research and Asset Management and became the king of the stock market in about five years. The stock market was surging in an unprecedented way and so was Harshad Mehta's fortune. He was flamboyant and his lifestyle announced that he had arrived. Staying in a 15,000 square feet penthouse with a mini-golf course and swimming pool, a fleet of expensive cars made him not only a role model but also a darling of the stock market.

The pin which burst the bubble was an article by Sucheta Dalal on 23 April 1992 in the *Times of India*. The story explained the technique used by Mehta to manipulate the market. Though few financial experts felt the transactions of the Big Bull to be categorized as fraud was not fair, he took advantage of a few loopholes in the banking system. RFD and BR are two abbreviations that need to be deciphered to understand the fraudulent bank transactions engineered by Mehta. RFD (Ready Forward Deal) is a secured short-term loan of a fifteen-day-period between two banks. The transaction is against government securities (GSec) and instead of doing the transaction directly, a set of brokers were involved between the two banks. The borrowing bank sells the government securities to the lending bank and after the tenure, buys it back at a price decided before the transaction (which included interest and brokerage). The banks never knew who was the borrowing or the lending bank. When deals were made through a broker, it would not be possible for the lending banks to find out where the loans were being moved to. Similarly, the borrowing banks too would not be concerned where the loans would be coming from. The dealings were both done only with the broker. The two banks would not even know with whom they have dealt. The loans were viewed as loans to the brokers and loans from the brokers. Brokers were indispensible. The brokers started using BR (Bank Receipt) instead of actual government securities. So, as long as a lending bank would get its money back with interest, then all the parties were happy.

Now the operation was simple. Take the money from the bank, put it in the stock market, manipulate share of your choice, book profit and return the money to the banker. A case in point is the share of ACC which zoomed from Rs 200 to Rs 9,000 in three months. A few favourite shares of Mehta were of Sterlite and Videocon. Part 2 of his game plan was also unveiled; along with public sector banks, he started operating with Bank of Karad and Metropolitan Co-operative Bank. Now fictitious BRs were issued by banks, money was taken and again returned after using it in the stock market. After the story of Sucheta Dalal, all hell broke loose, which ultimately led to the arrest of Harshad Mehta in November 1992. About 76 criminal cases and more than 600 civil suits were filed against Harshad Mehta. He came out of custody, started writing columns, and giving stock market tips. He was sentenced to five years of rigorous imprisonment in 1999. Harshad Mehta died on 31 December 2001. The decision of the Supreme Court on the petition challenging his sentence came on 14 January 2003 which was upheld by a split decision of 2:1 where one of the three judges pronounced him not guilty. The death brought an end to all the pending criminal cases but civil suits are still going on. These cases are defended by his brother Ashwin Mehta, who graduated in law primarily to defend all the pending cases. Ashwin is confident that someday he will settle all the cases and everyone's liability will be paid. The biggest amount that is outstanding is of the Income Tax Department comprising mainly accrued interest and penalties.

Harshad Mehta was arrested in November 1992 and came out on bail after 111 days in custody. He called for a press conference on 16 June 1993 with the country's top lawyer Ram Jethmalani by his side. He gave details of how the money was paid. According to Mehta, as per the advice of Rao, he handed over the suitcase with 67 lakh rupees to Ram Khandekar, private secretary of the prime minister. The balance amount of Rs 33 lakhs was given a day after as he was not able to arrange the total amount of Rs 1 crore on the day he met the prime minister. As per the interview given to *India Today* (15 July 1993), Harshad Mehta recounted that Satpal Mittal, Congress MP and father of Sunil Mittal of Bharti Telecom, took him to the prime minister. Satpal Mittal told Rao the logic of bringing Rs 67 lakhs as it was a lucky number for them. Mehta played a video in which he gave details of how the bribe money was put in an oversized suitcase as it was doubted that so much of money could not be packed in a suitcase. He also gave an audiotape in which he was talking to Sunil Mittal. It is also strange that neither Harshad Mehta for levelling charges on the prime minister for taking the bribe, nor Rao who was charged for accepting the bribe were convicted. The allegation of Harshad Mehta that money was paid to P. V. Narsimha Rao was examined by the Joint Parliament Committee (JPC) set up to probe into the banking transaction and stock market activities in August 1992. The JPC was headed by Ram Niwas Mirdha. He, along with George Fernandes, Jaswant Singh and other members of the Joint Parliament Committee, cross-examined Mehta in July 1993. The recommendations of the JPC were neither accepted completely nor implemented. Considering the way the stock market was manipulated, the Security and Exchange Board of India (SEBI) was formed to regulate the money market.

There are a series of charges levelled on Rao. A scam that rocked the Indian political and financial world during the tenure of Narasimha Rao was the Hawala Scandal, also called the Jain Diaries case or the Hawala Scam. This Hawala Scam showed a nexus between politicians, bureaucrats and criminals, who were recipients of money from unlawful sources. The Jain brothers were arrested in the Hawala Scam in 1995. Charges were levelled against Narasimha Rao that he had received a bribe and he also tried to influence the inquiry. It was an US $18 million bribery scandal that implicated some of the country's leading politicians.

There was also an allegation by a well-known NRI pickle manufacturer Lakhubhai Pathak of making a payment of $100,000 to the controversial Godman Chandraswami on the insistence of Rao. Pathak was promised a contract for the supply of newsprint and paper pulp in India though Rao was acquitted in 2003.

One case which is still fresh in the minds of people who follow Indian politics is St Kitts, though this was not during his tenure as prime minister but when he was foreign minister in Rajiv Gandhi's government. To malign V.P. Singh, who was emerging as a prime challenger to Rajiv Gandhi, a conspiracy was hatched by K.K. Tiwari, minister of state for external affairs along with Chandraswami and a group of people. Narasimha Rao as minister for external affairs played a key role in this conspiracy. By way of forged documents, a bank account was opened in Saint Kitts in the name of Ajeya Singh, the NRI son of V.P. Singh. It was alleged that a deposit of US $ 21 million was made in his account. The CBI investigated the case and Rao was arrested on the charge of conspiring to harm V.P. Singh's image by forging documents. He was later released on bail in October 1996 creating another record of becoming the first prime minister to be arrested in India on criminal charges. In this case, also, he was acquitted in 1999.

Narasimha Rao also deserves far greater credit for transforming India than what's accorded to him. Reorienting India to flourish in the new world was a distinct political challenge. It is rightly said that 'If Jawaharlal Nehru "discovered" India, it can reasonably be said that P.V. Narasimha Rao reinvented it.' We need to look into the work of Prime Minister Narsimha Rao which changed the destiny of the country. India's Foreign Exchange Reserve (Forex) was at an all-time low of $ 1.2 billion in 1991 and half of it by June 1991. It could hardly last for three weeks' payment of very essential imports. India was on the verge of defaulting on IMF loans. Left with no other option but to take an emergency loan by pledging 67 tons of gold at collateral security. The first trench of 20 metric tonnes of gold confiscated by the State Bank of India known as the sale and purchase option to raise the US $ 200 million was made. Chandrashekhar was the prime minister and Yashwant Sinha his finance minister. As soon as voting was over, the gold was transferred between 21 and 31 May 1991 by air from Mumbai to London and deposited in the Bank of England and the Union Bank of Switzerland. The whole operation was done secretly as it was done in the midst of the 1991 General Elections. During the election, Rajiv Gandhi was assassinated and later, when the nation came to know of this gold pledge, it was felt as if national wealth had been sold. Indicative of the state of the country's economy, even the van carrying the gold from the bank to the airport broke down en route.

As soon as Rao took an oath of office as prime minister, the top most priority was to rescue the sinking Indian Economy. I.G. Patel, ex-governor RBI, who served as the director of the London School of Economics was the prime minister's choice for finance minister. He refused to take up the challenge. It was clear to Rao that he needed a specialist, an economist with international exposure who understood not only international and national economy, macro and micro-paradigms but also bureaucracy and above all, the Indian people. For the first time, a non-political economist Dr Manmohan Singh was entrusted the job of reviving the economy as the finance minister of India. The second trench of 46.91 tonnes of gold was transferred to the Bank of England and Bank of Japan between 4 and 18 July 1991 to raise the US $ 400 million. To steer the nation on a new path of development, Rao kept the ministry of industries with him. The nation witnessed the end of Licence Permit raj. Liberalization, privatization and globalization of the Indian economy started, putting India on the new path of the market-driven economy. This economic model was very different from Nehru's model of the mixed economy. The country was opened up for foreign investors. The equity market was reformed. In 1994, more scientific National Stock Exchange (NSE) started functioning.

Two important personal landmarks of **Rao** which will be almost impossible to surpass by any politician are—one he was a polyglot and knew **seventeen languages in which** he could read, write and speak fluently. Second, he was the only Indian politician to win parliament elections from four different states of India—Hanamkonda of Telengana, Nandyal of Andhra Pradesh, Ramtek of Maharashtra and Brahampur of Orissa. The two other politicians to come anywhere close to him are Sharad Yadav the veteran socialist, who had represented Lok Sabha from three different states—Jabalpur of Madhya Pradesh, Badaun of Uttar Pradesh and Madhepura of Bihar and V.K. Menon who had represented the Lok Sabha from North Mumbai in Maharashtra, Midnapore in West Bengal and Trivandrum in Kerala. Rao as prime minister took two important decisions, which are not much talked about but are certainly a landmark in the democratic traditions of the country—Subramaniam Swamy who was in opposition was made chairman of Labour Standards and International Trade. Never in the past has any prime minister appointed an opposition leader with the rank of a cabinet minister. Another proof of his statesmanship was to send an opposition leader Atal Bihari Vajpayee to represent India at the United Nations, Geneva conference. Two important diplomatic initiatives of Rao which go unnoticed are—the opening of the Israel embassy in India and the Indian embassy in Tel Aviv, a departure from the age-old pro-Arab stand. To improve relations with China, he distanced himself from the Dalai Lama and Tibet issues.

The story will not be complete without another unique record to his name, not as prime minister but as Congress party president from 1991 to 1996. Congress faced the maximum split during his presidency. In 1994, the All-India Indira Congress (Tewari) was formed, which was led by N.D. Tewari, Arjun Singh, Natwar Singh and Rangarajan Kumarmaanglam. In Karnataka, S. Bangarappa, after being replaced by V. Moily as chief minister, formed the Karnataka Congress party in 1992. In Tamil Nadu, two groups left Congress to form new parties—first in 1994, V. Ramamurthy formed the Tamizhaga Rajiv Congress and in 1996, before the elections, G.K. Moopanar formed the Tamil Manila Congress. Also, in Arunachal Pradesh, Gegong Apang left Congress in 1996 to form the Arunachal Congress. The last to leave Congress in 1996 was Madhav Rao Scindia to form the Madhya Pradesh Vikas Congress.

Rao's term both as prime minister and Congress

president was the turning point in the history of India. Till then, India had single-party domination. Congress was all-powerful. All the other opposition parties were put under the umbrella of being non-Congress parties. The anti-Congress sentiment was broadly the binding factor for the opposition parties which had a broad spectrum from left-wing Communist parties to right-wing BJP and with Socialists somewhere in the centre. The left-right spectrum of politics completely changed in the 1990s. Not only did the Congress suffer organizationally but the Janata Party and later, the Janata Dal also fragmented into regional parties, controlled by different families. On 4 October 1992, Mulayam Singh Yadav formed the Samajwadi Party (SP) now controlled by his son Akhilesh Yadav. In 1996, Ajit Singh formed the Rashtriya Lok Dal, which is now under his son Jayant Chowdhury. The Indian National Lok Dal of Devi Lal (popularly known as Tau) was controlled by his son Om Prakash Chautala but the third and fourth generation of Tau don't see eye to eye. Sons of Om Prakash Chautala, Abhay and Ajay Chautala, have different parties controlled by their sons. In 1997, two more offshoots of Janata came up with Lalu Yadav forming the Rashtriya Janata Dal (RJD), which after his conviction in the Fodder Scam case, is run by his wife Rabri Devi and their sons Tejasvi and Tej Pratap. In 1997, Naveen Patnaik formed the Biju Janata Dal (BJD). The leftover of the Janata Dal called the JD(U) over a period of time was further divided to form the Lok Janshakti Party (LJP) of Ram Vilas Paswan, which is now controlled by his son Chirag Paswan. Deve Gauda's party, Janata Dal (S) is run by his son H. D. Kumarswamy. So, all these parties are now family-run parties with an area of influence restricted to their states. What an irony that all these founders of so many Janata parties/*dals* throughout their career talked of the Gandhi-family-domination of the Congress. It was their battle cry not only to fight but end the control of the Gandhi-Nehru family over Congress. Ironically, all of them are now promoting dynastic politics.

The chapter will not be complete without talking about BJP and the Samata Party. The formation of BJP in 1980 was more or less a reincarnation of the old Jana Sangh. During Rao's regime, many opposition leaders left the Janata party and formed their family enterprises in their states. The only exception to it was the formation of the Samata Party by George Fernandes in July 1994. Twenty-two sitting MPs from Janata Dal came out to form the party. Though the maximum leaders were from Bihar, still the party had an all-India character. In UP, Chandrajit Yadav, Harsh Vardhan, Mohan Singh, Harkewal Prasad were leaders with a strong base. In Orissa, ex-speaker Rabi Ray, in Haryana—old-timer Mani Ram Bagri were strong leaders. In Bihar, Nitish Kumar became the face and his Kurmi caste gave the critical mass against the Yadav–Muslim combination of Lalu Yadav. Abdul Ghafoor, popularly known as Chacha Ghafoor, became the state president of the Samata Party in Bihar. In 1995, Samata went for Bihar assembly elections with the confidence of forming the government. The final tally was JDU led by Lalu–167, BJP–41, Congress–29, CPI–26, JMM–10 and Samata–7. After testing the waters, George Fernandes and Nitish decided to go with BJP. This one decision certainly changed the course of history. After the Babri Masjid demolition, BJP was looking for a partner with the credential of being a secular party with a socialist-leaning. The election of 1996 was fought jointly by BJP and Samata. Later, George Fernandes was made Convenor of NDA. So, it was during the rule of P.V. Narasimha Rao that both in the government as prime minister and also as Congress president that BJP marched to replace Congress as the central party of the country with an all-India footprint. During his tenure, Hindu nationalists, a fringe force in Indian politics a mere decade ago, occupied the bulk of opposition seats in parliament, poised to banish the secularism that had been the foundational basis of Indian nationalism.

Chapter-12

Ram Kahaani

Demolition of the Babri Masjid, Rise of a New Social Identity

6 December 1992, Sunday

Rama, the most widely worshipped Hindu deity, is the embodiment of chivalry and virtue and conceived as a model of reason, correct action and desirable virtues. The indelible influence of Lord Ram reverberates in every part of India and his connect with India and Indians is so deep that the term – *'Ram kahaani'* is used for one's own story. But Ayodhya (meaning 'unconquerable' in Sanskrit), the birth place of this *'maryada purshottam'*(a perfect man with high moral values) has become a land of dispute and Ram Mandir in Ayodhya is embroiled in a political, historical, and socio-religious debate for decades. We are going to talk about the story of Ram Mandir. It is said that Mir Baqi, who was a commander of the Mughal emperor Babur was responsible for building a mosque in 1528 after destroying the Hindu temple there and named it Babri Masjid after his king Babar. The first reported communal riot between Hindus and Muslims due to this structure was in 1853. The disputed structure was called Babri Masjid and in the late twentieth century, radical Hindus started calling it

Ramjanmbhumi. For Hindus, the whole of Ayodhya is sacred but Ram is also connected in a much stronger way with *Ramchabutara* (Ram's platform) and *Sita charan chinh rasoi* (kitchen with Sita's footprint). Since we are dealing with the post-Independence events, the status of the masjid was that it was built near *Ramchabutara*, which was believed to be the place where Ram was born. Babri Masjid was the property of Waqf and namaaz (Muslim way of offering prayer) was held there by the Muslims.[1] We got independence in August 1947 and for the next two years, the focus and all resources were diverted to reduce the unenvisaged pain and agony of Partition. The radical Hindu outfit after the murder of Gandhi was confident that no one of the statures of Gandhi was going to come to stop them from realizing their dream of a Hindu Rashtra. Mahatma Gandhi could keep the various factions in Congress together but with his demise, the element of restraint disappeared. The fight between the power blocs in Congress came out in the open. The secularists in Congress were led by Jawaharlal Nehru. Govind Vallabh Pant, the Prime Minister of the United Provinces (the term used for chief minister till the Constitution was implemented in 1950) was a staunch follower of Soft Hindutva.

The real story of Baba Abhiram Das placing the idol of Ram in Babri Masjid on the night of 22–23 December 1949 with the help of District Magistrate K.K. Nair and City Magistrate Guru Dutt Singh was forgotten over a period of time. The historical facts associated with the contrived appearance of the idol in 1949 had slipped into obscurity. The claim of the All India Hindu Mahasabha and Rashtriya Swayamsevak Sangh (RSS)—that the idol had never been planted and Lord Rama had manifested *Himself* at *His* place of birth—gained ground among devout Hindus, largely delinking Abhiram Das from what he had done in the dark hours of that fateful night—the myth of 'divine exercise' was reinforced over a period of time. The demand for a Ram Mandir had to be channelled into a people's movement; therefore, it was necessary to whip up religious fervour by claiming that *Ram Lalla* (Lord Ram in form of child) himself appeared at his birthplace. Twenty-second December 1949 is the Winter Solstice, meaning it is the shortest day of the year or the longest night. This gives more time to perform those activities at night which the people were hesitant to perform during the daytime. Abhiram Das (later known as 'Ramjanmbhumi *udharak*' or '*udharak* baba', the saviour of the birth place of Lord Ram) was named the prime accused in this case which remained inconclusive. The main strategist for placing Ram *Lalla*w as Mahant Digvijay Nath, the head of the Gorakhnath Temple in Gorakhpur, which is one of the most sacred religious seats of Hindus. It is very close to Ayodhya. Mahant Digvijay Nath's name appeared prominently in the Gandhi murder case but was later let off. K.K. Nair the then-district magistrate of Faizabad was his close friend. The elaborate plan would not have been possible without the local administration's help. The city magistrate Gurudutt Singh was a known Hindu Rashtra sympathizer. Though he was a provincial civil service officer, he refused to kowtow to his colonial masters. He refused to wear the customary hat favoured by the British; instead, he preferred to put on a turban in the true Hindu tradition. He was more than eager to implement the plan of putting the idol of Ram *Lalla* inside the mosque where regular namaaz was held. The president of the Uttar Pradesh unit of the Hindu Mahasabha.[2] Mahant Digvijay

Nath soon after became the All India General Secretary of the Hindu Mahasabha. The plan had the tactical support of Hanuman Prasad Poddar, the man who was the trustee of Geeta Press.[3] Abhiram Das after taking a dip in the Saryu river proceeded with the idol of Ram *Lalla* to be placed in Babri Masjid. A word about Saryuji, as it is popularly called is the name of the river Ghaghra but as soon as it touches the city of Ayodhya, the name is Saryu and as it leaves the shores of Ayodhya it gets its original name Ghaghra.[4]

Constable Barkat Ali of the Uttar Pradesh Police was to relieve constable Sher Singh for the night duty at the Babri Masjid entrance. It is not clear if there was some secret understanding between Sher Singh and the five carriers of the Ram idol but Sher Singh woke up Barkat Ali about one hour after the scheduled time of his duty hours. This was after the idol of Ram *Lalla* was placed inside the structure. Barkat Ali, in order to escape punishment for late reporting of duty, found it more convenient to report that the idol of Ram miraculously appeared by itself and he saw the area under the central dome bathed in a golden light. The news of Ram *Lalla* reached Delhi and surprisingly, instead of Patel who was the home minister, it was Jawahar Lal who sent a wire (telegram) to Govind Vallabh Pant on 26 December to remove the idol immediately. He was greatly perturbed by the idol being placed in a mosque. Religious frenzy as an aftermath of Partition was slowly subsiding and Nehru did not want communal poison to spread. The action of Hindu sadhus and their sympathizers could add fuel to the religious fire and destroy the secular fabric of the nation. Nair, who was District Magistrate, Faizabad and Gurudutt Singh, who was the City Magistrate, communicated to the government that removing idols from the site would invite trouble that would be difficult to control. Nehru kept on writing letters to Pant for removing the idol but it suited the chief minister to settle the internal power struggle of the Congress so that followers of Nehru were weakened. The First Information Report (FIR) No. 167/49 lodged by Sub-Inspector Ram Dube at Ayodhya Police Station on 23 December 1949 under section 147, 148 of the Indian Penal Code narrates the details of how the idol was placed:

The FIR manuscript reads:

First Information Report (FIR), of 23 December 1949

Copy of the report (of the) Station Officer (S.O.) dated 23 December 1949, u/s 147/295/448 Taazirate-Hind (IPC), regd. By Pandit Shri Ram Dubey, Senior Sub-Inspector, In-charge Thana (PS) Ayodhya, Faizabad

against

(1) Abhey Ram Das (2) Ram Shukla Das (3) Sudarshan Das R/O Ayodhya Faizabad and other 50 to 60 persons names and addresses not known of Thana Ayodhya.

According to the information of Mata Prasad, Constable No. 7:

That at about 9 in the morning when I reached Janmabhumi, I came to know that a group of 50 to 60 persons have entered the Babri Masjid by breaking open the locks of the compound and also by scaling the walls and staircases and place an idol of Shri Bhagwan in it and scribbled sketches of Sita, Ram Ji etc. in saffron and yellow colours on the inner and outer walls of it. That Hans Raj, the Constable No. 70 stopped them (to *doso*) but they did not care. The PAC Guards present there were called for help. But by then the people have already entered the mosque. Senior District Officials visited the site and ran into action. Later on, a mob of five to six thousand people gathered and tried to enter into the mosque razing religious slogans and kirtans. But due to proper arrangement, nothing happened. Committers of crime (Mujrimane-Waqe) Ram Das, Shukla Das, Sudarshan Das with 50 to 60 persons names not known have desecrated (*napak kiya hai*) the Mosques by trespassing the mosque through rioting and placing idols in it. Officers on duty and many other people have seen it. So the case has been checked. It is found correct.

Sd/-S.O.
(Head Muharrir)[5]

On 27 December 1949, K.K. Nair, ICS (Deputy Commissioner, Faizabad) also wrote to Bhagwan Sahai, Chief Secretary of Uttar Pradesh that it was 'an illegal position created by force and subterfuge'.[6] A civil suit was also filed in Faizabad court for the ownership of the disputed plot No. 583. The administration locked the door on the grounds that the area was disputed and the matter is sub judice.

It is interesting to note that within six months, Gurudutt Singh resigned and became the president of the Bhartiya Jana Sangh, a newly formed political party with the idea of Hindu Rashtra as the core philosophy. He later contested the election and also became a Member of Legislative Assembly (MLA) in Uttar Pradesh. The second bureaucrat K.K. Nair, who was a close friend of Mahant Digvijay Nath, also resigned and became Member of Parliament (MP) on the Jana Sangh ticket in 1967 from the nearby district Bahraich. His wife Sakuntala Nair became the lone Hindu Mahasabha MP from Gonda (West) in the first Lok Sabha election of 1952. She was a member of Uttar Pradesh Vidhan Sabha from 1962 to 1967. She won the Lok Sabha election held in 1967 and 1971 from Kaisarganj on a Jana Sangh ticket. So, husband and wife both were MPs for the fourth Lok Sabha in 1967. Even his driver fought and won an MLA seat on a Jana Sangh ticket.

The battle in the court continued at its pace, where Hindus and Muslims claimed ownership of the site. The court locked the gate of the mosque in which the idol of Ram *Lalla* was placed. On 3 March 1951, the civil judge of Faizabad allowed limited access to Hindu *pujaris* for routine worship of idols. Rajiv Gandhi became the Prime Minister of India in 1984 by sheer fate when Indira Gandhi was assassinated. He was the grandson of Jawaharlal, the man who tried his best to get the idol removed so that status quo was maintained. Rajiv was naive and unaware of the complexities of running the party and government. His core advisors were the likes of Arun Nehru—sharp and intelligent but far removed from ground reality and so their advice also lacked political understanding and maturity. One such case was the amateur handling of the Shah Bano case.

In 1978, Shah Bano, a 62-year-old filed a case against her husband Mohd Ahmad Khan, a leading lawyer of Indore for maintenance of herself and her children as per Section 123 of the Code of Criminal Procedure, 1973. Both had got married in 1932 and Khan subsequently had a second marriage. They had five children and Khan asked her to live separately, gave her irrevocable *talaq* (divorce) and refused to pay maintenance after the period of *iddat*.[7] Khan contested the case supported by the All-India Muslim Personal Law Board arguing that courts cannot interfere as it would violate the Muslim Personal Law Application Act, 1937. The case after travelling through different courts reached the court of Y.V. Chandrachud, the Chief Justice of India. In 1985, the Supreme Court gave the landmark judgement upholding the decision of the High Court that gave orders for maintenance to Shah Bano. The rights of Muslim women regarding matters of marriage and divorce were dealt with by the *sharia* and were outside the purview of regular courts. The case was considered a milestone as it was a step ahead of the general practice of deciding cases based on the interpretation of personal law. It also considered the need for implementing the Uniform Civil Code.

Arif Mohammad Khan, who was the modern reformist Muslim face of Rajiv Gandhi's government, gave a seventy-minute-long speech in the parliament after the Supreme Court verdict hailing the decision as a major step in restoring the dignity and equality of women. The vote managers and election specialists of the Congress party started advising Rajiv Gandhi that this one decision of the Supreme Court was going to alienate Muslims from voting for the party. The traditional vote bank of Congress consisted of Brahmins, Muslims and Scheduled Castes on the strength of which they won a series of elections since Independence. Now, these doctors of vote bank politics predicted that Muslims were going to desert the Congress and hence the fate of the party in the election under Rajiv Gandhi was doomed. They feared that the Congress would face decimation in the polls ahead. Muslim conservatives, armed with religious zeal, forced Rajiv Gandhi to overturn the decision of the apex court. Rajiv Gandhi, who neither had the charisma and vision of Nehru nor the will and ability of Indira to read the pulse of the Indian voters, succumbed to the pressure. He capitulated before the Muslim fundamentalists and brought in a law in 1986 that overturned the Supreme Court verdict. The Muslim Women (Protection of Rights on Divorce) Act, 1986 was passed in the parliament on 5 February 1986. This bill was part of the understanding with the Muslim leadership, which is dealt with at length in the following para. This law overturned the verdict of the

Supreme Court. Shah Bano's lawyer Danial Latifi challenged the act in court but the validity of the new law was upheld. This one act of parliament worked not only against the equality of women but in the long run, it worked against the Congress in vote bank politics. Predecessors of the Nehru-Gandhi family were infamous for their minority appeasement but Rajiv Gandhi took minority appeasement to a whole new unprecedented level. He was accused of giving in to orthodox, fundamental and radical Muslims who said that the judgement conflicted with the *sharia*. The anti-climax of the case was when Shah Bano withdrew the maintenance claim filed by her.

To portray himself as the custodian of secularism of India, his conciliatory and appeasement moves gave birth to communal politics, which was never seen before in the history of independent India. During the course of messing up the Muslim vote bank, another set of doctors specializing in the Hindu vote bank advised Rajiv that if something drastic was not done, he would lose the Hindu vote bank as he would be seen as someone upholding the interest only of Muslims. So, a team of vote-bank specialists led by Arun Nehru decided to open the locked doors of Ramjanmbhumi and allow Hindus to perform puja (rituals as per Hindu customs and traditions). A deal was struck with the Muslim leaders that they would not raise a voice of protest and in return by an act of parliament, the decision of the Supreme Court in the Shah Bano case would be over turned. Veer Bahadur Singh was the chief minister of Uttar Pradesh. The district magistrate (DM) and superintendent of police (SP) of Faizabad were directed to tell the district court that no law-and-order problem was expected if the doors of Ramjanmbhumi was opened to the Hindus. On 25 January 1986, Umesh Chandra Pandey, an advocate applied that the public must be permitted to have *darshan* from inside and the lock placed by the government in 1949 should be opened. On 28 January 1986, the munsif magistrate of Faizabad Harishankar Dubey rejected the application of advocate Chandra Chand Pandey for opening the locks of Ramjanmbhumi. Another application filed in the court of the district judge by Umesh Chandra Pandey was connected with the application of an old pending case no. 2/1949 and listed it for hearing immediately on 1 February. On 1 February 1986, K.K. Pandey, who was the district judge of Faizabad, gave the verdict to open the gates at 4.40 pm. He gave this verdict based on the verbal views of DM and SP. He did not take any written affidavit. The district administration implemented the judgement with a speed unheard and unseen before and opened the locks of the gate at 5.20 pm, within forty minutes of the judgement. That was unlocking the gates of discord.

The regular bhajan and rituals immediately started at Ramjanmbhumi by the devotees. Even the government television channel Doordarshan telecast the opening of the gates. Judge Krishna Mohan Pandey had mentioned that it was divine inspiration that prompted him to order the opening of the locks. He said that he was inspired to open the gate from a langoor (black monkey with a longtail). He mentioned that before this judgement, Hanuman[8] as a langoor came in his dream and on the day of judgement, the said langoor not only came to his house but throughout the day sat outside the court without food and again visited his house in the evening after he pronounced the judgement. So, in 1986, we were presented with a fait accompli thanks to 'divine inspiration'. As already agreed, the Muslim Personal Law Board never opposed this decision of Rajiv Gandhi and accordingly on 5 February, the Muslim Women

Bill was passed in the parliament. The announcement to reverse the Supreme Court judgement on the Shah Bano case and the removal of the locks happened within two weeks. Most people considered this as a balancing act and they hoped that now both Hindus and Muslims would feel satisfied. In the presence of the Union Home Minister Buta Singh and Uttar Pradesh Chief Minister N.D. Tiwari, the *shilanyas* (laying of the foundation stone) of the temple was performed near the disputed site under the supervision of the Congress party which was pursuing a soft Hindutva line. This attempt of the Congress to appease the fundamentalists of both communities gave the BJP a platform that ensured its future electoral successes. It led to successful communal polarisation. The rise of the RSS–BJP–VHP combine and their emergence later as the principal parties of Indian politics can be traced back to these complex political events.

The political wisdom of Rajiv Gandhi failed to check inter-group politics and rivalry within the Congress party. He made several mistakes while preparing the right recipe for vote management. Arif Mohammad Khan– the defender of the Supreme Court decision in the Shah Bano case in the parliament, Arun Nehru—the architect of unlocking the disputed structure and freeing Ram *Lalla* and V.P. Singh– who launched investigations into kickbacks on defence contracts and embarrassed the party, left Congress. The coming together of the troika was not altogether unexpected. The three saw themselves as victims of Rajiv's manoeuvrings. In July 1988, V.P. Singh won the by-election from the Allahabad parliamentary constituency when Amitabh Bachhan resigned as MP and said goodbye to politics. This was the election when Kanshi Ram also fought first time as a Bahujan Samaj Party (BSP) candidate and stood third with about 70,000 votes. The Vishwa Hindu Parishad (VHP) convened Dharma Sansad presided by Paramhans Ram Chandra Das at Prayagraj (Allahabad) during Magh Mela in February 1989.[9] Saints decided to perform *shilanyas* and *shilapujan* on 9 November 1989. The significance of 9 November was that it was *devuththan Ekadashi*.[10] The VHP tactically chose this day because thousands of devotees assemble in Ayodhya on this day. They also gave a call that each village and individual should donate a brick with Ram embossed on it. The bricks were intended to be used for constructing the temple. On 17 October 1989, the Union Home Minister Buta Singh of the Congress party permitted VHP for the *shilanyas* on 9 November 1989. During the run-up for *shilanyas*–the Ramshila *pujan* was organized in villages which led to communal riots in many parts of the country. The worst-affected city was Bhagalpur in Bihar where riots started on 24 October 1989 in which about 900 people died and among the dead, majority were Muslims.

The Dharma Sansad in February 1989 declared the details of the momentous *shilanyas* ceremony on 9 November 1989. Paradoxically this was also the day when the Berlin Wall was brought down and East and West Germanies were united.[11] However, this date brought conflict and disunity in our country. On 11 June 1989, the BJP was quick to seize the opportunity by incorporating the demand for the Ram temple in its agenda at the National Executive meeting held in Himachal Pradesh. The VHP till then was not a part and parcel of BJP. Indira Gandhi had no hesitation in associating with the VHP. In 1983, on the invitation of the VHP, she launched *ekatmata* or the Ganga Jal Yatra.[12] The general elections of 1989 were round the corner and for the BJP, this was going to be the election which would decide their very existence. Their poll managers worked out a pre-poll seat adjustment with the National Front led by V.P. Singh as convenor and N.T. Rama Rao as president of the front. N.T. Rama Rao's Telugu Desam Party, the largest opposition party of thirty seats got only two seats in the 1989 elections when there was a V.P. Singh wave. V.P. Singh united the entire disparate spectrum of parties. He was supported by the left and the right to keep out the Congress. The spectrum of parties entering the pre-poll alliance against Congress led by Rajiv Gandhi had communist parties on one end of the spectrum and the right-wing BJP on the other end of the spectrum. Instead of directly negotiating the seat-share, both the communist and BJP were comfortable having the National Front in between to iron out the rough edges. The BJP with just two sitting MPs in the outgoing 1984 Lok Sabha skilfully manoeuvred, managed and negotiated to contest for 224 seats whereas the National Front (less communist) with about fifty sitting MPs in the outgoing Lok Sabha fought only on 241 seats. The rest of the seats went to the communist parties and others. The Janata Dal/National Front government led by V.P. Singh was a fragile minority government of 143 members supported by two ideologically opposite groups of the right to left – the BJP and communists. The BJP achieved a spectacular increase from winning only two seats in parliament in 1984 to capturing 85 seats in 1989; the two communist parties and their left front allies got fifty-one seats.

A new term coined during the 1989 general elections by the National Front was 'seat adjustment'. The word alliance was not used. This was a win-win situation for all the parties. V. P. Singh, while negotiating this with Rajju Bhaiya of RSS in the presence of Prabhas Joshi of *Jansatta* newspaper in Mumbai, said in no uncertain terms that by embarking on a seat adjustment instead of an alliance, Muslim voters would not leave the Janata Dal and the BJP Hindu voter would be happy that the party they were voting for had nothing to do with Muslims. If it was not too harsh, the voter was fooled or taken for a ride.

On 24 June 1988,Veer Bahadur Singh who was the chief minister of Uttar Pradesh, was made the union minister of communication, and old experienced Brahmin face N.D. Tewari replaced him as chief minister on 25 June 1988 to consolidate Hindu votes. The clinching evidence that the Congress was desperate to use the Hindu majoritarian agenda as its campaign plank was the occasion of the launch of the party's poll campaign. Congress leaders were keen to harness the political advantages opened by the Ayodhya controversy even if that meant brushing aside secular principles. Rajiv Gandhi launched the election campaign for 1989 from Ayodhya on 3 November 1989 assuming that the Congress was the rightful candidate for taking the credit for liberating Ram *Lalla*. Rajiv also announced in the rally that the Congress would bring back Ram*rajya*.[13] The word coined for the Congress Hindu-centric campaign was *soft Hindutva*. The Congress never realized that the issue had already been hijacked by the BJP (one can say snatched or stolen). Initially, no main stream party including the BJP dared to touch this issue for political gains. But later, the BJP assessed the political relevance of this issue and with their well-calibrated efforts took it up in a big way. The Ram Mandir issue proved to have a large catchment area and took the BJP on the path of electoral success.

Rajiv Gandhi lost the 9th Lok Sabha elections held in 1989. V.P. Singh, with the support of the BJP, formed the government. Narayan Dutt became the last Congress chief minister of Uttar Pradesh and in the last thirty years, the Congress is reduced to seven MLAs and one MP from the state in 2020. The power equation in Janata Dal was not settled and Chandrashekhar was giving tactical support to Mulayam Singh Yadav, the chief minister of Uttar Pradesh whereas Lalu Prasad Yadav, the chief minister of Bihar, had the patronage of V. P. Singh. The National Front government implemented the Mandal Commission report on 7 August 1990, which provided reservation to the backward classes and it was the main theme of V.P. Singh's Independence Day speech on 15 August 1990 from the ramparts of the Red Fort. V.P. Singh was positioning himself as the champion of the backward classes and minorities so that he could secure a committed vote bank. The whole country witnessed violent agitation against the implementation of the Mandal Commission and on 19 September, Rajiv Goswami, a student of Delhi University put himself on fire.

The VHP announced the construction of Ram Mandir from 30 October 1990. The BJP was busy addressing its vote bank and Lal Krishna Advani decided to take out his 10,000 km Rath Yatra (a bus converted as a mythological chariot) from Somnath to Ayodhya to muster support for the construction of the temple. The move of Advani was called 'Mandal versus *Kamandal*'. The journey started on 25 September 1990 with the plan of reaching Ayodhya on 30 October to join in the declared Kar Sewa of the VHP. Intelligence reports were confirming the fear that if Kar Sewaks reached Ayodhya they would damage Babri Masjid. Mulayam was positioning himself as the protector of Muslims to garner minority votes. His statement – '*Parinda bhi par nahi maar sakta*' (even a bird cannot reach Ayodhya what to talk of Kar Sewaks) was a relief for Muslims. It was common knowledge that Advani would not be allowed to reach Ayodhya. Mulayam had planned to detain him to further consolidate his position among Muslims. There was another serious contender for Muslim leadership—V.P. Singh himself, and in order to take away the initiative of Mulayam, he advised Lalu Yadav, the chief minister of Bihar to arrest Advani in Bihar. Lalu had planned to arrest Advani in Sasaram, who had left the Rath Yatra midway to attend an important meeting in New Delhi and was returning by train to resume the yatra from Dhanbad. But the plan was leaked and to avoid any law-and-order problem, the programme was shelved. Lalu now planned to arrest him at Samastipur but the plan was kept secret. He called Sudhir Kumar, district magistrate of Dumka to keep the Masanjor guest house ready the next day as he would be coming there. The district magistrate of Samastipur R.K. Singh and the deputy inspector-general of police (DIG) Rameshwar Oraoan were summoned and were asked to stay back. Advani had left Patna and was sleeping in the Samastipur guest house on 23 October 1990 when he was arrested and flown by state helicopter to the Masanjor guest house. When Advani became the home minister during the NDA rule, he chose R.K. Singh to become a joint secretary in his department.[14]

The arrest of Advani triggered the mood of the Kar Sewaks, who defied government orders and assembled in Ayodhya in large numbers (estimated 40,000–50,000) on 30 October 1990—the day of Kar Sewa. These Kar Sewaks reached the disputed site and when they started damaging the structure after hoisting a flag on the dome, police opened fire to disperse them. Eleven died in police firing. The agitated Kar Sewaks decided to reassemble on 2 November

1990. It is alleged that on that day, after lathi charge and tear gas, police opened fire on the agitators when they were about two kilometres away from the disputed structure. This was done on the direct orders of Chief Minister Mulayam Singh Yadav. The action of the police to open fire without first going for water cannon or rubber bullets resulted in a lot of deaths. It is estimated that more than fifty people died due to agitation all over India. This action of Mulayam got him the title of 'Maulana Mulayam'. The commissioner of Faizabad Madhukar Gupta, who was in charge of the government arrangement, was the first cousin of Ashok Singhal, the VHP head.

As expected, the BJP withdrew its support to the National Front government and V. P. Singh resigned on 7 November 1990 after 343 days as Prime Minister. Chandrashekhar became the prime minister for a brief period with the support of the Congress. On the petty issue of the Haryana government keeping surveillance on Rajiv Gandhi, Congress withdrew its support to Chandrashekhar and the country faced mid-term elections in 1991. The second Janata experiment of opposition parties not only failed but the result was diametrically opposite to the objective of its formation. Instead of uniting opposition parties, it gave birth to splinter groups in many states. Rajiv Gandhi was assassinated and the Congress, which was not in the reckoning, managed to get 244 seats and formed the government. The BJP got the formula of winning elections—an issue of construction of Ram Mandir, which gave them 120 seats in the Lok Sabha. Advani, the poster boy of Rath Yatra, became the leader of opposition relegating V.P. Singh's Janata Dal with 69 seats.

In 1991, in the Uttar Pradesh assembly elections, the BJP got a clear majority and Kalyan Singh became the chief minister. Different events were organized by various Hindu parties, and groups, with Ram Mandir as the central theme. The Kalyan Singh government acquired 2.77 acres of land of the disputed structure and gave it to the Ramjanmbhumi Trust on lease, at a rent of Re 1 per year. As expected, the move was challenged in the High Court which stayed the order and directed the state government to stop any permanent construction on the acquired land. The decision of the High Court was challenged in the Supreme Court. The VHP declared that suspended Kar Sewa would resume from 9 July 1992 and to circumvent the order of the High Court, the term used for the Ram Mandir 'construction' was changed to Ram Mandir 'repair'. More than 50,000 Kar Sewaks assembled in Ayodhya on 9 July and a platform was made as a symbolic start of the Ram Mandir construction. The BJP took a stand that it was done by Hindu saints and they had nothing to do with it and the central government should directly talk to them without involving the state government. On 23 July 1992, Hindu Saints and Narasimha Rao met and Kar Sewa was stopped for ninety days. The first and only official effort between the VHP and the Babri Masjid Action Committee (BMAC), where the government was also involved, started. The central minister P. R. Kumarmanglam was representing and coordinating on behalf of the central government. On 30 October 1992, the VHP announced in the Dharma Sansad that talks had failed and 6 December 1992 would be the date of Kar Sewa. Though after this, the VHP and BMAC again met on 8 November 1992 and the BMAC announced that it had no agenda to discuss and resolved the issue. Prime Minister Rao and Chief minister Kalyan Singh met to resolve the issue and a meeting of the National Integration Council was called on 23 November. The meeting was boycotted by the BJP. On 26 November, the Uttar Pradesh government filed its affidavit in the Supreme Court reassuring and promising that nothing would happen to the disputed structure during Kar Sewa. Because of this affidavit, Satya Narain Reddy, the governor of Uttar Pradesh, who was summoned to New Delhi, went back to Lucknow and the plan to sack the Kalyan Singh government and protect the disputed structure under the central rule was also shelved.

The High Court verdict was also awaited. The two leaders of the BJP—Atal Bihari Vajpayee and Lal Krishna Advani on many occasions expressed their view that delay in the High Court judgement was also one of the reasons for demolishing the structure. The argument was if the land was given to them, then there would have been no issues even if the court verdict had not been in their favour. The construction of the mandir would have commenced by altering the site or design or at the place where during Congress rule, the *shilanyas* had been held. In the High Court, the case came up on 30 November giving hope of a verdict, then was pushed to 4 December and again for 11 December.

The government of BJP led by Kalyan Singh had given the confidence to Kar Sewaks that whatever be the law-and-order issue, the police would not open fire. On Gita Jayanti Day,[15] that is 5 December 1992, Atal Bihari Vajpayee addressed the Kar Sewaks in Lucknow. The master orator's tone was sarcastic, his words were controversial and his body language was buoyant. His speech smacked of complicity and was laden with innuendo, allusions and imagery. He informed the Kar Sewaks that the court had stopped the construction of a permanent structure but there was no restriction on bhajan-kirtan. He further added that it was not possible to stand for long hours and do bhajan-kirtan, so one had to sit. He further explained that if one had to sit, the place had to be cleaned. All the sharp stones had to be removed from the area and the ground levelled. It had to be made fit for sitting. Arrangements for a yajna[16] had to be done. It is still not clear what Vajpayee meant by those 'sharp stones' and 'levelling of the ground'at the disputed site at Ayodhya but the fact is that the sixteenth-century Babri mosque was demolished the very next day. On 6 December, except for Vajpayee, the top leaders of BJP–Advani, Murli Manohar Joshi, Vijay Raje Scindia, Pramod Mahajan and Uma Bharti were all present in Ayodhya. For the first time, the official RSS bigwig—H.B. Seshadri, K.C. Sudarshan and Moropant Pingle were camping in Ayodhya since 3 December 1992 overseeing the preparation. It was clear that BJP leaders were prepared for an apocalyptic event at Ayodhya. More than 2 lakh Kar Sewaks descended on Ayodhya for the event. The auspicious time (*muhurta*) was at 12.15 hours; the published programme was puja and symbolic construction at Ram *chabutra*. The Kar Sewaks started gathering; not an inch of land in the notified area of 46 acres of land was without a Kar Sewak. After performing the routine puja, the door of Ramjanmbhumi/Babri Masjid was closed for the last time around 11 am. By noon, the crowd was out of control; the police barricade was broken and more than 200 Kar Sewaks climbed the three domes and a strong frenzied crowd of about a lakh surrounded the domes. The stage for the VHP and BJP leaders was erected 300 metres from the disputed site in Ram Katha Kunj Park overlooking the domes. Advani and Ashok Singhal's repeated appeals not to destroy the main dome as the idol of Ram *Lalla* was resting inside were not heard by the crowd. The three leaders Uma Bharti,

Sadhvi Ritambhara and Acharya Dharmendra were openly inciting the crowd to demolish the structure by coining new slogans. A few of the slogans coined by them were

> *Gandhi bolo Jai Shri Ram, Jinnah bolo Jai Shri Ram, Mullah bolo Jai Shri Ram*
> *Ram Naam satya hai, Babri Masjid dhvast hai*
> *Ek dhakkaa ur do, Babri Masjid tor do*

Photographs taken after the demolition show a jubilant and excited Uma Bharti on the stage climbing on the back of Murli Manohar Joshi in full public view. In five hours of Kar Sewa, all three domes were razed to the ground. The idol of Ram *Lalla* was taken away by someone in the melee and to date, it is not recovered. Raja Vimalendra Pratap Mishra gave new idols and the same were placed in the temporary mandir (which was a tent shed). By 7 pm, bhajan kirtan started in front of Ram darbar in the temporary mandir.[17]

It will be interesting to know the activity of individuals and institutions who failed to protect the disputed structure. To start with the district administration, the Director General (DG) of Indo-Tibetan Border Police (ITBP) asked permission from the district magistrate to move two battalions around 1 pm to protect the structure but was told that the permission would be given by the magistrate of that specific area. The DG kept on looking for the elusive magistrate who remained untraceable. The then District Magistrate (DM), R.N. Shrivastav and Senior Superintendent of Police (SSP), D.B. Rai are on record that DIG (Deputy Inspector General) CRPF (Central Reserve Police Force) Malik asked for one magistrate and PAC (Provincial Armed Constabulary) Company to guard every company of CRPF. The district officers say it was ridiculous to ask for fifty gazetted officers, fifty magistrates and the most hilarious demand of PAC to protect the central police force. Kalyan Singh, after giving an affidavit in the Supreme Court, was at his residence basking in the sun.[18] Initially, it is said that he was hurt as he was not taken into confidence by the BJP leadership and wanted to resign immediately but was stopped by Advani to get the crucial few hours to complete the task. His immediate resignation would have passed the decision-making from the state to the central government and it was apprehended that the centre could stop the demolition midway. Advani in his autobiography *My Country My Life* has written that it was the 'saddest day of my life'.[19] Prime Minister Narsimha Rao decided to close himself alone and was briefed by one or two people on the development and remained indecisive. But it is widely believed that it was his decision—'not to take a decision'. It is alleged that instead of immediately terminating Kalyan Singh, he waited till the new idols were placed and then the state government was sacked but Kalyan Singh by that time had already resigned. The advocate of the Uttar Pradesh Government K. Venugopal was asked to explain in the Supreme Court that evening. He told the court, 'My clients misled me and I am ashamed.' The three defined arms of our Constitution—the Legislature, Judiciary and Executive not only failed to protect the monument but their neutrality for times to come will always be doubted.

Notes

1. An Islamic endowment of property to be held in trust and used for a charitable or religious purpose
2. An organization formed in 1915 to protect the rights of Hindus as an answer to the formation of the Muslim League in 1906 to defend the rights of Muslims.

3. A well-known publishing institution started in 1923 by Jaya Dayal Goyanka and Ghanshyam Das Jalan for printing of Hindu religious text books.
4. In the Hindi heartland, the name of any river is taken with a lot of reverence, and *ji or mata or maiya* is added after the name as a mark of respect.
5. Verbal source
6. Letter manuscript mentioned in the book *The Babri Masjid Question, 1528–2003 – 'A Matter of National Honour'*, vol. 1, 215, by A.G. Noorani, Delhi: Tulika Books, 2020 (Paperback). A. G. Noorani is a famous lawyer and Constitution expert.
7. As per the Muslim personal law, the three months after divorce/ death is called *iddat* after which the woman is free to marry.
8. A Hindu monkey-god known as the favourite devout of Lord Ram
9. Magh Mela is an annual Hindu festival on the banks of rivers. It is believed that by taking a holy dip during the month of Magh, one can wash away all their sins and it is also a gateway for attaining *moksha*.
10. The Hindu gods awaken after four months' recess; during these four months no auspicious work is done as it is believed that the gods are resting.
11. The Berlin Wall was a concrete structure separating East and West Germany; it was built by GDR (the German Democratic Republic) and part of the Eastern Bloc in 1961 and remained like that during the Cold War. It was a physical wall which separated it from western Europe. Willy Brandt termed it the Wall of Shame.
12. In 1983, VHP started a series of pilgrimage to promote and gather support for Hindu polity.
13. A concept of governance in which a state takes care of the poorest of the poor with no discrimination on the basis of caste, colour, creed or sex.
14. R. K. Singh also served as home secretary during the United Progressive Alliance (UPA) regime when Chidambaram was the home minister. After retirement, he fought elections from Arrah and became a BJP MP, and in the second Modi government, he is the union energy minister. Rameshwar

Oraoan resigned, became Congress MP from Jharkhand in 2004. He served as union minister with Manmohan in the UPA government and is currently minister in Jharkhand.

15. The day Sri Krishna narrated the Gita to Arjuna on the first day of the war at Kurukshetra.
16. A Hindu ritual performed before the fire.
17. It is considered that Ram, Sita, Laxman and Hanuman make Ram Darbar; many Hindus keep this Ram Darbar in the form of idols or pictures in their homes, place of worship, etc.
18. Hemant Sharma, 2020. *Ayodhya: The Battleground*. Delhi: Rupa Publications India.
19. L. K. Advani, 2008, *My Country My Life*, Delhi: Rupa Publications India.

Chapter-13

Pokhran II

From 'Smiling Buddha'to 'Operation Vijay'

11 May 1998, Monday

The former President of India Dr Abdul J. Kalam had mentioned in his book *Wings of Fire*[1] his visit to NASA's Wallops Flight Facility, Maryland in the United States. During this visit, he saw a painting showing Tipu Sultan's army fighting the British forces with rockets, which was proof of Indian research and development that kept us ahead of Europeans in the field of warfare innovations. Tipu Sultan is the only Indian king to die on the battlefield while defending his motherland from the British forces.[2]

To understand the Indian nuclear programme, it will be prudent to look back into the formation of the club of five super powers and the path they followed. These five super powers are the five permanent members of the UN Security Council—the US, Russia, China, France and Britain—are all nuclear powers. They prevent the other countries from testing nuclear weapons and prevent the spread of nuclear weapons and technology but they themselves are engaged in or have plans to modernize their nuclear arsenal and related facilities. During World War II, Germany was working on nuclear weaponry. To counter this, Project Manhattan was launched. Project Manhattan was a code name for the American-led effort to develop a functional atomic bomb during World War II. The project was a collaboration among USA, UK and Canada. Their first test was conducted on 16 July 1945. The USA also became the first and the only nation to use this new found discovery. The USA, in less than thirty days of the test, dropped bombs named *Little Boy* and *Fat Man* on Hiroshima and Nagasaki on 6 and 9 August 1945 respectively. This action of the US can never be justified. There was no logic for the use of this bomb as Hitler was dead on 30 April 1945 and for all practical purposes, the allied forces were the winners and in control. The justification given by America was that it had the desired effect of ending World War II and the Japanese agreed to sign the peace treaty. Most of the debate over the atomic bombing of Japan focuses on so many unanswerable questions like whether it was necessary to use an atom bomb or why to use two and not just one? In the race for supremacy to dominate the world, the USSR successfully tested its nuclear device called RDS-1 on 29 August 1949. The United Kingdom tested it on 30 October 1952, France on 13 February 1960 and finally, China entered the club in 1964.

Before choosing Pokhran to conduct the nuclear test, a site in the Telangana region was identified but it had habitation within 25 sq. km. So, it was not chosen. The Andaman Islands gave the isolation required for the nuclear test site but to camouflage, the movement of so many people was not possible. Pokhran had all the characteristics needed for a nuclear-testing site. The place is close to the Pakistani border. It is under army control—therefore routine defence exercise and movement of people do not attract any attention. The Pokhran range was 1,200 sq. km, which is much more than the required range. The place also has very little human population. The water table is very low so it is ideal for any underground test.

The first nuclear test was conducted on Buddha Purnima Day on 18 May 1974. It was termed a nuclear test for peaceful purposes. The code name of the operation was 'Smiling Buddha' and India became the sixth nation of the world to have nuclear capability. The journey after this test was very difficult. A determined and strong Indira Gandhi was responsible for taking this difficult decision of conducting Pokhran I. It was also the first confirmed nuclear weapons test by a nation outside the club of five permanent members of the Security Council, who opposed such tests. Indira's political career was on a decline after 1974. The nuclear program was left without any political leadership and basic management. India had to wait for 24 years to conduct its first weaponized nuclear warhead. A long hiatus in overt nuclear weapons development followed the 1974 test.

The 11th Lok Sabha which lasted for less than two years saw three prime ministers during this period. First, Atal Bihari Vajpayee became prime minister for thirteen days, followed by H.D. Deve Gowda and finally I.K. Gujral. Two attempts by Narasimha Rao in 1995 and 1996 to carry on the nuclear test were thwarted by the US government. They got the news in advance about India's plan to conduct the test and mounted international pressure due to which India had to withdraw. Way back on 16 October 1964 when China conducted a nuclear test for the first time, Atal Bihari Vajpayee as Jana Sangh member, told Rajya Sabha, 'The answer to an atom bomb is an atom bomb, nothing else'. When Pokhran I was conducted by Indira Gandhi in May 1974, Vajpayee was one of the first opposition leaders to hail and congratulate Indira for becoming the sixth nuclear power in the world. Nineteenth March 1998 was historic when Atal Bihari Vajpayee once again took an oath of office and became the prime minister.

Post Pokhran I, people and scientists involved with the nuclear test were getting impatient to carry on the test further as America was giving all the help and technology to Pakistan. China was also sharing the knowhow and it was only a matter of time for Pakistan to conduct the test. A meeting of Prime Minister Atal Bihari Vajpayee, the Defence Research and Development Organisation (DRDO) head A.P.J. Abdul Kalam and the Department of Atomic Energy (DAE) head R. Chidambaram was held on 8 April 1998. Besides Kalam and Chidambaram, the core team consisted of the Director of the Bhabha Atomic Research Centre (BARC) Anil Kakodkar and K. Santhanam, Mission Director. Nuclear test preparations began immediately after the meeting. The Indian Intelligence Agency had been aware of United States spy satellites detecting the Indian nuclear test preparations since 1995. The US kept a close vigil on the Pokhran site through their two KH-11 keyhole photo imagery. Therefore, the tests required complete secrecy to avoid any international hindrance. The Principal Secretary to the Prime Minister Brajesh Mishra was to coordinate everything from the government side from the PMO (Prime Minister's Office). No minister, not even Defence Minister George Fernandes was informed about this test, the only exception being Home Minister L.K. Advani.

A film on Pokhran II–*Parmanu*—is very close to the actual incident. Barring *filmy Tadka* (filmy drama) keeping in mind the box office to make the film commercially viable, it is close to reality. The Pokhran II nuclear test was assigned the code name *Operation Shakti.* It was decided that all the scientists and manpower involved would be wearing army uniform to deceive the spies in space as well as on the ground. The blind spots when the spy satellite was elsewhere were of three to seven hours with a frequency of two per local day.[3] The test was scheduled for May keeping in mind two major factors. First, the winds pick up speed during this month resulting in serious sand storms denying clear vision; tyre marks of the rolling trucks and other vehicles are also wiped out due to this. The second reason was, it becomes difficult for an infrared sensor to pick up images when the temperature rises above 50 degrees Celsius.

The nuclear device from the BARC Mumbai was airlifted and brought to Jaisalmer in trenches from different destinations and transferred to the site through different army trucks. On 10 May, three shafts, code-named White House, Taj Mahal and Kumbhkaran, were placed with the thermo-nuclear device (Shakti I), fusion device (Shakti II) and kiloton device (Shakti III) and sealed at 8.30 pm. India was ready for the big leap. George Fernandes, the three service chiefs, the foreign secretary were informed and the cabinet committee on security met on 11 May. A hurried press conference was called and Prime Minister Vajpayee informed the nation that India had performed the nuclear test at 3.45 pm. It was a defining moment for both—the country and Vajpayee, who was leading a precarious coalition under the National Democratic Alliance (NDA). All the top reporters covering science and technology were in Bengaluru attending a conference of the Council of Scientific and Industrial Research (CSIR). Murli Manohar Joshi, Minister of Science and Technology, who was also in the conference stopped the proceedings to break the news.

On 13 May 1998, India wrapped up Pokhran II after conducting two more tests Shakti IV and Shakti V.

The international community led by the USA made a lot of hue and cry. Many sanctions were imposed. The complete philosophy of India taking up Pokhran II can be found in the reply given by Dr A.P.J. Abdul Kalam when on 18 May 1998, Sunday, he was briefing the press. When some foreign correspondent asked him justification of a poor country like India to go for Pokhran II he said – 'India has always been a nation under attack in its long history, surrounded by hostile neighbours, and it requires a strong deterrence. In contrast, the US has never been attacked and had had the least threat, but possesses the highest number of nuclear weapons. Was it justified?' (*Business Line*, 2018). As expected, Pakistan also conducted nuclear test Chagai 1 on 28 and Chagai 2 on 30 May 1998.

In May 1998, both India and Pakistan conducted nuclear tests and over the next twelve months, these two rival nations went from making one of the most significant peace overtures to fighting the world's first and only hot conflict between two nuclear powers. *These twelve months in 1998–99 transformed the India-Pakistan rivalry. Nuclear weapons have since ensured a certain deterrence and demonstrated that they may not be used in the resolution of political disagreements.* Soon after the tests, Advani confidently proclaimed, 'India's decisive step to become a nuclear-weapon state has brought about a qualitatively new state in India-Pakistan relations, particularly in finding a lasting solution to the Kashmir problem. Islamabad has to realize the change in the geostrategic situation in the region and the world.'[4]

Advani couldn't have been more wrong. Islamabad did realize but in a very different way. Kargil war is the cogent comprehension of what the Pokhran tests meant for Pakistan and its approach for Jammu and Kashmir.

To understand Operation Vijay in 1999, when we reclaimed our pickets in Kargil from Pakistani infiltrators, we have to briefly go through the history. It is a unique example in world history that India and Pakistan got independence first and borders were created later. On 17 August 1947, India and Pakistan borders were established by the Radcliffe Line, in the name of the Chairman of the Border Commission. The two nations have a common border of 3,323 km called by different names. In the state of Jammu and Kashmir (from October 2019 called union territory of Ladakh and Jammu–Kashmir) the India–Pakistan border of 1,222 km can be categorized into three sections; the Siachen glacier located in India running from Indira Col to NJ 9842 has neither the Line of Control (LOC) nor an international border defined; an 830 km-stretch of LOC runs from NJ 9842 to the southern most point on the west of the Chenab and the rest is the international border. The three Indian states south of Jammu and Kashmir with defined international borders are Punjab (425 km), Rajasthan (1,170 km) and Gujarat (506 km).

Two nations created in August 1947 entered into a state of war to have control over the unified state of Jammu and Kashmir which was amalgamated with India by the ruler Raja Hari Singh. An agreement between military representatives of India and Pakistan regarding the establishment of a ceasefire line in the state of Jammu and Kashmir, popularly known as the Karachi agreement, was signed on 27 July 1949. It was supervised by the United Nations Commission for India and Pakistan (UNCIP) established by the Security Council Resolution 39 of April 1948 and Lt General S.M. Shrinagesh (later Chief of Army) signed on behalf of India. Other members of the Indian delegation were Major General K.S. Thimayya (later Chief of Army), Brigadier Sam Maneckshaw (later Field Marshal of Indian Army) and Major S.K. Sinha, Aide-de-camp (ADC) of General Shrinagesh (later Lt General; he was one of the brightest officers of the Indian Army not made Chief of Indian Army by Indira Gandhi as he had refused to attack the Golden Temple). Major General W.J. Cawthorn (an Australian soldier) signed on behalf of Pakistan. Hernando Samper and M. Delvoie signed on behalf of the United Nations Commission for India and Pakistan (UNCIP).

The 830-km ceasefire line was drawn from the southern most point, west of Chenab to NJ 9842, the northern most point. The China border was about 65–75 km from NJ 9842, separated by the Siachen glacier. The Shimla Agreement was signed on 3 July 1972 (at 0040 hrs midnight of 3 July, though the actual agreement is dated 2 July 1972).[5] By this agreement, the ceasefire line was converted to a Line of Control (LOC). The agreement again was silent on the Siachen glacier (maybe it was considered to be barren and inhospitable for any human habitation).[6]

The access to Siachen from the Pakistan side is not very steep as compared to India and if it was occupied by Pakistan and China from the Aksai Chin side, it would have a common border.[7] General Zia ul Haq after executing Zulfikar Ali Bhutto in 1979 turned his attention on Siachen. He started sending expeditions to the glacier to plan its occupation. Sometime in early April 1984, the Research and Analysis Wing (R & AW) passed on information to Indian defence that the Pakistani army had ordered for uniform and equipment for use in the snowclad area. On further probe, intelligence reported that the anticipated date for the Pakistani army to occupy Siachen was on 17April 1984.

Lt General Prem Nath Hoon born in Abbottabad in Pakistan (Bin Laden was hiding in Abbottabad when US forces killed him in May 2011), was General Officer Commanding-in-Chief (GOC-in-C) of Western Command. He was to command Operation Meghdoot to occupy Siachen. The delay was due to the non-availability of fighting gears for snow. The temperature goes down to minus sixty degrees Celsius in Siachen.

The required snow-protection kit, equipment and ammunition arrived on 12 April and on Baisakhi Day, that is 13 April 1984, Operation Meghdoot commenced. Ladakh Scout and 4th Kumaon occupied Bilafond La, Sia La and Gyang La and since then, our soldiers are occupying these posts paying a heavy price. Many lives were lost at the time occupying the glacier due to hostile weather. On average, two soldiers die here every month.

After Pokhran II and Chagai 1 and 2, both India and Pakistan were facing many sanctions from the world community. Especially five nations who had nuclear capability and were permanent members of the Security Council with veto rights of the United Nations were against the two countries. Atal Bihari Vajpayee and his Pakistani counterpart Nawaz Sharif had many common problems and to break the ice, Vajpayee took the historical Lahore Bus Journey on 19 February 1999. The visit to Lahore by an Indian Prime Minister was after a gap of ten years. Some groups in Pakistan protested this initiative of Vajpayee and Sharif, though Indians stood behind their prime minister. Vajpayee took with him people from different walks of life like Dev Anand, Javed Akhtar, Shatrughan Sinha, Kapil Dev, Mallika Sarabhai, Kuldip Nayar, etc.

For the inaugural run of the Delhi–Lahore bus service named Sada-e-Sarhad (Call of the Frontier),Vajpayee's initial programme was to just cross the Wagah border and come back. But Sharif insisted, *'Dwar tak aye ho, Ghar nahin aaoge?'* (You have come to the door, won't you come inside?). The main reception was organized at Lahore Fort. Shariff entrusted the arrangement of the venue to Salima Hashmi, daughter of poet Faiz Ahmad Faiz, who was the principal of the National College of Arts. When Vajpayee visited Minar-e-Pakistan, the symbolic icon of the creation of Pakistan he wrote in the visitor's book: 'A stable, secure and prosperous Pakistan is in India's interest. Let no one in Pakistan be in doubt. India sincerely wishes Pakistan well.'

The treaty signed by the two prime ministers and the subsequent Memorandum of Understanding (MOU) signed by K. Raghunath and Shamshad Ahmad, foreign secretaries of India and Pakistan respectively on 21 February 1999, was known as the Lahore Declaration. It was ratified by the parliaments of both nations. It was agreed to implement the Shimla Agreement and a clause defining how both nations should respect each other as the development of nuclear weapons brought added responsibility to both nations towards avoiding conflict. The extra mile which Vajpayee walked established India as a nation not hungry for war, a nation which wanted to live peacefully with her neighbours and wanted to resolve mutual disputes with no third-party (USA) intervention. General Parvez Musharaff, Chief of the Pakistani Army, boycotted this event.

After 1984, many plans were made by Pakistan for adventure in Siachen but it always got postponed due to some reason or the other. Siachen remained a thorn for Pakistan's establishment and haunted the military as well as their politicians. The Pakistan Army is headed by a four-star general. Chairman of Joint Chiefs is normally the seniormost head of the Army, Air Force and Navy. In India, we have Chief of Defence Staff since 2019, a position held by a five-star general. Nawaz Sharif sacked General Jehangir Karamat, Chairman of the Joint Chiefs and Army Chief in October 1998, and made Parvez Mushraff an artillery officer and a four-star general as Army Chief. He superseded two generals. General Mushrraf summoned Lt General Mahmood Ahmad, Lt General Mohd Aziz and Major General Javed Hasan in November 1998, and a plan for Kargil was initiated. Nawaz Sharif has maintained that the operation was conducted without his knowledge. But this has been challenged by some opinion-makers in Pakistan. It is said that Sharif was briefed about the operation from time to time by the army. As per the standard practice of the last fifty years, Indian soldiers had been regularly vacating the bunkers and posts located on the LOC Drass Kargil sector during the harsh winters of Kashmir. They occupy it again once the winter season is over. In the winters of 1998–99, as per the plan of the generals, these empty bunkers and posts numbering about 132 were occupied by the Pakistani army throughout 100 km. The NH 1, a distance of 316 km from Leh to Zozila pass, which connects Srinagar, was the lifeline of the entire Ladakh region. The Kargil war was reported extensively by media, both electronic and print. We will touch on some salient events and incidents of the Kargil conflict. The National Democratic Alliance (NDA) led by the Atal Bihari Vajpayee government lost the trust motion brought against them by the narrowest margin possible. The trust fell by 270 votes against and 269 in favour. Vajpayee was the caretaker prime minister. Pakistan strategists thought it to be the best time to execute the conspiracy. On 3 May 1999, a few shepherds carrying binoculars to manage their herd in the Drass sector reported some suspicious activity to the Indian army. Twenty-two-year-old Lt Saurabh Kalia, who had passed out from the Indian Military Academy (IMA) in December 1998 had joined the 4th Battalion Jat regiment. He went on a recce on 15 May 1999 with five soldiers never to come back. The missing of the entire recce party also raised doubts. In the meantime, war broke out and their badly mutilated bodies were handed over after twenty-two days. There were visible marks of torture on their bodies. In gross violation of the Geneva Convention, the Pakistani army subjected Captain Kalia and his soldiers to horrendous torture during which their eardrums were pierced with hot iron rods, eyes punctured, limbs were chopped off, teeth broken and skull fractured. The autopsy of the bodies also revealed that they were burned with cigarette butts. It was confirmed that it was not a Mujahedeen adventure as claimed by Pakistan but a full-fledged army operation. The planners in Pakistan miscalculated two things—first, they were confident that by occupying an advantageous vantage position, the Indian army would not be able to strike back. Secondly, they thought that if they disrupted NH 1, the lifeline to Ladakh would be strangulated but they failed to understand that in that case, India would have no option but to strike back. The over confidence of Pakistan that they have a nuclear arm and can bulldoze their way was also ill-founded. They lacked the basic understanding that after Nagasaki-Hiroshima, even the US had never used nuclear weapons, not even during the humiliating withdrawal from Vietnam. Recently, even North Korea with all the rhetoric and threats never used its nuclear arm.

One hundred and thirty Bofors guns deployed proved to be the most effective strike weapon of Kargil. Eighteen grenadiers, one Naga, two Rajputana Rifles started the formal infantry attack on 22 May 1999 and from a routine border skirmish, it was now a full-fledged war. After the recapture of Tololing on 13 June, Prime Minister Vajpayee visited Kargil. The war lasted for about two and a half months.The Air Force later joined the Army to clear the Pakistani troops occupying Indian territory. India never wanted to scale up the war and so the brief of the Air Force was specific—be inside Indian air space, destroy the Pakistani post and break the supply chain. A couple of war veterans consider the capture of Point 5140 as the turning point of the war. The hero of 5140 was Vikram Batra of 13 JAK Rifles, commissioned as Lieutenant in 1997 from the Manekshaw Battalion in the Indian Military Academy (IMA). He completed the Young Officers (YO) course from Mhow in Madhya Pradesh and was awarded Alpha grading. He attended the Commando Course at Belgaum, Karnataka, where he excelled. He was awarded the highest grading – the Instructor's Grade.

The advance party of 13 JAK had reached Shahjahanpur, their new place of posting when they were redeployed to Dras, Kargil on 5 June 1999. On 19–20 June, a night assault was made to capture Point 5140, the highest point in the Tololing ridgeline. In the early hours of 20 June, around 4.30 am the transmitter heard the success signal of Vikram–*Yeh Dil Mange More.* The highlight of the 5140 operation was no casualty, barring some wounds. Vikram was promoted as Captain. The 13 JAK rifles were now moved to Mushkoh Valley and the next target was Point 4875. The post was critical as a stretch of 30–40 km of NH 1 highway was directly under the observation of the enemy. The assault started on 4 July. Vikram had a fever and was recovering from his wounds. The raiding party met with a surprise attack from the north of Point 4875 from Area Flat

Top and it was now certain that without capturing it, Point 4875 was invincible. The battle continued for three days. A group of fellow soldiers were stuck. Vikram volunteered to bring them back. The commander reluctantly permitted him as he was running temperature. On the night of 6-7 July, he started climbing the hill with twenty-five soldiers but finally had to resort to full day light frontal attack on the enemy who had occupied an advantageous position. The fighting was fierce and one of his soldiers hit by the enemy fire was lying in open. Subedar Raghu Nath Singh was closer to the injured man and started to move to bring him undercover. Vikram told Subedar Singh to hold on and himself went out in open telling him, 'You have children and family, I have no responsibility at home.' He had almost dragged the injured man undercover but at the last minute was hit by an enemy bullet to become a martyr on the battlefield. He was awarded the Param Vir Chakra, the highest battle honour.

A total of four soldiers were awarded the Param Vir Chakra in Kargil—Capt. Vikram Batra and Capt. Manoj Pandey posthumously, Hagldar Sanjay Kumar and Naib Subedar Yogendra Singh Yadav are still serving the Indian Army. The story of the bravery of the other three recipients is equally captivating and fascinating. Havildar Sanjay Kumar was also of 13 JAK Rifles and conferred the award for his bravery in capturing Point 4875. Captain Manoj Pandey of 1/11 Gorakha Rifles gave his life while attacking Jubar Top in Batalik Sector on 3 July 1999. Yogendra Yadav of 18 Grenadiers is now a profound speaker and delivers motivational lectures. His character was played by Hrithik Roshan in the film *Lakshya*.

Though the Indian Navy never engaged itself, it moved its vessels on the western coast and readied itself for an attempted blockade of Pakistani ports to cut off supply routes due to which Karachi, the main Pakistani port, came under pressure. The oil supply from the Gulf was threatened. Nawaz Sharif, after the war, is on record stating that Pakistan had only six days of oil stock left. Prime Minister Vajpayee contained the war in Kargil. His instructions were that India will not cross the LOC and this was the main reason due to which war continued for two and a half months. The Indian Air Force remained in a supportive role and did not engage in full-throttle combat. It wrote a new chapter—'Air warfare at High Altitude'. By the first week of July 1999, the Indian forces had broken the supply line of the Pakistani forces. Few Pakistani soldiers after the war admitted that for several days they survived only on sugar since the supply line was cut off.

Two interesting facts worth pondering are –The most hated person in Pakistan after Operation Meghdoot (Siachen), Lt General Hoon of the Indian Army, was born in Pakistan and the most hated person in India after Kargil, General Musharraf of Pakistan, was born in India. Pakistan was ruled by Prime Minister Nawaz Sharif who had a landslide victory in the 1997 general elections with his party Pakistan Muslim League (N) winning 137 seats of a total of 207, but he was not taken into confidence by their army. India at the time of Kargil was ruled by a caretaker prime minister who had lost in a no-confidence motion but the entire defence forces worked as per his command.

The action in the summers of 1999 was limited to Kargil with just one exception. A small contingent of forty-eight soldiers of the Indian Army under Brig. P.C. Katoch on 27 June 1999 seized control of Point 5770 (Naveed Top/ Cheema Top/Bilal Top), a post occupied by Pakistan. The nuclear threat of Pakistan did not work. The President of

USA Bill Clinton asked Pakistan to withdraw and praised India for showing restraint and keeping the conflict confined to Kargil despite Pakistani provocation. Brajesh Mishra, a security advisor to Prime Minister Vajpayee met the leaders of G-8 in Geneva on 17 June to apprise them of the ground reality and stand of India. Sharif was desperate to get some world support. While he was in China on a state visit, the regular media briefing in Pakistan on 27 June informed that he would be travelling to the USA to end the war. Sharif cut short his visit to China and came back. President Clinton was scheduled to go for a vacation but he postponed his holidays. Clinton wanted the Indian prime minister also to come but Vajpayee was a seasoned politician, he declined. Brajesh Mishra was sent to coordinate from the Indian side.

Nawaz Sharif reached Washington and met Bill Clinton on 4 July 1999 which was American Independence Day. In a few archives of the US media, the 4 July meeting is recorded as 'The Day a Nuclear Conflict Was Averted'. The apprehension of the use of nuclear weapons by the conflicting nations was of paramount concern to Clinton. It was clear to the world as to who the perpetrators of the war were, who showed restraint and which democracy was in control of its military. Pakistan was criticized by the international community for allowing its paramilitary forces and insurgents to cross the Line of Control. Pakistan's primary diplomatic response, one of plausible denial, linking the incursion to what is officially termed as the 'Kashmiri freedom fighters', was in the end not successful. Sharif was told in no uncertain terms that the only course left for him was to withdraw. The wordings and details of the declaration were discussed by the National Security Advisor of USA–Samuel Burger and his Indian counterpart Brajesh Mishra. Pakistan started withdrawing from 11 July 1999 and India gave the deadline of 16 July to complete the withdrawal from LOC. Nawaz came on television to explain Pakistan's withdrawal.

Officially, the war ended on 26 July 1999. The day has since been marked as Kargil Vijay Diwas (Victory Day). On 13 October 1999, the leader of the 13th Lok Sabha Atal Bihari Vajpayee took oath as the prime minister of India after his party and alliance won the general elections and remained in office for a complete five-year term. History is repeated in a diametrically opposite way. Pakistan again got a new ruler a day before on 12 October 1999, not through the power of ballot but the power of the bullet. In a military coup, General Parvez Musharraf became the head of government by overthrowing Sharif. Not only was the duly elected Prime Minister of Pakistan Nawaz Sharif taken into custody but the democracy in Pakistan was also imprisoned.

Notes

1. Arun Tiwari and A. P. J. Abdul Kalam, 1999, *Wings of Fire: An Autobiography of Abdul Kalam.* Universities Press.
2. Faisal Iftikhar, 2006. *The only King who died on the Battlefield: An Historical Novel Based on Truth.* Author House.
3. When satellites are unable to collect data accurately due to some reasons then the region is called a blind spot.
4. Praful Bidwai and Achin Vanaik, 1999, *New Nukes: India, Pakistan & Global Nuclear Disarmament*, Chapter 9, 187 Interlink Publishing Group.
5. 0See Chapter 5 of this book.
6. The lowest point of a ridge or saddle between two peaks, typically affording a pass from one side of a mountain range to another, is called a Col and in Siachen, the head of the glacier is called Indira Col.

   The Indira Col on the Siachen Glacier is located at a height of 5,753 metres. It is 3 km from Sia Kangri, the summit of which is called the 'tripoint', the point where the territories of India, China and Pakistan meet. The toe or snout is at 3,620 metres. The length from head to toe is 71–76 metres.

7. 'Sia' in the Balti language refers to the rose family plant widely dispersed in the region. 'Chun' refers to any object found in abundance. Thus, the name Siachen refers to land with an abundance of roses.

CHAPTER-14

No One Killed Sohrabuddin

Godhra Carnage and Gujarat Riots

27 February 2002, Wednesday

In my opinion, along with 30 January 1948, the day Gandhi was assassinated, 27 February 2002 is also an important date in the history of independent India. It changed the course of the history of the country. On the call of the Vishwa Hindu Parishad (VHP) Kar Sewaks from all over the country gathered at Ayodhya to take part in the Purna Ahuti Yagya, a ritual as part of the Ram Mandir movement. On 25 February 2002, after taking part in the ritual, one batch of 1,700 Kar Sewaks boarded the Sabarmati Express at Ayodhya for their destination in Gujarat.

At the time of the Godhara rail tragedy, the NDA government led by the BJP under the leadership of Atal Bihari Vajpayee was in power in the centre. In 2004, the poll strategists of the BJP called for early elections, six months ahead of schedule, given the good showing of the BJP in the assembly elections in the Hindi heart land states of Madhya Pradesh, Chattisgarh and Rajasthan. The other major stimulators for early elections were a buoyant market, a robust economy, good monsoons, political stability and no major allegations on the government. The slogan

'India Shining' was apt for going to elections and the BJP went to polls with the confidence of returning to power once again.

The defeat in the 2004 elections was shocking from the BJP perspective. There are two major components to it—mathematics and chemistry. The mathematics of elections is so complex that the best of brains fail to calculate the pluses and minuses because plus may not always be plus. The BJP in 1998 had 182 seats and 25.59 per cent votes, whereas Congress with 26.14 per centvotes had only 141 seats. Going for mid-term elections in 1999, the BJP had the successful Kargil Operation Vijay and also the sympathy of Atal Bihari Vajpayee losing the confidence motion by one vote. But the election result numbers have a different story to tell. In the 1999 elections, the BJP tally remained at 182 as in the previous election and surprisingly the vote percentage dropped from 25.59 per cent to 23.75 per cent. The Congress improved its vote share from 26.14 per cent to 28.30 per cent but the number of seats in 1999 dropped from 141 to 114. Though the BJP-led front NDA formed the government, on the ground, it had fewer votes as compared to the previous elections where they were not able to complete their term. Purely from the statistical viewpoint, the 2004 elections were more interesting. As already told, a confident BJP went to polls for the 14th Lok Sabha in 2004 seeking a second term based on the performance of the Atal Bihari Vajpayee government. A drop of BJP vote share by about 1.5 per cent (23.75 percent in 1999 and 22.16 percent in 2004) resulted in 138 seats (loss of 44 seats as compared to the seats in 1999). Congress, on the other hand, also lost its votes share by more than 1.75 per cent (28.30 per cent in 1999 and 26.53 per cent in 2004) but in the complex world of Indian elections, it improved its tally from 114 to 145. The difference in seats between the BJP and Congress was only 7 but Congress formed a government with Manmohan Singh as prime minister. What was the factor which came in the way of BJP to form a government despite mathematics being in their favour? The answer is to be seen in the chapters of chemistry and history. The single-most crucial factor for losing the election was Godhra (history), and smaller parties preferred to support the Congress because of the chemistry of future elections. None of the smaller regional parties wanted to be seen aligning with a right-wing Hindu party.

The 13th Lok Sabha which ran its full term established BJP as one of the major national parties along with the Congress. In my opinion, the contribution of one person who was not a BJP man and still was instrumental in getting them national acceptance in the political canvas of the country was George Fernandes. He was made convenor of the NDA and being a Christian knew that he could never be the king in the caste-ridden Indian politics but only a kingmaker. George was a born socialist and true secularist to the core. His style of politics had the romanticism of an activist always fighting for the oppressed. George started his political journey under the tutelage of D'Mello, the trade union leader of Mumbai. George Fernandes was mercilessly beaten up when he opposed the visiting Chinese Prime Minister Chaun En Lai. George Fernandes trounced S.K.Patil and reached the Lok Sabha in 1967. The twenty-day long railway strike from 8 May to 27 May in 1974 is recorded as the largest industrial action in the world, in which on the call of George Fernandes, more than 17 lakh (1.7 million) railwaymen took part. During the Emergency, it was George who planned explosions through dynamite to be heard. It was something similar to Bhagat Singh's assembly bomb incident where he too believed that 'It takes a loud noise to make the deaf hear'. He was caught and the case is now popularly known as the Baroda Dynamite case. As industry minister in 1977, IBM had a CAG (Comptroller and Auditor General of India) report against it, and also as per the new FERA (Foreign Exchange Regulation Act) rules, equity was to be diluted which IBM refused to adhere to and therefore was asked to leave. Coca-Cola was also asked to share its secret formula and dilute its stake as per the new policy. On refusal, they were also shown the door. George had the conviction and courage to ban the entry of Dhirubhai Ambani by an administrative order in Udyog Bhawan. The hero of a generation of youth lost a lot of old-time die-hard followers when he aligned himself with the BJP. George Fernandes's choice was questioned by his admirers when he made a political transition from being a consistent defender of civil and trade union rights and secular values to becoming a consistent ally of the BJP. But new friends and equations were to be formed. As NDA chairman, he was able to defend the policies of the BJP which were till then not acceptable by an average Indian. I was in Delhi with George when the news of the Babri Masjid demolition on 6 December 1992 came. He was not only sad but was furious about this act of the BJP and its leader. Who knew that in about six years he would change his stance? His support to the BJP began the process of legitimizing the saffron party as a principal political power and a party of governance.

Manohar Joshi, another non-BJP person from Mumbai in the 13th Lok Sabha, needs to be mentioned before we move to the Godhra incident. The Telugu Desam Party (TDP) with twenty-nine seats in the 1999 elections was the second-largest party in the NDA after the BJP. Its nominee

G.M.C. Balayogi was made the speaker becoming the first Dalit speaker. (He was also the speaker in the 12th Lok Sabha). Balayogi died in a helicopter crash on 3 March 2002. The new incumbent to the post of the speaker was Shiv Sena's Manohar Joshi, ex-chief minister of Mumbai. He was a confidante of Bal Thackeray and was held responsible by the Sri Krishna Report for inciting the 1992–93 Mumbai riots. He termed the report as 'anti-Hindu, pro-Muslim and biased'. He had to resign from the post of Chief Minister of Maharashtra when an RTI (Right to Information Act) activist Vijay Kumar Ghor made public the information of favour shown to his son-in-law in the Pune Housing Complex Land Scam Sundew. The verdict of the High Court went against the developer and was upheld by the Supreme Court as well. The appointment of Manohar Joshi as the speaker clearly shows that the BJP was learning fast to keep the coalition partners content. On one end of the spectrum, the post of the speaker which was till then occupied by people with a spotless political career, was given to Manohar Joshi, an extreme right-wing politician, who had resigned from the post of chief minister due to an allegation of favouritism. The other end of the spectrum was occupied by George, the eternal rebel, who put all his goodwill of the past to wash the blots of religious fanaticism at the cost of losing his credibility.

Godhra tossed quite a few questions that are yet to be answered with finality. The first question 'Did the fire break from inside the train or was the bogey set ablaze from outside?' The answer to this one question can decide whether the tragedy was a planned ghastly attack or an accident.

The Sabarmati Express with Kar Sewaks started from Ayodhya on 25 February and was running late by four hours. It reached Godhara at 7.43 am on 27 February 2002. After the usual halt, the train started moving but the driver had to stop at the signal as the chain was pulled multiple times. The train was attacked by a mob of about 1,000 to 2,000 people. The three-tier sleeper coach S6 was set alight and people were trapped inside. Fifty-nine people including 27 women and 10 children were burnt alive and 48 were injured. Out of these 59, only 4 were reserved passengers. Nineteen bodies remained unidentified and 35 burnt bodies were identified by the government (the figure of 59 in many records is shown as 58). Two commissions of enquiry were set up; one by the state government and the second by the Indian Railways, which is under the central government. On 6 March 2002, the Gujarat government set up a commission of inquiry to investigate the incident and submit a report, the chairman and sole member of which was retired Gujarat High Court judge K. G. Shah. Later the scope of the commission was enlarged to look into the post-Godhra riots of Gujarat in 2002. It was alleged by human rights organizations that Justice Shah was close to Narendra Modi; therefore, an impartial inquiry would be doubtful. As a result, the government reconstituted the commission and a retired judge of Supreme Court Justice Nanavati was also inducted as chairman, and the Shah Inquiry Commission was rechristened Nanavati-Shah Commission. Justice Shah died all alone in his flat in Ahmedabad in 2008 before the submission of the report. As per the provision of the commission, another retired judge of Gujarat High Court, Justice A. H. Mehta was appointed in his place. Now the inquiry commission is known as the Nanavati-Mehta Commission. For the human rights activists, the name of Mehta too was not reassuring as he was the same judge who had granted bail to Babu Bajrangi, the main accused of the Naroda Patiya riots in which 97 Muslim were killed on 28 February 2002 in the post-Godhra riots. After 24 extensions by the state government, the commission submitted its report in two parts. The first part of the report dealing with the Godhra train burning was submitted in September 2008. The report observed that the burning of the Sabarmati Express S6 coach was a 'planned conspiracy'. The second part dealing with post-Godhra riots was submitted when Narendra Modi had moved from the Gujarat chief minister's residence in Gandhi Nagar to the Prime Minister of India's residence in New Delhi on 26 May 2014. The trial court gave its verdict in February 2011 convicting 31 people. Eleven were sentenced to death and 20 got life imprisonment and 63, including the alleged conspirator Maulvi Umarji, were acquitted. The High Court in October 2017 upheld the judgement of the lower court with one change commuting the death sentence of the eleven accused to life imprisonment. The court also directed the Gujarat government and railways to pay Rs 10 lakh compensation to all the victims. Was it ethical for the Nanavati-Mehta Committee to submit its report to the chief minister of Gujarat instead of the governor since the inquiry itself was to examine the role of the state government? This is a question that will always remain unanswered. The accused and judges were the same and even the investigation machinery was getting its infrastructure and financial support from the government. Justice Nanavati, Shah or Mehta – none of them thought to take the version of Narendra Modi, the chief minister, by summoning him to appear before the commission. Critics say the findings of the commission were along expected lines as the report was influenced by the government.

When Laloo Prasad Yadav became railway minister in

the UPA government in 2004, Justice U. C. Banerjee, a retired judge of the Supreme Court was appointed to investigate the incident in September 2004. Justice Banerjee submitted its interim report in January 2005 terming the incidentas an accident setting aside the theory of pre-planned conspiracy. The report was challenged in the Gujarat High Court by Tulsidas Bhatia, who was injured at the Godhra Station in the burning train. The Gujarat High Court pronounced its verdict in October 2006—stating that the investigation was unconstitutional, illegal and null and void and also directing that the report should not be tabled in the parliament. Various independent agencies went for investigation and inquiry at various levels and at different times.

The Godhara incident was the trigger for the Gujarat riots of 2002. Apart from the loss of human lives, the property damage was incalculable.

Now we come to the second question—what was discussed in the meeting at the chief minister's residence on the evening of 27 February 2002? How many meetings were held on that fateful evening? One meeting or two? There are many different versions and theories which are in circulation regarding the meeting which was the first official, joint reaction of the government which decided the way the Godhara train tragedy was to be tackled. The meeting not only decided the fate of Gujarat but the future of Indian polity as well. We will examine questions raised by the then stakeholders of the Gujarat government which are not answered the way it should have been. The answers that were given in the court of law and room of inquiry committee still have a lot of gaps, doubts and thus, we can say that these burning questions remained unanswered.

The Supreme Court of India in March 2008 appointed

a Special Investigation Team (SIT) led by R. K. Raghavan, former Director of the CBI to enquire into the 2002 Gujarat riots. In 2009, the scope of the SIT was enlarged to examine the role of Modi and sixty-two other people. Sanjiv Bhatt appeared before the SIT and gave evidence in 2009. He was MTech from IIT Mumbai, had cleared his civil services examination in 1988 with a top rank and chose the Indian Police Service (IPS). He had a meritorious service record.

Let us examine charges levied by Sanjiv Bhatt and how he finally fell foul of the establishment. He filed an affidavit in the Supreme Court that in the meeting chaired by Chief Minister Narendra Modi in the evening of 27 February 2002 officials were told that Hindus should be allowed to vent their anger against Muslims. This was the turning point of the Gujarat riots and he had also been present in the meeting. The affidavit by Sanjiv Bhatt was filed in the Supreme Court on 14 April 2011, nine years after the tragedy. The reason for the delay also gives rise to the suspicion that the intention was not humanitarian but biased. Bhatt's action apart from being a whistle-blower and a good Samaritan seems to be more at a personal level. It is thought that he had 'an *axe* to *grind' against* the Modi government. Though Bhatt explained that he had wanted to testify in front of the Nanavati Commission but had been denied an audience. He was summoned by the Nanavati-Mehta Commission in May 2011 after filing his affidavit and still maintains that the documents crucial for an impartial inquiry were not provided which would enable him to authenticate his final affidavit before the commission. Also, the documents were never examined by the commission. The Supreme Court appointed the SIT to examine the charges. The SIT concluded that Bhatt's claims to have attended the meeting himself were not true and accordingly charges are also baseless. Bhatt had alleged that he went to the residence of Modi to attend the meeting along with K. Chakraborty, the then director-general of police (DGP). The car of the DGP in which Bhatt and Chakraborty were riding was driven by Tarachand Yadav and the car of Bhatt which was following the DGP's car was driven by Constable K. D. Panth, who also signed the affidavit. Panth was one of the six witnesses of Bhatt. Constable K. D. Panth dared to file an FIR on 24 June 2011 against Bhatt, an IPS officer with twenty-three years of service; this clearly shows that he had the backing of influential and powerful people who wanted to silence Bhatt. Panth in his FIR alleged that he was forced to sign the letter and on the day of the incident, he was on leave. DGP Chakraborty also refutes charges of Bhatt but his driver Tarachand Yadav confirms that Bhatt travelled with the DGP to chief minister's residence and Panth was following in Bhatt's car. The SIT found other allegations of Bhatt also without any basis.

In the 2011 affidavit, Bhatt had also accused Tushar Mehta, the then Additional Advocate General of Gujarat (who was subsequently made Solicitor General of India by the Modi government). Tushar Mehta and Sanjiv Bhatt were very close friends since 1980 and used to go for family vacations together. Shweta, wife of Sanjiv Bhatt maintains that Tushar Mehta was not very tech-savvy and Bhatt used to help him out with the computer. In other words, he had access to Mehta's email account. Sanjiv claims that the ticket for their vacations in Goa in September 2009 and the USA in March 2010 were booked by him through the email account of Tushar Mehta and during that period he saw the SIT emails in Mehta's account. Bhatt alleged that Gujarat's Additional Advocate General Tushar Mehta through an informer in the SIT leaked information to the Modi government. In August 2011, Mehta lodged a complaint after Bhatt filed his affidavit in Supreme Court in April 2011 that his email account was hacked by Sanjiv Bhatt. On his friendship, Mehta's stand is that something happened during the US trip after which their friendship broke. He refused to divulge the reason as to why their friendship ended calling it a personal affair.

The R.K. Raghavan—led SIT submitted its report in November 2010. It was examined by the Supreme Court-appointed amicus curiae, Raju Ramachandran. Based on Ramachandran's recommendation, the Supreme Court asked SIT to conduct a self-review. The self-review was submitted in April 2011 and it was again referred to Ramachandran for consideration. By the time, the affidavit of Bhatt was already filled in the Supreme Court but was not accepted.

Sanjiv Bhatt was suspended on 8 August 2011 on fabricated charges like 'unauthorized absence from duty', not appearing before an inquiry committee and using his official car while not on duty. He was removed from service after serving twenty-seven years in the Indian Police Service. If the government starts suspending officers on the grounds of misusing their official cars, there would be hardly any one left to carry on the work of the executive!

Bhatt was arrested on 30 September 2011 after the investigation was carried out based on the FIR filed by constable Panth. He was granted bail on 17 October 2011. Law enforcement in Gujarat left no stone unturned to ensure that Bhatt was incarcerated. In November 2012, Bhatt along with six policemen was charged for a twenty-two-year-old case of custodial death of Prabhudas Vaihnani. At one point in time, the government had moved for the closure of the 1990 custodial death case but the state took a U-turn and withdrew the application of closure after Bhatt became vocal and accused the chief minister of complicity in anti-minority riots in the state. Bhatt was removed from IPS on 19 August and was pronounced guilty in the custodial death case. He was sentenced for life on 20 June 2019.

Now we again go back to the 27 February 2002 meeting at the chief minister's residence. The decision to bring charred dead bodies of the Godhra victims to Ahmedabad was opposed by the police and administrative officers. Looking at the 'sensitive' and 'tinderbox-like' situation in Ahmedabad, it was felt that bringing the bodies could lead to serious repercussions. But in the absence of any official account of the meeting, there is no proof as to who decided to take the bodies to Ahmedabad. Various statements can be found in bits and pieces by different people. It is said that on the objection of one or two sane voices, the majority of politicians present were unanimous that it would help the BJP in the forthcoming elections. On 28 February, the dead bodies came in an open truck from Godhara. Instead of handing over the bodies to the relatives of the dead, they were handed over to the Vishwa Hindu Parishad (VHP) leaders. In form of a procession, the bodies were taken out on the streets of Ahmedabad. The procession of dead bodies moved in at least sixteen areas of Ahmedabad and till then, curfew was not imposed in the city. After providing all the fodder for communal riots, the desired results were achieved. The riots went on for three months in Ahmedabad but Gujarat witnessed communal unrest for more than a year. Official figures say 1,044 were dead, 223 missing and 2,500 injured. The figure of 1,044 dead had 790 Muslims and 254 Hindus but the actual figure must have been much more. The loss of property was immense.

The encounters and killings in Gujarat post-Godhra opened up a ghastly Pandora's box of how a communalized hate-prone atmosphere can manufacture its own brand of killers in the governance. Political protagonists were 'eliminated' and killed in cold blood. And the regime was clueless to all this bloodshed. After all the 'prized' encounters, the police officers boasted of having dented a terror plan to eliminate the top political leadership of the state. Even several years after Godhra, the ghosts of these encounters and killings return to haunt.

The murder of Haren Pandya, former home minister of Gujarat in 2003 might have silenced his voice as desired by the conspirator and propagator of this gory killing but lots of people in governance will always be under a cloud of suspicion. The present political scenario might prevent people to openly take names of the suspects but someday the truth will emerge. Haren Pandya, Home Minister of Gujarat was a close confidante of Keshu Bhai Patel, erstwhile chief minister of Gujarat who handed over the reins to Narendra Modi in October 2001. Haren Pandya was elected from the Ellis Bridge constituency of Ahmedabad from where the last Congress MLA was elected in 1975. After that, it has remained with the BJP. Pandya had *complex dynamics* with Modi. He was a formidable political rival for Modi. The clash between the two started when Modi was in search of a safe assembly seat to contest after he was appointed chief minister. He wanted to run from Pandya's constituency, Ellis Bridge—a very safe seat for the BJP. But Pandya refused to yield to Modi's wishes. Pandya was also an old-time RSS worker, well-rooted in the BJP and Ahmedabad politics, and failed to understand that 'Modi never forgets, and never forgives'. Vajubhai Vala vacated his seat of Rajkot II, another safe seat which the

BJP (Jana Sangh) has been winning since 1975 with only one exception of 1980. Narendra Modi got elected from Rajkot II by-elections and Vajubhai Vala became the Governor of Karnataka in 2014 and continued after the 2019 elections as well. Haren Pandya had claimed that he was a lone voice among leaders who opposed the display of dead bodies in Ahmedabad after the Godhra tragedy. Pandya was stripped of the high-profile Home Ministry and given the revenue portfolio by Modi. Pandya had to resign from the ministry in August 2002. He was denied a ticket in the 2002 assembly elections. Modi shifted to the Ahmedabad—Maninagar seat in the 2002 regular assembly elections. Haren Pandaya remained critical of Modi's leadership. He was a strong leader with clout and was privy to a lot of classified information. He found the post-Godhra riots to be cynically induced and the violence unleashed during riots sickening.

On 26 March 2003, Haren Pandya was murdered in Ahmedabad when he had gone for his daily morning walk. He was found shot dead in his car where his body was lying for more than two hours. A criminal conspiracy to eliminate Pandya was evident and the top BJP leadership came under fire both at the centre and state. It was disparaging that two self-styled men of the twenty-first century frequently compared with Sardar Patel were holding key positions when Hiren Pandya was murdered—Lal Krishna Advani was home minister of India and Narendra Modi was the chief minister of Gujarat when their party colleague was killed in broad daylight. Haren Pandya's father accused Narendra Modi of his son's killing. The case of murder was registered and an investigation was carried out by the CBI. In 2007, a special Prevention of Terrorism Act (POTA) court sentenced the main accused from Hyderabad, Asgar Ali, to life imprisonment, while eleven other convicts were handed out imprisonment ranging between ten and five years. The Gujarat High Court in August 2011 dropped charges of murder but retained charges of criminal conspiracy and attempt to murder. *The High Court's judgement noted that the CBI investigation had been 'botched up and blinkered' and 'misdirected'.* Though in July 2019, the Supreme Court again reversed the High Court decision and the accused were charged with murder.

Another case which had garnered a lot of attention is the Sohrabuddin encounter. His encounter blew up into a political storm of enormous proportions. This case is also linked to the Haren Pandya murder case and till today raises doubts in the minds of people. Sohrabuddin was a person with a criminal background. He had more than sixty cases against his name. His criminal activity network was extended to Rajasthan, Madhya Pradesh and Gujarat. He was primarily running an extortion racket and collecting money from marble-mine owners, traders and contractors. When things became hot in these states, he shifted base to Hyderabad in Telangana (then Andhra Pradesh). It is alleged that Sohrabuddin first approached Asgar Ali of Hyderabad to kill Haren Pandya but subsequently when he backed out, the job was entrusted to Tulsiram Prajapati, who carried out the execution. On the night of 23 November 2005, while travelling in a public bus from Hyderabad to Sangli in Maharashtra, Sohrabuddin and his wife Kausar Bi were arrested by the Gujarat Anti-Terrorism Squad (ATS). Both were brought to Ahmedabad. Sohrabuddin was encountered by the police on 26 November 2005 in Ahmedabad and the FIR of the alleged encounter was written by Ravindra Makwana of Gujarat police who was doing the duty of Police Station Officer (PSO) at the ATS office. After the encounter, it was alleged that he had links with Dawood Ibrahim, a terrorist organization and ISI (Inter-Services Intelligence) of Pakistan.

Gujarat saw many encounters after the Godhra tragedy, which resulted in several enquiry commissions, SIT, CBI and court-monitored investigations. But in a majority of the cases, the accused got an acquittal. Sohrabuddin's family approached the Supreme Court for investigation of his encounter and also to know the whereabouts of Kauser Bi who was not traceable from the day of the encounter. The Supreme Court directed the state government for CID (Criminal Investigation Department) enquiry which was done by Geeta Johri, an IPS officer of the Gujarat cadre who later served as the DGP of the state.

Sohrabuddin's wife Kausar Bi was detained by the police along with him. She disappeared and was untraceable since 26 November 2005. While hearing the habeas corpus petition in the Supreme Court, the Gujarat government's counsel K.T.S. Tulsi and Hemantika Wahi told the court– 'She has been killed'. The fact of killing Kauser Bi was disclosed during the custodial interrogation of the three IPS officers alleged to be involved in the Sohrabuddin encounter. The report was submitted in court in sealed cover confirming that the mortal remains of Kauser Bi had been burnt. She had been kept in a farm house near Ahmedabad and later strangled to death and cremated near Illol at the farm of IPS officer Vanzara. Sohrabuddin's brother Rubabuddin Sheikh's request for a CBI probe into the episode was opposed by the Gujarat government because the SIT (Special Investigation Team) investigation was going on and three senior IPS officers D. G.Vanzara, Rajkumar Pandian of the Gujarat cadre and M. N. Dinesh Kumar of Rajasthan were already arrested. Ravindra Makwana who was the PSO at the ATS office at the time of the Sohrabuddin encounter testified in his statement to CBI later that ATS Sub-inspector Balkrishan Chaubey had raped Kauser Bi before she was killed. The question still to be answered is why was Kauser Bi killed? She was not a terrorist, nor was she a culprit in any case. Her only fault was that she was married to a person who was encountered. The custodians of the Constitution in Gujarat have yet to answer this question.

Was it Tulsiram Prajapati who killed Haren Pandya? The *DNA* newspaper carried a story with this heading on 30 August 2011. Who was Tulsiram Prajapati? He was an associate of Sohrabuddin and as written in the *DNA* newspaper, it was alleged that after Asgar Ali refused to carry out Haren Pandya's killing, Sohrabuddin turned to Prajapati, who carried out the execution. After the UPA government returned to power in 2004, there were apprehensions that Sohrabuddin could be investigated. It was then decided to eliminate Sohrabuddin. Tulsiram Prajapati who was also arrested was made the witness of the Sohrabuddin encounter and sent to Udaipur Jail. On 27 December 2006, Prajapati was taken out of Udaipur Jail by the Rajasthan—Gujarat Police and he was also encountered on 28 December 2006 at Banskantha district near Sarhod—Chapri on the Gujarat Rajasthan Border. In the series of coincidences, Dahyaji Gobarji Vanzara, the encounter specialist of Gujarat was transferred just thirteen days before by the then Home Minister of Gujarat Amit Shah. In contract killing, it is not very uncommon to eliminate the people and links who were part of the chain in executing contract killing so that the identity of the main conspirator is never revealed. The alleged conspirators at whose behest Pandya was killed began to lose confidence in Sohrabuddin and Tulsiram. The encounter killings of

Sohrabuddin and Tulsiram were a result of unease among the conspirators when their equations began to worsen. The Supreme Court finally handed over the probe to CBI in January 2010. The CBI filed a chargesheet against thirty-eight persons including Amit Shah, the Gujarat home minister and Gulab Chandra Kataria, the then Rajasthan home minister. Kataria, an old BJP politician, who became the leader of opposition in Rajasthan in 2019 when Congress formed their government. He was a home minister in the BJP government led by Vasundhara Raje from 2004 to 2008 and again from 2014 to 2018. He hailed from Udaipur where Tulsiram Prajapati was lodged in jail. The most controversial role was of Amit Shah who was charge-sheeted by the CBI for the killing of Sohrabuddin, Kauser Bi and Tulsiram Prajapati. Shah was described by the CBI as the 'kingpin of the case'. Amit Shah was the blue-eyed boy of Chief Minister Modi, though he was made only a minister of state but was entrusted the key portfolio of the state including home. At one point in time, he was in charge of twelve departments. The phone call details of Shah were given by the CBI to the court showing how he was in constant touch with the police officers supervising the encounter when the accused was in their custody. Though Shah argues that he was in routine touch with those officers as home minister. Amit Shah was arrested on 25 July 2010 in the Sohrabuddin case and remained in judicial custody till 29 October 2010 for about 100 days. Chidambaram was the home minister at that time. It is said that in 2019 Chidambaram was held for about 106 days in custody to square up the game of *chor-sipahi*.[1] It is alleged that CBI and ED (Enforcement Directorate) acted on the direction of their present boss. The Congress has called the CBI move against Chidambaram as political vendetta.

On 30 October 2010, the Saturday Supreme Court bench of Justice Aftab Alam and Justice Lodha heard the petition of the CBI at the residence of Justice Alam and passed the famous order of banishment *of* Amit Shah from Gujarat–thus barring Amit Shah to enter Gujarat, from where he got the adjective '*tadipaar*' (banished from the state). This was done due to serious apprehensi on that Shah's release on bail by the Gujarat High Court would virtually give him licence to influence witnesses in the case given the political clout he enjoyed in the state. The CBI was represented by K.T.S. Tulsi, who vehemently opposed the bail of Amit Shah. The manner and timing of his granting of bail and release from the jail were questioned. The CBI itself showed uncanny haste in moving the apex court on Friday night itself within hours of the High Court granting bail. Amit Shah was granted bail by the Gujarat High Court on Friday (29 October 2010), considering on Saturday and Sunday, courts are closed and any appeal against the bail would not have been heard before Monday. He was released from jail at 10 pm in the night. This violated the jail manual barring the release of inmates after sunset. The trial of Sohrabuddin, Kausar Bi and Tulsiram Prajapati was clubbed by the court in April 2012. In September 2012, Amit Shah was granted bail by the Supreme Court and allowed to enter Gujarat keeping assembly elections in view, which Shah contested and won.

Another interesting person is Advocate K.T.S. Tulsi, who became Rajya Sabha member in 2014 as a nominated member of the Congress government. After the retirement of jurist K.T.S.Tulsi from the Rajya Sabha, the vacancy was filled up by former Chief Justice of India Ranjan Gogoi. He was nominated as a Rajya Sabha member by the BJP government. Tulsi got elected as an unopposed Congress candidate from Chhattisgarh in 2020. His Wikipedia account shows that he represents Robert Vadra in the DLF land case. Ironically, the same advocate appeared on behalf of the Gujarat State in the Supreme Court accusing the centre of playing politics in the criminal case. The state government Counsel K.T.S. Tulsi made the allegation that the central government was trying to turn a case related to the 2005 killing of Sohrabuddin Sheikh in Ahmedabad into an 'election issue'. The Gujarat government was opposing the CBI enquiry. As per the directive of the Supreme Court, the CBI enquiry was done and the charge sheet was submitted and the same advocate was then defending the CBI and central government and casting doubts on the state government. In Wikipedia, it is mentioned—Tulsi refused to represent the Gujarat government in the Sohrabuddin encounter case.

On the request of the CBI, the Sohrabuddin case was transferred by the Supreme Court from Gujarat to Mumbai on 27 September 2012 on the grounds that the trial in Gujarat may not be fair. The apex court said, 'We are convinced that to preserve the integrity of the trial, it is necessary to shift it outside the state.' The Supreme Court also directed that no judge would be transferred not only during the trial but till judgement was pronounced. The state government in Gujarat was of BJP led by Modi and in Maharashtra, it was the Congress government. Narendra Modi took oath as Prime Minister of India on 26 May 2014. *Outlook* magazine in its February 2015 issue states, 'On June 6, 2014, Utpat had made his displeasure known to Shah's counsel and, while allowing an exemption for that day, ordered Shah's presence on June 20. But he didn't show up again.'[2]

J.T. Utpat, the trial court judge, the story noted, 'fixed

the next hearing for June 26. But on 25th, he was transferred to Pune' (ibid.). This was in violation of a September 2012 Supreme Court order, that the Sohrabuddin trial 'should be conducted from beginning to end by the same officer'; 'court records suggest Amit Shah had never turned up even once—including on the final day of discharge' despite the order of the Supreme Court (ibid.).

After Utpat's transfer, Brijgopal Harkishan Loya took charge to preside over the CBI special court in June 2014. According to the *Outlook* story, 'significantly, one of his last noting stated that Shah was being exempted from personal appearance "till the framing of charges". Loya had not harboured the thought of dropping charges against Shah even when he appeared to be gentle on him'(ibid.). According to the lawyer Mihir Desai, who represented Sohrabuddin's brother Rubabuddin—the complainant in the case—Loya was keen on scrutinizing the entire charge sheet, which ran to more than 10,000 pages, and on examining the evidence and witnesses carefully. 'The case was sensitive and important, and it was going to create and decide the reputation of Mr Loya as a judge,' Desai said. 'But the pressure was certainly mounting.'[3]

Loya, who had given an exemption to Amit Shah from an appearance in the court, was visibly annoyed during a hearing on 31 October 2014 when he came to know that Amit Shah was 1.5 km away in Mumbai to attend the swearing-in of the BJP government. Loya stated that exemption applied only when Shah was not in the state. The next date of hearing was fixed for 15 December 2014. Loya went to Nagpur to attend a wedding and died on the night of 30 November 2014. The death is still under suspicion. *The Caravan*, *The Wire*, *The Indian Express* carried out a detailed story. The post-mortem report is also not without controversy. The fact that it was not the police but RSS activist Ishwar Baheti who handed over Judge Loya's cell phone to the family, and that too, after 3-4 days, also raises some serious questions. Ishwar Baheti's claims to be Judge Loya's friend is contested by Loya's father and sister. If Ishwar Baheti was a friend of the deceased, why did neither his sister nor his father know who he was? Suspicions were raised on why instead of sending the body to Mumbai, it was sent to his village. Loya's sister Anuradha Biyani made an explosive claim that Mohit Shah, then the chief justice of the Bombay High Court, had offered her a bribe of Rs 100 crores in return for a favourable judgment. Surprisingly this allegation was not contested by Mohit Shah. Loya's father Harkishan also alleges that offers were made to deliver a favourable judgement.

After Loya's death, M. B. Gosavi was appointed to the Sohrabuddin case. Gosavi began hearing the case on 15 December 2014. This date had been fixed by Judge Loya. M. B. Gosavi heard the defence lawyers arguement for three days to discharge Amit Shah of all the charges, while the CBI, the prosecuting agency, argued for fifteen minutes. M. B. Gosavi concluded the hearing on 17 December and reserved his judgement. As alleged by Anuradha Biyani that Chief Justice Mohit Shah had also told Loya that if the judgement was delivered before 30 December it would not be noticed as some explosive story would shadow the discharge judgement news. On 30 December, Judge Gosavi upheld the defence argument that the CBI had political motives for implicating the accused. With that, Amit Shah along with sixteen others were discharged. The story of Mahendra Singh Dhoni's retirement also came on 30 December 2014 and as expected the limelight and focus were on Dhoni and the news of Amit Shah's discharge had a value of small ticker somewhere at the bottom of the television screen. The judgement itself said that the CBI was used for political motives. The persons and parties accused by CBI in Sohrabuddin's case were now the new bosses. Amit Shah named 'kingpin' by CBI got discharged without going to court even once during the trial. The elite Central Bureau of Investigation once again proved itself not just as a 'caged parrot' but also the one with its 'wings clipped'. The other twenty-two accused also subsequently got acquittal and no one killed Sohrabuddin, Kauser Bi and Prajapati.

Communal violence is often a deliberate product of human design. It is seemingly provoked by national and religious sentiments. This is evident from recurring inter-religious conflicts in India. To achieve durable harmony, it is essential to impart lessons of reconciliation at the grassroots level. While there were numerous attempts to provide relief and rehabilitation post-Godhra riots, none of them was specifically aimed at reconciliation. The absence of unequivocal condemnation from the leaders and complete silence over the loss of lives tends to legitimize the violence. This can set a dangerous precedent. When rank communalists entrench themselves across layers of governance, then there is not a single window of secular justice and hope. While people grapple with bestowing the right label to suit the country's collective consciousness, there is little doubt that terrorizing events like Godhra are an outcome of a calculated and systemic assault on India's pluralistic values and its social and secular fabric. People are not prepared to see the weakening of India's foundations and social structure. The state and the institutions associated with it should be the initiators and facilitators of the peace process. The government cannot abdicate the responsibility to mediate peace between the estranged groups. Lessons of the Gujarat riots are quite loud and clear. Will we go down in history as people endowed with knowledge but bereft of wisdom and *'raj dharma'* and will power to correct our course of action?

Notes

1. A game where two players act as thief and police, and the role is reversed so that both the players get a chance to act as thief and police.
2. 'The Curious Case of Amit Shah'. *Outlook*, 16 February 2015. Available at: https://magazine.outlookindia.com/issue/11379 (accessed on 30 January 2021).
3. Ibid.

Chapter-15

'Mgnrega' The Game Changer

UPA Returns to Power 2009: Rise of Rights

26 November 2008, Wednesday

The United Progressive Alliance (UPA) government went for polls in 2009, after completing its full five-year term. The Congress asked for vote based on their performance. The prime minister was teased and targeted by opponents as '*Maun* (silent)-Mohan' Singh. In about sixty years of democracy, for the first time, India was led by a person who was an economist, a planner and a professional but not a mass leader. Manmohan Singh was not a traditional politician and had little understanding of the political ground reality. He lacked charisma and in the matter of getting votes, he had no pull. The only other non-traditional prime minister had been I. K. Gujral. His less-than-one-year term (which includes his term as interim prime minister as well) in the office cannot be compared to Manmohan Singh.

Elections for the 14th Lok Sabha in 2004 were fought on the slogan of 'India Shining' where the BJP was over confident of forming a government for the second term. The loss of the BJP also permanently smashed the long-time desire of L.K. Advani to become prime minister. It was Advani who had built the party from two seats in the 1984 elections to 182 seats in the 1999 elections and formed the government. The critical mass of voters was built around the famous Rath Yatra of Advani. Govindacharya, the ideologue of the party, was shown the door when he called Atal Bihari Vajpayee *mukhota* (face) only, which was a fact as it was Advani who was instrumental in building the BJP after 1980.

There were two major reasons for the victory of the Congress in the two elections of 2004 and 2009, besides the mistakes, arrogance, haste and anti-incumbency of the BJP-led opposition. For the 2004 elections, the Congress organization, which was supposedly weak, worked to get the desired numbers. Secondly, in this election, one person who made the difference was Sonia Gandhi. She was able to maintain the cohesion of the party and galvanize it. For the 2004 elections, most of the political *pundits* felt that it was not the Congress, which won the elections but it was the BJP that lost them due to wrong strategies and slogans such as 'Shining India'. For the 2009 elections, the Manmohan Singh government was tested and voters gave them the second term. The Congress party organization had hardly any role to take the credit for this victory. The Congress leader who emerged as the largest contributor to this victory was no doubt, Rahul Gandhi. His detractors attribute this victory to Manmohan Singh but one must remember that though Singh never became a liability for the party even today he is not a mass-based leader who can spin votes in favour of the Congress. Rahul certainly had some charisma to make the Congress win in 2009.

In 2004, the Congress fought elections without a national alliance. They entered into a state-wise poll pact with the regional parties. The Communist Party of India (Marxist) (CPM) and Communist Party of India (CPI) fought the election on their own in Kerala, West Bengal and Tripura but in Punjab and Andhra Pradesh, they directly entered into a poll pact with the Congress. In Tamil Nadu, the Congress and communist parties were part of the Democratic Progressive Alliance (DPA) led by the Dravida Munnetra Kazhagam (DMK). As a post-poll agreement, the UPA was formed with Sonia Gandhi as its chairperson. The communist parties withdrew their support to the UPA1 in protest when the India–United States Civil Nuclear Agreement was signed. This proved to be the most fatal decision of the communists. There decline started from there after losing West Bengal—the only state of some influence is Kerala. To survive the vote of confidence in 2008, the Congress floor managers in the parliament got help from Amar Singh of the Samajwadi Party. In the history of general elections in India, the 2009 elections will be remembered for crystallizing some on going processes and introducing some major, unique shifts. On the process side, based on the 2001 census, 499 parliamentary constituencies out of 543 were redrawn as delimited electoral constituencies. For the first time, the election process was going to be supervised by two different Chief Election Commissioners of India (CEC). The first phase of polling for 124 constituencies was held on 16 April 2009. Chief Election Commissioner Gopalswami retired and Navin Chawla took over as CEC on 21 April 2009 to supervise the rest of the election.

On the political side, the first change was the announcement of a prime ministerial candidate by the major alliances. The NDA led by the BJP started this practice. On 11 December 2007, about one and a half years before the election, Lal Krishan Advani's name was announced as the prime ministerial candidate. His name was ratified on 23 January 2008 by all the NDA constituents. In a parliamentary democracy, the elected members of the parliament are supposed to elect their leader. Voters' choice certainly gets affected when a party names a person as a prime ministerial candidate before the elections. The prime ministerial candidate becomes the focal point and the central issue. People vote overwhelmingly on the name and image of the prime ministerial candidate. In other words, the voters start focusing more on the candidate instead of electing the best representative from their area. In subsequent elections, it was observed that people with very little grass roots work got elected in the name of Narendra Modi, the prime ministerial candidate of the BJP since the 2014 elections. Manmohan Singh, on 24 January 2009, went for cardiac bypass surgery in the All-India Institute of Medical Sciences (AIIMS), Delhi. To counter the NDA pre-poll announcement of the prime ministerial candidate, a section in the UPA projected the name of Sharad Pawar as their candidate. Sonia Gandhi wanted to stop speculation and bickering within the UPA. So, it was for the first time in the history of Congress that on 6 February 2009, she announced the name of Manmohan Singh as the prime ministerial candidate in the official Congress party magazine, *Sandesh*.

Other than NDA and UPA two more fronts fought the 2009 elections. The third front, an initiative of the communists wanted non-Congress, non-BJP parties to come under one umbrella. The alliance had 109 MPs before the elections. Mulayam Singh Yadav almost became the prime minister in 1998 when he was upstaged by Lalu Yadav, the leader of his caste. In the 2004 elections, he had thirty-six seats and had ex-BJP chief minister Kalyan Singh with him. His confidante and political architect Amar Singh was in full form. The Bahujan Samaj Party (BSP) was on the downhill due to the anti-incumbency of the Uttar Pradesh chief minister Mayawati. Thus, Mulayam Singh Yadav saw the opportunity to become the prime minister. The Samajwadi Party of Mulayam Singh, the Rashtriya Janata Dal (RJD) of Lalu Yadav and the Lok Jan Shakti Party (LJP) joined hands when they failed to reach an understanding with the Congress. This front had sixty-four MPs with them. The Congress emerged as the single-largest party with improved performance. The verdict can be termed as 'people's approval' of the policies of UPA-1 led by Manmohan Singh. Another game-changer was NREGA (National Rural Employment Guarantee Act). It will always be debated whether it helped the Congress to win the elections or not.

The Congress improved its vote share from 26.7 per cent to 28.6 per cent and managed to win 206 seats as compared to 145 seats from 2004. This is the best performance of the Congress from the eleventh to the seventeenth Lok Sabha. This election is the classic case study of how a multi-party democracy works. In a few states, it was pure arithmetic which worked in favour of the Congress. Congress also got help from the presence of some key individuals in the election arena. In Andhra Pradesh, Chiranjeevi's Praja Rajyam Party fought forty seats and cornered 15.6 per cent votes without getting any seat. The Congress vote share came down by 2.6 per cent when compared to the last election. It had 41.6 percent votes in 2004 and in 2009, it came down to 39 per cent votes but the number of seats increased from 29 to 33. Uttar Pradesh, the largest state of the country, acknowledged as the 'kingmaker' worked in favour of Congress where they secured 22 seats (initially 21seats; later the Firozabad seat vacated by Akhilesh Yadav of the Samajwadi Party to retain Kannauj was grabbed by Raj Babbar of Congress). The plan of Mulayam to bring Kalyan with him proved counter productive. Besides the Yadavs, the Muslims were the main block voters of the SP. They deserted SP and voted for the BSP and Congress, thus improving their performance. In Maharashtra, Raj Thakeray-led Maharashtra Navnirman Sena (MNS) contested elections which came as a blessing for the Congress. The MNS fought 11 seats in the Mumbai—Konkan region; as a result, the BJP–Shiv Sena lost 8 of these 11 seats. Congress with 19.61 per cent votes was less by 4 percent than what they got in 2004. But they increased their tally by 4 seats and got 17 seats.

One more factor which had a role in the final verdict was NREGA. Fifth September is the birthday of the second President of India, Sarvpalli Radhakrishnan. Every year, this day is celebrated as Teachers' Day. Teachers are remembered, felicitated and as a mark of respect, functions are organized in most of the educational institutions of the country. On 5 September 2005, the president gave consent for the Mahatma Gandhi Employment Guarantee Act empowering the villages and giving every villager the right to work. The proposal which was mooted by the P.V. Narsimha Rao government in 1991 to give a minimum job guarantee for unskilled manual labour completed its journey and the act was gazetted on 7 September 2005. Though we still celebrate Teachers' Day on 5 September, on this day the *daridra narain*[1] living in villages also got the right to get at least 100 days of job every year.

The scheme NREGA which is now rechristened as Mahatma Gandhi National Rural Employment Guarantee Act (MGNREGA) was initially implemented in a few districts and subsequently from 1 April 2008, it was extended to all the districts of the country. It guaranteed 100 days of employment to unskilled manual labour in each household within five kilometres of their village. It was compared to the famous slogan given by Indira Gandhi in 1971—'*Garibi hatao*'. This slogan was the clinching factor for her victory. In the same way, NREGA proved to be the game-changer for the Congress in 2009. But there was a major difference. *Garibi hatao* was only a slogan and a promise for a better future. But NREGA was a promise fulfilled and delivered. The Congress was asking voters for a second term based on their actual performance. Any government seeking votes in an election has to take care of anti-incumbency, but surprisingly, the vote share of the Congress improved by 2 per cent as compared to the 2004 elections. NREGA changed the sentiments in rural India. That this scheme energized the whole of rural India can be proven by looking at Kalahandi, a backward parliamentary constituency of Orissa. It had become synonymous with poverty, hunger and starvation. This constituency had last elected a Congress MP in 1991. After losing four elections in a row, the Congress candidate won in 2009 after almost two-and-a-half decades of the introduction of NREGA. This indicates that the NREGA was a revolutionary initiative.

The MGNREGA scheme was ridiculed by the BJP when they were in opposition. But they continued with this scheme when they came to power. It is the largest social security scheme in the world. On many occasions, the World Bank has praised it for rural development. Initially, the big landlords in villages were not happy with the scheme because not only did the labour wages go up dramatically but the availability of labour force to work in the fields also became scarce. The scheme, which was a boon for rural labour, was ironically perceived to be full of corruption and malpractices. The 1985 remark of Rajiv Gandhi that only 15 paise out of 1 rupee reaches the beneficiary in the welfare scheme was quoted for MGNREGA scheme too. It must be understood that the scheme is path-breaking and very innovative. The allegation of corruption is because of the faulty implementation of the scheme.

Another landmark Act of UPA-1, which may not have got votes for the party, but it certainly empowered the common man on the street was the Right to Information (RTI) Act passed in 2005. The RTI is a weapon that is used to check the sufferings of the citizens. Two leaders who started their public life as RTI activists—Arvind Kejriwal and Manish Sisodia—ultimately became Chief and Deputy Chief Minister of Delhi respectively.

The election issues on which political parties appeal for votes have also changed in the twenty-first century. In recent times it is convenient for the ruling party to ask for votes on emotional issues rather issues based on performance. One incident which changed a lot of narratives for the country was the Mumbai Attack of 26 November 2008. The attack was done by Lashkar-e-Taiba, a terrorist group based in Pakistan. It started on Wednesday, the 26th, and continued for four days till 29 November. There was an urgency to stop any such future terror attacks. For this purpose, the National Investigation Agency (NIA) was established. It is under the central government and has wide powers. It was established in February 2009 just before the general elections. The agency can directly deal with terror-related crimes anywhere in India without informing or taking permission from the state government. The noteworthy point is that the Mumbai attack was telecast live on the national television nonstop for four days. Pakistan was the perpetrator of the attack and nationalist feeling was at its highest but nowhere during the election campaign, the Mumbai attack was made an issue to vote in favour of Congress. On the other hand, the Pulwama attack was the core issue around which the poll campaign of BJP was built for the 2019 election. The biggest decision which changed the course of the economy of India was demonetization (8 November 2016) but it was nowhere mentioned by the ruling party during its election campaign.

Over the years, there have been subtle changes in the nationalist tone and now it has no links with the ideology of the original nationalist cause. It has become a partisan effort. The ten-year journey of nationalism from 2010 till 2020 has been more of a radical, aggressive political ideology/campaign. From being a national emotion, it has become the property of one political party.

Notes

1. The almighty in the form of the poorest as addressed by Gandhi.

CHAPTER-16

Main Hoon Anna

India against Corruption, Advent of the Aam Aadmi Party

28 August 2011, Sunday

Implementation of the Mandal Commission and Babri Masjid demolition changed the political structure of the country. Political parties and electorates aligned themselves based on caste and religion. No agitation was witnessed on the national scale to change the system against corruption after Jayaprakash (JP) led Sampurna Kranti, which led to the imposition of Emergency. The movement to end corruption in public life led by JP was against a specific party, that is, the Congress and against a specific leader, that is Indira Gandhi. Two decades after the Emergency, people were fed up not just with a particular political party or person but all the parties and politicians were under the scanner.

Kisan Baburao Hazare, a flower-seller in the Dadar area of Mumbai became Anna Hazare by 1990. Coming from a poor background, he had to leave school after seventh grade as his family was not able to pay his tuition fees. Hazare joined the army in 1960 as a driver. He had two miraculous escapes—the first one was in 1965 during the Indo-Pak war.

He was posted in the Khemkaran sector when during an attack by the Pakistani forces, he was the lone survivor. The second escape was when he was posted in Nagaland and during an insurgency operation, he was the lone survivor. Hazare interpreted his miraculous escapes as a sign that his life was intended for a bigger role. He was influenced by the teachings of Vivekanand, Gandhi and Vinoba Bhave.

In 1975, after his stint with the army, he came back to his native village, Ralegan Siddhi in Ahmad Nagar district of Maharashtra. Ralegan Siddhi was just another drought-prone, poverty-stricken village and Anna made it his lab for experimenting and implementing various methods of irrigation and getting a stable income for the farmers. He then also took up various social reforms, such as the prohibition of liquor and tobacco, the establishment of the Grain Bank, ban on cutting trees and drugs, etc. He remained unmarried and the village temple became the centre of all activities. He was conferred the Padma Bhushan by the Government of India in 1992 for his contributions to society.

In 1991, he launched the 'Bhrashtachar Virodhi Jan Andolan' the people's movement against corruption. With this, he graduated to a bigger role in cleaning the rampant corruption in politics. The first agitation in 1991 was against local forest officials. The state-level movement was against Gholap, the social welfare minister in Manohar Joshi's cabinet in Maharashtra in 1997. Gholap filed a defamation suit against Hazare. Hazare was arrested, released, again arrested and sent for three months' imprisonment. All parties barring the ruling Shiv Sena and BJP supported Anna and as a result, he was released and Gholap had to resign.

In 2000, Anna led the first mass movement which

galvanized the entire state of Maharashtra to enact a revised RTI Act, which subsequently became the base document for the 2005 Right to Information Act (RTI). Next in 2003, the Nationalist Congress Party (NCP) ministers of Congress–the NCP Government of Maharashtra were in the firing line of his anti-corruption campaign. The most lethal weapon he discovered during this movement was, fast unto death. His fast started on 9 August 2003 and ended on 17 August when Chief Minister Sushil Kumar Shinde appointed a one-man inquiry commission of retired Justice P.B. Sawant. Three ministers had to resign when Justice Sawant submitted his report in 2005 indicting them. Three trusts headed by Anna Hazare were also named in the report. The commission's report levelled serious charges against Hazare for using the money of the trust for his birthday celebrations. But Congress took no action against him.

Anna's entry into the national scene was triggered when the union government on 20 July 2006 proposed an amendment in the RTI Act. Anna's fast unto death from 9 August 2006 ended on 19 August when the government agreed to withdraw amendments. After a long struggle, in 2006 itself, Anna Hazare made the Maharashtra government implement the Regulation of Transfers and Prevention of Delay in Discharge of Official Duties Act. This act ensured that government servants would be transfer red after three years of posting. It also regulated delays in the clearing of files *within* a specified time. Though the act exists, it is not implemented. It proved to be just an announcement.

The lifetime achievement for which Anna Hazare will be remembered came in 2011. Different social and political activists and groups were working in different parts of the country for Lokpal. It was conceived that an impartial person should be appointed to look after the interest of the common man and especially enquire into the corruption charges of the Legislature, Executive and Judiciary. Eminent people like Medha Patkar, Santosh Hegde, Shanti Bhushan, his son Prashant Bhushan, Arvind Kejriwal, Kiran Bedi and many more joined hands and Anna Hazare was made their leader. On 5 April 2011, he started his fast at Jantar Mantar in Delhi with the demand of forming a Joint Committee of the government and members of civil societies. Sri Sri Ravi Shankar, Baba Ramdev also came in support of Anna Hazare. In line with the announced policy that no politician should be allowed to come on stage, Uma Bharti and Om Prakash Chautala were denied to address the protestors.

The protest had an All India support. People staged dharnas, observed fast, took out candlelight marches and rallies in Bengaluru, Mumbai, Chennai, Lucknow, Ahmedabad, Guwahati, Shillong, Aizwal, etc. The government accepted the demands on 8 April 2011 and a ten-member joint committee was formed. Five ministers–Pranab Mukherjee, Chidambaram, Kapil Sibbal, Veerapa Moily and Salman Khurshid were the government nominees, and the civil society members of the joint committee were Anna Hazare, Santosh Hegde, Shanti Bhushan, Prashant Bhushan and Arvind Kejriwal. Anna ended his 98-hour fast on 9 April 2011 giving a deadline of 15 August 2011 to pass the bill.

In between, Ramdev became politically active and formed a political party named Swabhiman Bharat in 2010. Ramdev had declared to fight elections on all the parliament seats. He also started his movement for the Lokpal Bill. He announced a hunger strike against black money and corruption at Ramlila Ground from 4 June 2011. The permission was taken to organize a yoga camp for 5,000 people but the numbers were more than 50,000. Negotiations were going on between Ramdev and the government but he suddenly withdrew from the discussions citing breach of trust. The government acted and Ramdev was arrested when he was trying to escape from the Ramlila ground wearing female attire of salwar, kurta and dupatta. He was sent to his ashram in Haridwar by plane. He was banned for fifteen days from coming to Delhi.

The negotiations in the Lokpal committee came to a deadlock when in the draft bill, the government wanted to keep the prime minister, Judiciary, and lower bureaucracy out of the purview of Lokpal. On 6 June 2011, the civil society members boycotted the drafting committee meeting to press the inclusion of all categories under the law's purview and also to protest against the arrest of Ramdev on 5 June. Another demand of the group was to live telecast all future meetings of the committee. The cabinet approved the bill on 28 July 2011 keeping all the three categories, on whom objection was raised, out of the purview of Lokpal. Now two sets of draft bills were considered–one that was approved by the government and second that was prepared by the civil society members.

Anna Hazare was arrested hours before the start of his fast on 16 August 2011 along with his supporters. He was granted bail on giving a personal bond which he refused. He was transferred to Tihar Jail in Delhi. The entire country protested and the ruling Congress party was also divided on this issue. It is also said that Congress vice-president Rahul Gandhi met the prime minister Manmohan Singh and conveyed his displeasure on his arrest. He was released but he refused to leave Tihar Jail till permission to protest was not granted. Ultimately permission to protest at Ramlila Ground was given. Anna Hazare left Tihar on 20 August 2011 to start his fast.

This high-profile fast in August 2011 held a lot of future possibilities and was going to change the future politics of India in an unprecedented manner. The public pressure on the government was enormous. This ultimately resulted in the unanimous passing of the Lokpal Bill in the Parliament. After 288 hours, Anna Hazare ended his fast on 28 August 2011. He drove straight to Medanta Hospital in Gurgaon with Arvind Kejriwal by his side. The campaign of Lokpal was fought under the banner of India Against Corruption (IAC) which was a loose organization with a core committee of twenty-four members. By the time the Lokpal bill was passed, another group within the IAC emerged as Team Anna.

Team Anna drew inspiration from the Egyptian protestor Khaled Saeed who died in 2010, which led to the 'We Are All Khaled' campaign. Team Anna's campaign in India was known as 'I Am Anna Hazare', which was similar to the 'We Are All Khaled' campaign from the Egyptian uprising. Another symbolic mark of being Gandhian was the Gandhi cap which made a comeback after about 60 years of Gandhi's death. Now all the political outfits use the iconic Gandhi cap; only the colour of the cap changes with the party. It is very interesting to note that there are very few pictures of Gandhi wearing the Gandhian cap and the secret is revealed by Nafees Siddique, a Rampur-based historian and writer. In 1919, Gandhi came to Rampur in Uttar Pradesh to meet the Nawab, Sayyid Hamid Ali Khan Bahadur and came to know that as per the royal tradition, he had to cover his head with a cap. Since Gandhi was not carrying any cap, Abadi Begum, mother of the Ali brothers, who had led the Khilafat movement gifted him a handmade cap–with pointed ends and a wide band. Gandhi wore this cap for the first time. This Gandhi cap became the symbol of Gandhi and Gandhian philosophy. The Gandhi cap became a part of the Congress dress and a symbol of the freedom struggle. According to Siddique, at some point in time, the British rulers tried unsuccessfully to impose a ban on the immensely popular Gandhi caps.

It is generally said that Anna was backed strategically by the RSS/BJP to target Congress. In October 2011, Ajay Chautala was the first candidate to be backed by Anna's outfit—India against Corruption for the Hisar parliamentary by-election. Anna appealed to defeat Congress. Arvind Kejriwal, Manish Sisodia and Kiran Bedi actively campaigned for Chautala. At the time of the election, an investigation was going on regarding the Teachers Recruitment Scam case of 2008 in which Ajay Chautala and his father Om Prakash Chautala were convicted and sentenced to ten years' imprisonment in 2013. In the agitation against Congress, Anna extended open support to Yoga Guru Baba Ramdev, who has now turned into a businessman. All the issues of protest raised by Ramdev against the Congress government are still relevant. In some instances, the situation has deteriorated during the BJP rule but the yoga guru chooses to remain silent.

India Against Corruption (IAC) was a heterogeneous group consisting of different individuals. Each individual had their agenda. The only common binding factor was the anti-Congress crusade. Two views emerged during this agitation to enter into the political arena directly or remain apolitical and work as a pressure group. Anna himself was sceptical about organizing huge funds that were a primary requirement of electoral politics. The other group led by Arvind Kejriwal, Shanti Bhushan, Prashant Bhushan, Manish Sisodia, Yogendra Yadav, Kumar Vishwas, Anand Kumar were of the view that, to bring meaningful change in the corrupt system direct entry into politics was inevitable. The debate went on and officially in September 2012 Anna and Kejriwal parted ways. The Aam Aadmi Party was formally launched on 26 November 2012. It is a historic date as it was on 26 November 1949 when the Indian Constitution was adopted. The Delhi state election was the first election fought by AAP in 2013. Out of seventy seats, BJP won thirty-four, AAP twenty-eight and Congress eight. In a strange turn of events, AAP and Congress joined hands and Arvind Kejriwal became the chief minister with a wafer-thin margin. As expected, Kejriwal had to resign after forty-nine days. But somewhere, his alliance with the Congress also proved that electoral politics is all about gaining power and making compromises. Principles, ethical conduct, integrity, issues or values are not important. The AAP came into existence opposing and criticizing the Congress party and its government. But they joined hands with the Congress without any qualms to form the government. The hidden ambition and agenda of the party came to the forefront.

The 2014 general election was fought well by AAP. It roped in activists from all over India to contest the elections. Kejriwal challenged Modi in Varanasi and Kumar Vishwas contested against Rahul Gandhi. The elections were keenly fought. The campaigns were well organized. But the votes polled may not tell the real story. During the campaign, Modi and Rahul Gandhi both had to pay more attention to their respective constituencies. The BJP contested the maximum seats–487, Congress–464 and AAP contested 432 seats. AAP in its first election won four seats from Punjab thus surpassing the figure of BJP by 100 per cent. The BJP in its debut general elections in 1984 had won only two seats. The AAP also created another record by for feiting the security deposits in 413 seats. It surpassed the record set by Jaigurudev Doordarshi Party in the 1991 elections when 321 candidates had forfeited their deposits. The Delhi Assembly Elections of 2015 broke many myths and established that the roots of democracy are much deeper than they appear. The AAP swept the poll by winning 67 seats out of 70 with BJP getting 3 and Congress, which ruled Delhi for 15 years, drew a blank. The AAP government concentrated on four core areas, that is, electricity, water, education and hospitals, and they delivered results. The BJP swept the polls in the 2019 general elections with a massive mandate for the second term. The Delhi state elections in 2020 were keenly fought. Amit Shah personally supervised the campaign of BJP. The AAP was seeking votes based on their performance and BJP was fighting on the time-tested communal basis. The speeches of Kapil Mishra, Parwesh Verma and Amit Shah were directed against the minorities. Delhiites again voted maturely and AAP got 62 seats whereas BJP with full-throttle campaign managed to secure only 8 seats. Delhi's election is proof of the maturity of Indian democracy with all its shortcomings. If you govern well and keep the welfare of the masses in mind then people will rise above the divisive *politics of* religion, caste, and other narrow considerations. Voters reward the party for its track record of delivering better services.

An interesting factor worth knowing is the drop in the level of corruption during AAP's rule in Delhi. In the 2013 elections, the statistics of 66 candidates, who fought elections in 2008 too gives us some idea. The assets and wealth affidavits filed by them at the time of elections indicate that during five years from 2008 to 2013, their wealth grew by 259 per cent (Rs 7.53 crore) on an average. In the 2020 Delhi elections, the growth during the 5-year-period was a meagre—13 per cent (Rs 92.12 lakh). Despite some shortcomings of AAP's rule in Delhi, it must be noted that the elected representatives were by and large not corrupt. They were more connected with the common man and their policies were more people-oriented.

The year 2012 will always be remembered as a year of mass awakening when the man on the street decided enough is enough and stood against the wrong practices of the society, government and the state. Instead of choosing the right and the ethical path, our political leaders choose to serve their selfish interests. After the half-cooked Anna Agitation, which culminated in AAP, 2012 witnessed the Nirbhaya Protest. A 23-year-old physiotherapist intern, hailing from Ballia along with her friend from Gorakhpur, boarded the bus around 9.30 pm after watching the evening show of the movie–*Life of Pi*. She boarded the bus at Munirka for Dwarka in Delhi. It was a private bus operating under the contract of the Delhi Transport Corporation. The bus with tinted glasses was used for charter services and was not supposed to ply on that route. Six people including the bus driver Ram Singh were on a fun trip and had looted an unsuspecting carpenter before luring Nirbhaya to board the bus. Nirbhaya was raped, beaten brutally by all six before being thrown on the road. Her friend was beaten severally and a blow by an iron rod made him unconscious. He was also thrown on the road. She was seen by a passer-by and a police vehicle brought her to the hospital. The rape assault was so brutal that her abdomen, intestine and genitals were damaged. A wheel jack handle was penetrated after rape damaging her uterus and intestine. During the trial, it came out that her intestine was physically pulled out by one of the culprits by hand. After eleven days and many surgeries, she was shifted to Singapore on 27 December where she died on 29 December 2012. According to paper reports, the decision to shift her to Singapore was taken by the government on the insistence of Delhi chief minister Sheila Dixit. It was more or less certain on the 27th after her fifth surgery that she would not survive. To dilute the impact of immediate public backlash after her death, she was sent by air ambulance to a super-speciality hospital in Singapore.

All six culprits were caught and sent to jail. One of the culprits was seventeen years and six months old on the day of the crime. He came under the category of juvenile and was sentenced to three years' imprisonment in a remand home. This juvenile was the person who made the call and lured Nirbhaya to board the bus before raping her. He was a free man after three years. The identity of this juvenile who was an equal partner in the gory crime was not only protected but as per the law of the land got some monetary assistance also to start a new life. Dr Subramaniam Swamy filed a *petition* before the High Court, challenging the release of the juvenile rapist. Dr Subramaniam Swamy said that because of his age he should not be spared for the heinous crime. But the law of the land helped him evade stringent punishment. During the trial, Ram Singh officially committed suicide in jail in March 2013. The remaining four were found guilty by the trial court and were sentenced to death in September 2013. By Indian standards, it was a very fast trial. The High Court confirmed the death sentence and the case went to the

Supreme Court. All the tricks of the trade were used to delay the execution of the death sentence but finally, on 20 March 2020, all four were hanged to death in Delhi.

The protest against the rape and in support of Nirbhaya started in Delhi in a modest way but in a few days, it took the entire country by storm. The Delhi protestors were lathi-charged. Water cannon and tear gas were used to dispel the protestors. Sheila Dikshit, Chief Minister of Delhi called her state–Delhi the rape capital of India. Manmohan Singh, portrayed as one of the silent prime ministers had to come on television and address the nation. In his appeal to bring peace, he reminded that being the father of three daughters he shares the trauma of Nirbhaya's parents. The case invoked an unprecedented response in the form of protests from the common man. At the government level, lots of changes were made and the Criminal Law (Amendment) Ordinance, 2013 was passed for faster and effective trials. The public discourse on crime against women issues gave moral courage and strength to women to report acts of crime against them. It was reported that the numbers of foreign female tourists in the following year fell by 30-40 per cent.

Seventy years after the 1942 Quit India movement, which was the turning point for the Britishers to leave India when the common man was united, in the 2012 protest—Anna and Nirbhaya failed to unite the nation. The biggest factor for unity in 1942 was the leadership of Gandhi. In 1942, when Congress gave a call—Quit India against Britishers then the RSS, Muslim League, Ambedkar and communists preferred to stand with the Britishers. Gandhi never termed them as traitors either in his writings or his speeches. At the time of Independence, Gandhi insisted that leaders like Ambedkar and Shyama Prasad Mukherjee must be a part of the making of free India. The Constituent

Assembly and the first cabinet of India is a testimony for this. Today any voice of dissent, any kind of opposition, and any question raised towards the government or against a political party are termed anti-national. Like JP's call of Sampurna Kranti (total revolution) in the seventies, India once again missed the opportunity given by the protests of 2012 to clean the system. Strong leadership was not there, sympathizers had their agenda and India would again have to wait for true independence.

Chapter-17

India 'Modi' fied

Modi Sweeps India, Headline Management Begins

26 May 2014, Monday

Narendra Modi took an oath of office as prime minister of India on 26 May 2014. The people of India who had voted for Modi comprising 31.34 per cent (the National Democratic Alliance vote share was 38.5 per cent) and also people who had not voted for Modi comprising 68.66 per cent had high hopes from Modi. Though the BJP had a clear majority (BJP won 282 seats) but as mentioned before, the vote percentage was 31.34 per cent, which is the lowest share for a party to form a majority government in India since the first general election after independence. This statistical fact shows just how fragmented the vote is. The swearing-in ceremony was held in the forecourts of Rashtrapati Bhavan. It was the beginning of the gala events which became the trademark of Modi rule. The heads of state from all the SAARC (South Asian Association for Regional Cooperation) countries attended the function and a lot of people considered it the revival of the Panchsheel doctrine of Nehru.[1]

The story of Modi becoming the fifteenth prime minister

of India can be divided into two parts. Part one deals with the events at the centre and the follies of the UPA-2 government. These mistakes could have been by design or by accident under the accidental Prime Minister Manmohan Singh, but they proved to be very costly. Part two of the story tells us about the meticulous planning by Team Modi.

The ruling UPA coalition led by Congress had nothing to offer for the 2014 elections. Though the economy was doing reasonably well, due to Narendra Modi's aggressive and frenzied election campaign, all the achievements and development under the UPA government stood discredited. There were many achievements, such as India had successfully hosted the Commonwealth Games, and despite criticism, the Mahatma Gandhi National Rural Employment Guarantee Act, 2005 (MGNREGA) had put some money in the hands of the rural poor. Manmohan Singh had completed two terms, played the role given by the Congress party exceedingly well but he did not grow as a leader who could get votes. The poll managers and strategists of the Congress party were confident that despite scams and anti-incumbency charges, they would manage to secure enough seats to form some coalition. Congress leaders thought that if after the Emergency in 1977, when the anger of the nation was at its peak, they could still win 189 seats, the charges against the government in 2014 were comparatively not so grave and could be easily managed. This was a huge error of judgement.

The *scam*-tainted UPA government was reeling under severe setback over corruption. The Commonwealth Games were supposed to be an event that would showcase India to the world. But very soon, the skeleton of successful Commonwealth Games started tumbling out. The Congress allowed scam after scam during its rule—the 2G Scam, the Coal Block scam, etc.—gave the impression that the UPA2 was steeped in corruption. Though Manmohan Singh's image was clean, he had no authority to take stern action against the erring ministers or officers. The beginning of the end of UPA-2 was a CAG Report on the Second Generation Spectrum Licence popularly known as 2G. Vinod Rai, who was the 1972 batch IAS officer was the Comptroller and Auditor General of India (CAG). On 16 November 2010, he presented the CAG report on 2G—quantifying the notional loss of Rs 1.76 lakh crores. The 2G scam was supposed to be the biggest scam of India; *Time* ranked it as second only to the Nixon Watergate scam in the history of the world. The Joint Parliamentary Committee (JPC) and CBI probed the 2G scam. In December 2017, the special court acquitted all the accused including A. Raja and Kanimozhi of DMK. The judgement said, 'Some people created a scam by artfully arranging a few selected facts and exaggerating things beyond recognition to astronomical levels.' The new government-appointed Vinod Rai, an architect of the 2G scam as the first chairman of the Banking Board in 2016, in recognition of the good work he had done. Later Supreme Court made him the interim chairman of the BCCI (Board of Control for Cricket in India), the richest cricketing outfit in the world.

Narendra Modi had a controversial and disturbing image after 2002 Godhara when he almost lost his chair. Atal Bihari Vajpayee reminded him of the *rajdharm* during the National Executive meeting of BJP held at Goa in 2002. It was certain that Modi would lose his chair. But thanks to the stand taken by Lal Krishna Advani that Vajpayee relented. Advani threatened to resign in the event of a change of leadership in Gujarat. Thus a new BJP fanatic icon was born who slowly acquired a larger-than-life image and captured the imagination of the voters. The next step for Modi was image makeover which was planned patiently and immaculately. Moniker 'NaMo' was carefully crafted for Narendra Modi. Just after Godhara, Grey Advertising was hired in 2003 to present the first version of vibrant Gujarat. The brief was specific and clear—to revive the image of Gujarat and Chief Minister Modi. The inaugural event was held around Navratri, keeping in mind the spirit of celebration during this joyous, festive season in Gujarat. All these efforts were to showcase Gujarat in front of foreign investors and attract foreign investments. The glitzy propaganda machine and the 'vibrant Gujarat' image helped build up the image of Modi. The mega event of the state—vibrant Gujarat—is now held biennially with a lot of pomp and show. More than the state or the party, the direct and the only beneficiary of this mega event was the individual named Narendra Modi.

A term—'Gujarat Model' was coined which became synonymous with progress and growth. It was considered a perfect model for the state where people were healthy, wealthy and happy. A reality check can be done—The per capita income of India in 2003–04 was Rs 20,871, Gujarat with Rs 26,992 was ranked ninth. In 2004–05, the all-India per capita income was Rs 23,198; Gujarat with Rs 28,846 stood at the eleventh position. During 2013–14 which was the last year of the successful Gujarat model and after which Modi was propelled from chief minister to prime minister, the per capita income of all India was Rs 79,118, Gujarat with Rs. 1,13,139 dropped down to the fourteenth place. People may debate and challenge these figures. Some economists may say it was calculated based on the current price, whereas some will say that it was based on the constant price. Statistical figures can tell completely different stories depending on when, how and who made it. Whatever might be the statistical jargon, it should be kept in mind that which ever method was applied remained the same for all the states. On close examination one may observe that the state had not delivered even an average performance on a lot of growth parameters during 2002–14. But the elaborate marketing strategies and the mega-events that were organized roped in the best in the trade.

The trend started by BJP in 2009, to announce its prime ministerial candidate before elections came in handy for Modi. For the 2004 elections, without any formal announcements, it was clear that Atal Bihari Vajpayee was the prime ministerial candidate of BJP and NDA. Congress had not announced any prime ministerial candidate. It was guessed that since Sonia Gandhi was the president of the party, she would be the prime minister if the party managed to get enough seats to form some coalition. The Italian origin debate started by BJP suited a few congressmen like Pranab Mukherjee and A.K. Antony. No one ever thought of Manmohan Singh. In 2009, L.K. Advani was the prime ministerial candidate. Rajnath Singh, the president of BJP had to issue a clarification that Advani wasthe prime ministerial candidate not only for BJP but also for NDA. The need for the statement arose when Bhairon Singh Shekhawat announced his desire to get back into active politics and fight elections from Rajasthan. He also made a statement that the prime minister is elected by the MPs. Rajnath Singh further clarified that after being the vice-president of the country and the presidential candidate it would not be proper if Shekhawat fought elections. The sitting prime minister Manmohan Singh was announced by Congress for the top job.

The issue of a prime ministerial candidate to be announced before the 2014 elections saw the power struggle between the old guards and the new emerging leaders. Under the weight of scams and corruption charges, UPA-2 was crumbling even before the elections started. The careful tactical support to Anna helped the BJP to raise the tempo of changing the corrupt government. Not only Lal Krishan Advani at the age of 74 saw it as his last chance to occupy the elusive prime minister's chair but many in the party also believed him to be the rightful leader. But Modi had different plans. First, he managed Nagpur (RSS headquarters). It is widely believed that Rajnath Singh, the party president and also an aspirant for the prime minister's chair was managed by one of the four cardinal principles of politics–*sam, daam, dand, bhed*. Modi with Amit Shah by his side was not ready to withdraw in favour of his guru who had always stood behind him. 'Machiavellian' thoughts on ruthless and emotionless leadership resonated and these thoughts were quickly implemented to ensure success. Modi received his birthday (17 September) gift four days in advance. On 13 September 2013, the parliamentary board decision was announced by Rajnath Singh. Narendra Modi was declared as the BJP prime ministerial candidate. Advani decided not to attend the meeting. He had wanted the party to not announce Modi's name as he felt that the forthcoming assembly elections of Rajasthan, Madhya Pradesh, Chhattisgarh and Delhi would get negatively affected. But all the suggestions given by Advani were overruled by the party.

After becoming the NDA's prime ministerial candidate, Team Modi worked on a three-pronged strategy. First, the projection of Modi as a decisive, no-nonsense leader. As a result, the elections of 2014 were in spirit more on the lines of the presidential form of election where people chose the prime minister and the party or MPs were non-consequential. Secondly, to build a campaign around the misrule and corruption to get rid of the Congress party led by the fourth generation of the Nehru-Gandhi family—the *Congress Mukt Bharat*. Thirdly, the most important strategy—election was carefully planned and decided on paper to the last step (instead of the conventional last mile) and executed with precision.

Ever since he became the chief minister of Gujarat, Modi's projected image was that of a decisive leader, one who delivers. On the contrary, Rahul Gandhi's image was that of a reluctant leader. The Congress party never came out with clear-cut announcements of its prime ministerial candidate. It was perceived that Rahul Gandhi would be the choice for the prime minister. The non-committed voters who were neither aligned to Congress nor with BJP were not ready to vote for an accidental or reluctant prime ministerial candidate. Thus this worked in Modi's favour. So Indian voters without realizing converted the election like a presidential form of election.

For strategic and organizational support, Modi had a stock-market trained politician, who always stood behind him. This man, who was hounded out of Gujarat for almost two years by a judicial order which in legal parlance is called—*tadipaar,* is none other than Amit Shah. Another man who changed the very dynamics and the rules of the game was PK (Prashant Kishore). He was a former public health specialist in the United Nations. PK left his job and joined Modi. He advised on various social and development issues. For the first time, PK involved himself completely in the micro management of the Vidhan Sabha elections of 2012 in Gujarat. This was when Modi was running for the assembly elections for the third term. Modi's complete trust in him was the reason that led to the creation of Citizen for Accountable Government (CAG) by PK in 2013. He took charge of campaigning and also managed the booths for the 2014 election. The various events which PK called models were developed and successfully implemented–*chai par charcha*, 3D rallies, Run for Unity, collection of used and old agricultural equipment from all over India for the making of the Sardar Patel statue, etc. are a few examples of such events.

Modi, a keen student of election and power politics, was able to read between the lines. In the past, two non-Hindi speaking prime ministers—Morarji Desai and Deve Gowda failed because they were not from the Hindi heart land. I.K. Gujral and Manmohan Singh became prime ministers, not on their own. UP has traditionally been the spring board for the prime ministers. Famed Indian prime ministers have historically contested elections from UP. Modi too decided to contest from Uttar Pradesh. Ganga Putra Modi arrived in Varanasi to fight the election. His best man Amit Shah was assigned a specific role to supervise the Uttar Pradesh elections. He was given free hand in deciding the candidates and the use of resources. The campaign of the Samajwadi Party (SP) and Bahujan Samaj Party (BSP) worked in favour of Modi. The Samajwadi Party fought elections against Congress but decided not to put any candidate against Sonia and Rahul, giving the impression that they were not against Congress. Mayawati had supported UPA-2 and it was perceived that her party would also go with the Congress. The net result was the anti-incumbency votes of Congress went to BJP instead of splitting between the SP, BSP and BJP.

The AAP was the joker in the pack. Arvind Kejriwal

decided to challenge Modi in Varanasi and Kumar Vishwas camped in Amethi to fight against Rahul Gandhi. Besides Varanasi, Modi filed his nomination from Vadodara too. This showed his level of confidence about Uttar Pradesh's seat. The selection of the Varanasi seat was done after scrutiny of past poll results. Post-Mandal, six elections were held from 1991 to 2009. Barring the 2004 elections, BJP had won five times from this seat. To further consolidate his position Apna Dal, a party championing the cause of Kurmi (a backward caste engaged in agriculture) was given two seats adjacent to Varanasi. Kurmi had a sizeable presence in the constituency. Along with Kejriwal of the AAP, the Congress, Samajwadi Party and Bahujan Samajwadi Party also fielded their candidates which suited Modi. Kejriwal in the run-up gave a good fight. Modi had to spend a considerable amount of time in Varanasi. Modi got, 581,022 votes, Kejriwal 2,09,238 votes and the remaining three of the Congress, SP and BSP together mustered 1,81,484 votes. It was certain that in a direct fight, results might not have changed but the margin would have been different. Now after about six years of witnessing BJP's election management techniques during the Modi era, it is not clear if apart from Kejriwal, the presence of the other three candidates was by design, strategy or party philosophy. Why did the opposition fail to put up a strong and consensus candidate in Varanasi is still a big question. Another interesting fact is that Modi spent the least as compared to the other four major candidates. The expenditure limit for a candidate contesting the Lok Sabha elections is Rs 70 lakhs. The details of expenses as given to the Election Commission was Ajai Rai of Congress–Rs 32,12,470, Arvind Kejriwal of AAP—Rs 22,72,000, Kailash Chaurasia of SP—Rs 9,74,707, V.P. Jaiswal of BSP–Rs

8,20,000 and Narendra Modi of BJP 5,83,099. As per the report of Nidhi Sharma published in the *Economic Times* of 2 March 2015, Rashtrapati Bhavan made an expenditure of Rs 34 lakhs during the swearing-in ceremony of Prime Minister Modi on 26 May 2014.

Though Rahul Gandhi won from Amethi defeating Smriti Irani by more than 1,00,000 votes, the game spoiler was Kumar Vishwas of AAP who got only 25,527 votes and finished a distant fourth. In his first election in 2004, Rahul got 66.18 per cent of votes polled in Amethi, which increased to 71.78 per cent votes in 2009. In the 2014 elections, Rahul's vote percentage was only 46.71 per cent, a phenomenal drop of 25 per cent when compared to 2009. Records may tell a different story but it was Kumar Vishwas who camped in Amethi for about five months and went on an intensive campaign. This was the main reason for the erosion of Rahul's votes. In 2014, Modi got 56.37 per cent votes and in the Modi tsunami of 2019, he got 63.62 per cent votes from Varanasi.

Social media, till then, was supposed to be a waste of time. For the first time, social media was used as a serious medium of the campaign by Team Modi. In the past, the use of technology in the agricultural sector had brought food to India. In the same way in the year 2014, all modern communication skills were used to bring votes for Modi. As a political leader, Manmohan Singh is a weak, somnolent communicator and by nature, he is a man of few words. In sharp contrast, Modi is a good public speaker and with his long innings as the Gujarat Chief Minister, he knows how to charm the audience. His biggest strength is he knows what his audience loves to listen to. He strikes a chord with the general public. Social media gave him a chance to communicate directly with the voters. He could greatly influence the first-timer voters through social media platforms. India had an estimated 80 million internet connections in 2014. Team Modi used Google Hangouts and Social Networks during the campaign to reach every nook and corner of the country. After the elections, Twitter India declared that there were whopping 58 million tweets from the start of the 2014 elections till the announcement of Modi's victory.

Though the Godhra used to haunt Modi, the same was used to his advantage. For the fence-sitter, non-decisive voters, he managed to portray himself as a successful chief minister who delivers. For the hard-core Hindu voters, it was their last chance to save the country from the leaders who styled themselves as secular but followed Muslim appeasement. In 2014, the estimated Muslim population was about 180 million (18 crores). Out of the 543 parliamentary constituencies, 218 seats have more than 10 per cent Muslim population. The breakup of the Muslim population can be given as—35 seats have 30 per cent plus Muslim population, 38 seats have 21–30 per cent Muslim population and 145 seats have 11–20 per cent Muslim population. After the emergence of the BJP, Muslims started voting en block. They have only one consideration in mind to support the party or a candidate who can defeat the BJP. The consolidation of Muslim votes helped the BJP, as it led to the consolidation of Hindu votes in reaction.

Muslims are about 14 per cent of the population. Going by proportionate representation they should have 76 seats in 545 seats of the Lok Sabha. *In 1980*, the *Lok Sabha had* the *maximum number* of *Muslim MPs* at *49*. As expected in the 2014 elections, due to the consolidation of Hindu votes, only 22 Muslims were elected. This was the minimum number since the first Lok Sabha. In the 2014 Lok Sabha elections, another record was set by the state of Uttar Pradesh from where for the first time there was no Muslim representation. In 2017, in Uttar Pradesh State elections, out of 403 seats in the Vidhan Sabha, BJP decided not to give the ticket to even one Muslim candidate. In the biggest state of the country which sends 80 MPs to the Lok Sabha, the minority appeasement was now countered with majority appeasement. Mercifully, in the 2019 Lok Sabha elections, BJP gave tickets to six Muslims, 3 each from West Bengal and Jammu & Kashmir. One of the candidates is Saumitra Khan, who defected from the Trinamool Congress and fought on the BJP ticket, won from West Bengal.

For the first time in 2014, India witnessed Team Modi work with focus and commitment only for winning the elections, for getting governance. They worked 24 x 7, 365 days a year. Team Modi thought with clarity, planned meticulously, and single-mindedly pursued the goal of winning elections. I had the privilege of working very closely with George Fernandes, a politician, who was a power house of energy, always busy, always multi-tasking, always working against time. A few of his political decisions can be questioned but even he had time for the finer aspects of life. He was a voracious reader and would write articles in newspapers, periodicals and personal letters to party colleagues and many others. He organized trade union activities, met a cross-section of people, engaged with human rights activities, protested for the rights of Tibet and Myanmar. The election was only a part of the bigger ideas of George. For Team Modi penning poems or writing articles seem to be a waste of time. In new India, the prime minister does not hold press conferences, the customary press does not travel with him on foreign tours. Modi enjoys monologue. Dialogue has become a thing of the past now.

The team is so engrossed with elections that each seat is discussed in detail, man to man marking of even opposition party candidates is done. I would like to share another personal story about my brother who was a sitting MP of Congress when run up for 2014 elections started. The Congress party prospects were not very great. Any novice could see the writing on the wall. A sitting member of parliament, the BJP came to his residence in Delhi and tried to persuade him to switch sides and fight as a BJP candidate. He reminded my brother of the shabby treatment given to him by the Congress party when the ticket for the 2009 elections was given to him. All types of allurements were offered. My brother chose not to take the offer, fought on the Congress ticket and lost. A small incident happened when my brother had filed the nomination and just before the last date of withdrawal, a senior Congress functionary came in my newspaper office in Lucknow, discussed the petty politics of UP Congressmen, and offered money for withdrawing his nomination at that juncture so that Congress would be left without a candidate. The money offered was sufficient to buy about half a quintal of gold. The point is the same tactics were applied to a few Congressmen who overnight switched sides, became MPs, or withdrew after the last date. For Team Modi, winning elections justifies all philosophies and principles.

Notes

1. See Chapter 3 of this book.

CHAPTER-18

Draconian Demonetization

What Did India Achieve?

8 November 2016, Tuesday

It was a normal trading session in the Bombay Stock Exchange on Tuesday, 8 November 2016. The Sensex closed with a gain of 132 points at 27,591. The evening was normal till after a cabinet meeting Prime Minister Modi appeared on televisionin a prime time address to the nation at 8.15 pm and everything changed—'*Mitron*'. The word '*Mitron*' became a precursor to bad news for large groups of people and it haunted the Indian public for quite some time. The 500-rupee notes and 1000-rupee notes were demonetized. The idea was to flush out black money from the system and eliminate the scourge of counterfeit currency that was circulating in the economy. It was estimated that out of a total of 15.41 lakh crore of 500 and 1,000 notes about 20 per cent were fake. It was widely believed that our cross-border neighbouring government was actively involved in printing these fake currencies. They were printed in their government press and were more or less as good as the original one.

One of the reasons propagated around this move was that demonetization would effectively neutralize terrorism and Naxalism. Prime Minister Modi in one of the many emotional speeches made an impassioned plea to the nation to bear the 'pain' for 'fifty days' after which he would end their hardship and resolve the problems of corruption, black money, etc. which would also mark the beginning of strong economy and employment for all. The Reserve Bank of India (RBI) issued guidelines that demonetized currency could be deposited till 31 December 2016. Though it should have been the legal right of the holder to exchange the currency, this new currency was made available with many strict rules and conditions. Each individual was initially permitted to make a one-time exchange of Rs 4,000 per day over the counter. The limit was increased to Rs 4,500 per day and subsequently reduced to Rs 2,000 per day. All exchange of notes was abruptly stopped from 25 November. The other condition was on cash withdrawal—it started with Rs 10,000 per day with an overall limit of Rs 20,000 per week. This was also changed and only on 13 March 2017, the restriction was withdrawn. The worst was ATM withdrawal starting with Rs 2,000 per day. The ATMs ran dry and empty ATMs were associated with a cash shortage. The machines were not calibrated for the size of the new currency which only added to the anxiousness and confusion of the public at large.

Long queues in front of banks were a common site leading to a lot of hardship that the common man was subjected to. The Indian public faced all this with utmost patience having only one hope that Modiji would end corruption with this masterstroke. The common man was happy forgetting his hardship because he was convinced that people, especially politicians with large unaccounted wealth, would be put to bigger hardships and the system would be cleaned. The banks were not prepared, the RBI was not prepared. The printing of new notes by the RBI started only in October. One major area which was wiped out by this one act of the Modi government was *streedhan*. In all Indian households—whether rich or poor, educated or illiterate, urban or rural—there was (we are not sure if it exists now or not) cash with the lady of the house, which only she was privy to and was spent on the needs of life. Women of the house keep bundles of cash stashed away in hidden biscuit tins or Tupperware containers, under sinks or at the back of wardrobe away from the prying eyes of husbands and other family members. It is security for a woman. This money over a while could be spent on school fees, marriage, hospital or medical bills, food, etc. Bank accounts are rare among Indian women, leaving them unable to deposit savings that many have preferred to keep secret from their spouses. This *streedhan* came into the knowledge of the people from whom it had been hidden for centuries, that is the male members of the family and half of the population was without any money of their own. With little access to reliable information and little experience of the banking system, women nationwide were thrown into a panic by Modi's announcement.

Among the many questions raised over the BJP government's move to invalidate high-currency notes is that of timing. Though the Modi government and the BJP always defend the decision of demonetization, the political grapevine says that one of the most important factors to announce this on 8 November was the Uttar Pradesh Assembly elections. The decision was aimed at hurting their competitors in a state where money power is crucial to electioneering. The Samajwadi Party under the leadership of young and energetic Akhilesh Yadav had given a fairly reasonable five-year rule. Prashant Kishore advised the

Congress for a comeback in this election, and Mayawati with over flowing coffers and a committed vote bank on her side was sure of displacing Akhilesh. Modi, till then, had not earned the reputation to win a state election on his own. The backroom operator who was calling the shots in the BJP subsequently showed to the world that winning and forming the government is the main objective and there is nothing wrong in using anything under your command to achieve this. The end justifies the means. If by some action or decision, the opposition is thrown out of gear, it must be taken. In Indian elections, money plays a very important role. Most campaigns run on illicit cash and money power is known to be used to woo voters. Though officially a limit is imposed, it is common knowledge that money spent directly and indirectly is much more. So, it was good tactics to bring a rule by which the opponent was stranded for want of resources despite having the money. Mayawati and Akhilesh's resources, especially dependent on cash, severely affected the campaign. The party in power at the centre which had prior information of demonetization prepared itself accordingly and naturally had the advantage.

Initially, all the banks and post offices were authorized to take a deposit of the old currency, but just after five days on 15 November, the government put an embargo on the district cooperative banks to receive deposits. This was done based on the widespread irregularity observed in these banks. It is important to mention about two banks that proved the idiom to make hay while the sun shines. These banks were the Ahmedabad District Cooperative Bank (ADCB) and the Rajkot District Cooperative Bank (RDCB). Amit Shah of the BJP was director of ADCB for many years and was also the chairman of the bank in 2000. The ADCB became the top bank in the country among the district cooperative banks to deposit demonetized currency worth Rs 745.59 crores. The RDCB whose chairman Jayeshbhai Vithalbhai Radadiya was cabinet minister of the state BJP government took the second position with a deposit of Rs 693.19 crores. Just for the record, a total of 370 district cooperative banks across the country deposited Rs 22,271 crore, an average of Rs 60 crores per bank. Another interesting fact is that in 2001 when for the first time Modi entered the Gujarat state legislature, it was from Rajkot.

The figures which were given after about two years told a very different story. Out of a total of Rs 15.41 lakh crore of currency (500- and 1,000-rupee notes), banks received Rs 15.30 lakh crores. This means that Rs 10,720 crore demonetized notes were not deposited which was the so-called black money. The RBI report in 2018 admitted that 99.3 per cent of the targeted currency was deposited. In the history of independent India, the first exercise of demonetization was done in 1978 by the Janata government and it was also linked with black money. The ordinance was passed on 16 January 1978 by which 1,000- 5,000-and 10,000-rupee notes were demonetized and the Bill became an Act on 30 March 1978. Though the people got a wider window, only 75 per cent of currency came back and it was presumed that 25 per cent of currency not deposited was black money.

The after-effect of this historical step is going to be long-lasting. The die-hard supporters of the ruling BJP party in private admit that the biggest mistake of the Modi-1 regime was demonetization. Production was hit negatively, the gross domestic product (GDP) started falling, unemployment increased and the economy was out of control. The Central Board of Direct Taxes (CBDT) report of 2012 stated that the black money in India is locked into

Benami properties, bullion and jewellery, and it was estimated that only about 6 per cent was in cash. The logic of going for such a big exercise is still unexplainable. The majority of the workforce in India is a daily wage earner. The rapid growth of the country saw urbanization and the first industry where many made their fortune and from where maximum labourers got their livelihood were builders and developers. This also became the first industry to take the hit and employment vanished resulting in unskilled labour going back to villages with no buying capacity.

The 2014 campaign of Modi was built around corruption and the poor state of the economy. This was the first and last election of India where people voted on the issues related to them—corruption and unemployment. Another promise which was debated after Modi came to power was to bring fifteen lakhs into the account of every Indian. Throughout his campaign, he emphasized that the black money stacked in foreign lands by corrupt (mainly politicians) would be brought back into the country. This promise was the clincher. He also added that the quantum of black money which would come from overseas would be sufficient for every citizen to have Rs 15 lakhs in their account. Now, this was tricky as people believed that this amount would come into their account whereas post-election this was contested by the BJP that such a promise of Rs 15 lakhs in each account was never made. Everyone, including die-hard supporters, agree that the promise to bring black money from foreign accounts was made but nothing happened. The BJP was looking for ways to wriggle out after being accused by political opponents of reneging on its poll promise.

The problem of black money in the Indian economy is not new. On the one hand, black money increases the purchasing power giving rise to higher demand, higher production, higher GDP but on the other hand, it also encourages undisclosed source of funds. It is widely believed that this undisclosed fund is mainly black money. Different governments tried to address this issue. In recent times, the 1997 Voluntary Disclosure of Income Scheme (VDIS) by Finance Minister P. Chidambaram gave defaulters immunity from the Foreign Exchange Regulation Act (FERA), Income Tax Act, Wealth Tax Act and Companies Act. It was designed as self valuation and disclosure. A huge number of 3,50,000 people participated and about Rs 7,500 crores came into government coffers. In the 2016 Union Budget, Finance Minister Arun Jaitley came out with another amnesty scheme which lasted from 1 June to 30 September 2016. The total declaration made was about Rs 67,382 crores by about 65,000 people. The major highlight was the declaration by Mahesh Shah from Ahmedabad, Gujarat who declared an undisclosed income of Rs 13,860 crores.

Another important decision that affected the economy was the implementation of the Goods and Services Tax (GST) which was imposed in true Modi style with an event. Let us discuss the basics of the GST. In 1996, Vishwanath Pratap Singh (V.P. Singh), the then finance minister in Rajiv Gandhi's cabinet, introduced the Modified Value Added Tax (MODVAT). Subsequently, in order to have one indirect tax in the country, which should be comprehensive, multistage and destination-based, various state governments worked together. The GST committee, under the chairmanship of Asim Dasgupta, finance minister of the CPM government of West Bengal, completed the ground work. In 2011, the CPM government was ousted from power by the Trinamool Congress. Asim Dasgupta had to resign from the chairmanship of the committee. The Modi government enacted the GST as an Act on 12 April 2017. Three midnight sessions of the parliament have been conducted since India's independence with the first such session marking the country's independence from the British in 1947. The two other sessions were held to commemorate the silver jubilee of India's independence in 1972 and to celebrate fifty years of freedom in 1997. All those occasions were celebratory. It was for the first time that a session was convened at midnight to mark the implementation of government tax reforms, the GST, which, whether has helped or burdened the common man is yet to be evaluated. The GST was launched in the midnight session of Parliament as the 101st amendment of the Constitution on the night of 30 June–1 July 2017. The opposition boycotted the session. Though it is said that India had one GST from 1 July 2017, after the Jammu and Kashmir State Assembly passed its GST Act on 7 July 2017, the entire nation came under a unified indirect tax regime.

The GST is imposed at various stages of the production process but refunded to all parties and finally collected from the point of consumption and not from the point of origin. So, taxes are paid in the state where goods and services are consumed not to the state where goods and services are produced. It replaced the central and state government tax on all goods except petroleum products, alcoholic drinks and electricity, which were not put under GST. The state tax, as in the past, was levied on these three categories. India adopted a dual GST model. Any transaction inside the state is treated as a single state transaction where CGST (Central GST) and SGST (State GST) are levied. Under GST, IGST (Integrated GST) is a tax levied on all inter-state supplies of goods and/or services and will be governed by the IGST Act. This IGST will be collected by the centre and the share of the state will be handed over to them. An eway bill is a permit needed for inter-state and intra-state transportation of goods worth more than a particular value. It contains details of the goods, the consignor, the recipient and the transporter. It came into effect from 1 June 2018.

The GST rates were revised multiple times. The slabs of tax kept on changing frequently. In the first three months, seven amendments were made. It is criticized as being too complex and is implemented poorly. It is said that out of about 115 countries in the world, India's GST rates are the second-highest. Delay in refunds is also a matter of concern for the firms paying advance GST. The initial hiccups of servers not working or a digital India still not ready to go paperless remains to be addressed. The only quantified positive effect of the GST is that the travel time of goods has reduced by about 20 per cent as all the toll booths on the highway are removed. The government stand is that in the long run, it would be beneficial for the business. The immediate effect of the GST is not very encouraging for the industry, especially for small and medium enterprises. Two factors that are held responsible for the fall in production and GDP are demonetization and implementation of GST.

We must know where we stand as compared to the world especially if we as a nation want to be the *vishwa guru* (world leader). In 2012, the United Nations started publishing the World Happiness Report of Nations. The report evaluates the causes of happiness and misery. It takes care of the positive and negative effects on life. The survey looks into unemployment, social support, freedom, corruption, health, education and good governance of the nations. In a 2012 report, a total of 156 countries were ranked for the first time. This report is now published every year (it was not published in 2014). In 2012, Denmark with a score of 7.693 was the happiest nation, and India with a score of 4.772 was in 111th position. We get more insight into which direction the country is heading when we look into the ranking of two more years. In 2015, in the first year of Modi's rule, Switzerland with a 7.587 score stood 1st and India with 4.565 points ranked 117th. In 2020, after six years of Modi's rule, India's world happiness ranking slipped to 144th position with a score of 3.573 points. For three consecutive years, Finland with a score of 7.809 is the best place to live.

Under Modi's rule, India is made to believe that we will be a five-trillion-dollar economy by 2024 (next general elections in India). Let us understand the roadmap. The GDP of an economy is the total value of all goods and services produced in that country within a year. For convenience, it is converted into US dollars for comparison. India is the fifth-largest economy in the world in 2019–20. The USA leads the pack with a nominal GDP of $21.3 trillion, China far behind with $14.2 trillion is second, Japan with $5.18 trillion is third. The only European country to make it to the top five is Germany with a nominal GDP of $4 trillion. It is ranked fourth. India which was behind the UK is now at fifth position with a nominal GDP of $2.972 trillion.

India with the large internal market, high saving rate and an inherent advantage of the possibility of growing any type of crop has the highest potential in the world economy. Till now, the country has witnessed a low level of the overall development. The first challenge is to develop a huge human resource which is the youngest in the world. It is the biggest strength of the country both in terms of capacity and capability. The country must invest in education and health care for a marked improvement. The enterprise, export, ease of doing business, law and order, and consumer spending must get a boost if India wants to reach a $5 trillion economy. Currently, if the GDP growth rate is 5 per cent, then the challenge is of governance. The best brains in the country must come together to make the road map.

In 2014, the formation of the BJP government at the centre saw a major change in the course of time. The journey from the 'BJP government' to 'Modi Raj' was complete by the time Modi went to the 2019 general elections. Not only the elections but even the government was run as a corporate entity. The emphasis on marketing and publicity was visible. Also, a core group was developed to clap and rant its support on every move of the government. Event management was the order of the day. The solid steel frame of the Civil Services is being shaken, stirred and given a make over like never before in its seven-decade history. This churn is part of a well-articulated agenda. The focus has shifted from governance and the officers selected for key positions are required to be loud event managers.

The event which can be described as the signature event of the Modi regime is certainly the installation of the Statue of Unity. In September 2013, the BJP announced Narendra Modi, the then Chief Minister of Gujaratas its prime ministerial candidate for the 2014 general election. On 7 October 2013, Modi announced the construction of the tallest statue in the world of Indian statesman and independence activist Sardar Vallabhbhai Patel. The statue was conceived to be 182 metres tall. The height of 182 metres was specifically chosen to match the number of seats in the Gujarat Legislative Assembly. This event was marked as the start of his tenth year as chief minister of Gujarat. The project of Gujarat became the project of India. The first major event kick-started by Modi's announcement of a nation-wide campaign to collect small pieces of iron from farmers for using it to build the proposed 'Statue of Unity' in the memory of Sardar Vallabhbhai Patel popularly known as the 'iron man'. This drive was used during the run-up to the 2014 parliamentary elections. It was claimed that a total of 135 metric tons of used iron was collected and after processing 109 metric tons of iron was used in the foundation of the statue.

The contract to design, construct and maintain was awarded to L&T for Rs 2,989 crores. The statue announced in 2013 by the chief minister of Gujarat was dedicated to the nation by the Prime Minister of India on 31 October 2018. Both the events were grand. This story shows how an event can be used to the advantage of the leader and party. It is a case to understand how Narendra Modi can use any event to his advantage. The Sangh Parivar has claimed ideological affinity with Patel for some time now whereas the latter was the one who was instrumental in banning the RSS when Gandhi was murdered. Ironically, Patel is being claimed by the BJP when he was himself a life long die-hard Congressman. Critics say that the BJP is trying to appropriate Patel's legacy and aura. It is ironic that when the organizations and groups supporting the BJP were giving a nationalist call to boycott Chinese goods, the Modi government got the bronze statue made in China. While Narendra Modi trots around the globe exhorting people of the business world to use India as a manufacturing hub, China was selected for a project close to the prime minister's heart. The project was inaugurated amidst controversy with so much fanfare. Any questioning voice was silenced and was termed anti-national.

The journey of event management of the Modi 1 regime started with Prashant Kishore calling the shots during the 2014 campaign. In 2019, when he was seeking elections, the services of the likes of Prashant Kishore were not required; in the last five years, the core team headed by Amit Shah had mastered this art of event management. Throughout the election campaign, the Congress President Rahul Gandhi used the slogan '*Chowkidar chor hai*' (the guard or watchman himself is a thief) as his hitting line on the prime minister. Instead of ducking this bouncer of Rahul Gandhi, it was used to the advantage of Modi with the event–'*Main bhi chowkidar*' (I am also a watchman). By the end of the five-year term, all the cabinet ministers were having a dedicated team for social media and accordingly all of them affixed '*chowkidar*' before their names. On 31 March 2019, despite the model code of conduct being in place, Prime Minister Modi organized an event of a live audience with his party workers, termed as *chowkidars* in 500 locations all over India. The Doordarshan, the government television channel, dutifully live-broadcasted this political event. This entire *chowkidar* campaign was designed by the social media team of BJP and executed by Gurugram (Gurgaon)-based company, ABM. Modi's virtual presence was made strong by the '*Main bhi chowkidar*' campaign. Modi surpassed Congress president Rahul Gandhi by a huge margin not just during the general election but also in terms of the 'hashtag battle'.

Just to have a bird's eye view of how the visit of foreign dignitaries visiting India was turned into events starts with the swearing-in ceremony of the prime minister on 26 May 2014. All SAARC (South Asian Association for Regional Cooperation) heads of state including Nawaz Sharif of Pakistan attended the swearing-in ceremony of the new cabinet in Delhi. After 2014, instead of having standard meetings with the visiting foreign dignitaries in Delhi or Agra, they were taken to see incredible India. Ahmedabad, the seat and source of the political power of Modi, was visited by President Trump of America, President Xi Jinping of China, Prime Minister Benjamin Netanyahu of Israel, Prime Minister Shinzo Abe of Japan. Varanasi, the parliamentary constituency of Modi, was visited by French President Macron and Japanese Prime Minister Abe even attended Ganga *aarti* in Varanasi where an event to transform Varanasi into Kyoto of Japan was held. President Xi Jinping of China had a one-to-one meeting with Modi in Mahabalipuram near Chennai.

In 2005, when Prime Minister Modi was the chief minister of Gujarat, he was denied the A-2 visa to travel to the USA. The B-1/B-2 visa previously given to him was also revoked. The denial and revocation of a visa were done under the US law by which foreign government officials responsible for severe violations of religious freedom become ineligible for the visa. Modi is the only person ever to be banned to travel to the United States of America under the IRFA (International Religious Freedom Act) provision of the US Immigration and Nationality Act. Modi with his Howdy Modi event in September 2019 also sets another record in his name. He visited the USA six times till 2019, making it the most-visited country in the world. During his first tenure as prime minister, he visited about sixty countries and made about ninety-five foreign visits. One of the most talked-about foreign visits of Modi will remain the Pakistan visit in December 2015. Modi, while returning from Kabul, made an unscheduled stopover in Pakistan to meet Nawaz Sharif on his birthday and for his granddaughter's marriage. He also touched the feet of Sharif's mother.

Modi's obsession with the USA was obvious when after taking over as prime minister in 2014, his team organized the biggest political event at New York's Madison Square Garden indoor arena in September 2014. A lot of concessions for NRIs were made in this address. Another huge event was organized in Sydney, Australia in November 2014. Modi's love for overseas events can be seen in the way event management teams were roped in for his event in Dubai in August 2015 and in London's Wembley in November 2015.

To sum it, the Modi government is just about event management and creating false impressions about the economy. The government is working as an event management firm. It dishes out untruths and boasts about its performance, economic management, and accomplishments. The government should realise that its divisive agendas will harm future generations. This government must address the burning issues of poverty and the marginalization of those at the bottom of the pyramid. Some monumental blunders have taken place and the government should transparently address these issues, listen to experts and all stakeholders with an open mind, and project serious intent to handle the crisis.

Chapter-19

Pradhan Sewak to Pradhan Senapati

Modi–Shah: The Unstoppable Electoral Juggernaut

30 May 2019, Thursday

The 2019 general election was held in April–May for the 17th Lok Sabha. Before this, out of sixteen, only eleven Lok Sabhas had completed their term of five years. The 4th (1967), 6th (1977), 9th (1989), 11th (1996) and 12th (1998) Lok Sabhas failed to complete their term. We were going for general elections after completing a full five-year term by four consecutive Lok Sabhas. In the past, state elections for the Vidhan Sabha and general elections for the Lok Sabha were held together. The last time India voted for the Lok Sabha and Vidhan Sabha together was in 1967. Since then, general elections and state elections are held separately.

Parliament needs to be an institution of accountability. But unfortunately, the performance of the government or opposition is never scrutinized or appraised for the concluding Lok Sabha and the elections are fought on entirely different issues. Before discussing the 2019 elections, some interesting facts about the 16th Lok Sabha can be discussed. Unlike the Rajya Sabha, which is a continuous upper house of parliament, the lower house Lok Sabha has a fixed term of five years. Every year, three Lok Sabha sessions are called–the budget session, the monsoon session and the winter session. So, any Lok Sabha which completes its tenure will have five budget, five monsoon and five winter sessions, that is a total of fifteen sessions. In the 16th Lok Sabha, by the time the Modi government took an oath, it was time for the monsoon session but the budget for 2014–15 was not tabled. Therefore, the first session of the Modi government was converted into a budget session. The 16th Lok Sabha had six budget sessions, four monsoon and five winter sessions.

We had ten Lok Sabhas completing their five-year term before the 16th Lok Sabha (2014–19). For parity, comparisons are now made only with the Lok Sabhas, which completed their full term. The average number of days the Lok Sabha was in session for the past ten full-term Lok Sabhas was 468 days in 5 years. The 16th Lok Sabha was in session for only 331 days in the five-year period. So, our parliamentarians of the 16th Lok Sabha in 52 weeks for 5 years, which is 262 weeks worked for about 1.27 days per week. We have not deducted the number of days when the house was not able to transact any business due to various reasons like walkout, disruption, obituary, etc. The second interesting data is that the past full-term 10 Lok Sabhas on an average worked for 2,689 hours in five years whereas the 16th Lok Sabha worked for only 1,615 hours. In other words, in 1,825 days (365 days for 5 years), the total number of hours our members of the 16th parliament worked for less than an hour every day. Out of this 1,615-hour duration, 16 per cent was lost in disruption in the 16th Lok Sabha. In the 15th Lok Sabha (2009–14), the disruption was for a staggering 37 per cent. These disruptions are generally attributed to opposition stalling proceedings of the house. The 16 per cent and 37 per cent can give some idea about the party that is more serious about the smooth functioning of the parliament or which party is a more serious opposition.

Another analysis will show the respect shown to the parliamentary traditions by the ruling party. In the past 10 full-term Lok Sabhas the average time given to legislative business was 675 hours or 25 per cent of the total time. During the 16th Lok Sabha, it was 480 hours and 32 per cent of the total time when the parliament was in session. During the 16th Lok Sabha, which passed 133 bills, only 25 per cent of them were sent to the Standing Committee as compared to 60 per cent and 71 per cent in the 14th and 15th Lok Sabha respectively. Most of the Lok Sabha members of parliament are members of one standing committee and one consultative committee of different ministries. Committees have cross-party representation and are great platforms for consensus building. The standing committee of a specific ministry scrutinizes, examines and suggests changes in the bills sent to them by the government but if the ruling dispensation considers these committees of no use or less use, they avoid sending bills to them. Another reason can be because the government does not want the bills to be scrutinized. We will sum up the topic with one small information—a bill must be passed by both the houses Rajya Sabha and Lok Sabha—to become an Act. If a bill is passed by the Rajya Sabha and is pending before the Lok Sabha, which is dissolved, the new Lok Sabha can pass the bill after voting. But if a bill is passed by the Lok Sabha and is pending in the Rajya Sabha, the bill will lapse as soon as the Lok Sabha, which passed the bill is dissolved.

Prime Minister Modi is not very enthusiastic about

attending the house when it is in session. The exact attendance of his presence in the parliament cannot be done as the prime minister is exempted from signing the attendance register. Members of Parliament (MPs), a part from participating in debates, have the privilege of asking different types of questions to the government. During the 16th Lok Sabha, about 1,42,000 questions were asked, that is, on an average 260 questions per MP. Thirty-one MPs asked zero questions. This non-questioning team was led by the then Congress President Rahul Gandhi, Sonia Gandhi, Lal Krishna Advani, Deve Gowda, Mulayam Singh Yadav to name a few. All these data are best analyzed by the ADR (Association for Democratic Reforms).

The preparation for the 2019 elections by Team Modi started the day results of the 2014 elections were announced. The performance in the 2014 elections by the party was spectacular in the Hindi heartland. In the 2019 elections, India had 29 states and 7 union territories, which makes a total of 36 out of which less than 20 per cent states (7) decided the fate of India in the 2014 election. Five of these states were in the north and two states were in south of the Vindhya ranges. Uttar Pradesh with 80 Lok Sabha seats, Maharashtra (48), Bihar (40), Madhya Pradesh (29), Karnataka (28), Gujarat (26) and Rajasthan (25) comprised a total of 276 seats – more than half of the total 545 Lok Sabha seats. In the 2014 elections, the performance of BJP and its allies in these 7 states was – Uttar Pradesh (73), Maharashtra (42), Bihar (31), MP (27), Karnataka (17), Gujarat (26) and Rajasthan (25), winning a total of 241 parliament seats out of 276 – about 87 per cent.

The decision of Modi to fight from Uttar Pradesh and put Amit Shah to focus in the state with the largest number of MPs was a pragmatic calculation. Uttar Pradesh, with

80 seats, plays a decisive role in the Lok Sabha elections. It is often said, to govern the country, it is important to perform well in Uttar Pradesh. This state has given India 9 prime ministers. In the run-up to the 2019 election, things were not very comfortable for the BJP in these seven states–2 were ruled by the BJP and 2 were ruled by the Congress; in 2 states the BJP had a coalition government and in 1 state, the Congress was part of the ruling front. The Uttar Pradesh BJP was in absolute majority led by Yogi Adityanath, the Hindutva face of the party but repeating the past performance was a far cry. The candidate of the BJP in the by-election in Gorakhpur from the seat vacated by Yogi was defeated by the Samajwadi Party. Mayawati and Akhilesh Yadav, two arch-rivals in Uttar Pradesh politics, decided to fight the election together. After all, it was an election of their survival. The Congress also placed their so-called *brahmastra* (a weapon which can destroy the opponent completely) in the form of Priyanka Gandhi. Shiv Pal defected from the Samajwadi Party and put up candidates all over the state. He was also trying to be a game spoiler for the opposition. The final count was that for the BJP and its allies, the tally came down to 64 from 73.

Gujarat, the stronghold of Modi, in the recent state election was contested very closely by the Congress with the help of three young leaders Hardik Patel, Jignesh Mewani and Alpesh Thakur. The Congress was putting all its effort to make a dent in Gujarat where the BJP was ruling for more than two decades. But the result was the BJP making a clean sweep of 26 out of 26 like in 2014.

In Maharashtra and Bihar, the BJP had a coalition government. Amit Shah was more cautious and large-hearted to offer more seats to the alliance partners namely the Shiv Sena and the Janata Dal (U) in these two states. The Shiv Sena, which had learn tthe lesson of fighting the Vidhan Sabha elections without an alliance, readily agreed to the formula of 23:25. That is 23 seats were for Shiv Sena and 25 seats for BJP. Asaduddin Owaisi of the All India Majlis-e-Ittehadul Musilmeen (AIMIM) joined hands with Prakash Ambedkar in Maharashtra and was able to split the vote of Congress and NCP. One has to understand the nitty-gritty of Indian politics to understand the role of some smaller parties who overtly stand against the policy of a party but help that party by cutting the votes of an opposition party. AIMIM falls in this category. Having a Muslim vote-bank-centric party, it positions itself as a vehement opponent of the BJP but puts the candidate and cut into the vote share of the party opposing the BJP and thus indirectly helping it.

The real bargaining and desperation of BJP were in Bihar. Nitish had fought the state elections with Laloo Yadav and the Congress to form the government in Bihar. Nitish was one person who was considered to be an alternative for Modi. Like Modi, he is from a backward caste. His Kurmi caste has a wider presence in the country. Nitish had a clean image and was called *Sushasan* Babu (good administrator). He had a wider acceptance than Modi in parties other than the BJP. Even in BJP, he had friends. He is an engineer whereas the degree of Modi is questionable. Above all, he was from the Hindi heartland and was capable of allying even with Laloo Yadav, his main adversary in Bihar politics. In the outgoing Lok Sabha, the BJP had 22 MPs, the Lok Jan Shakti Party (LJP) of Ram Vilas Paswan (6) and Janata Dal (U) had 2 MPs. Modi and Amit Shah desperately wanted Nitish on their side, for which they were ready to pay any price. Accordingly, an alliance of 17 : 17 : 6 seats were finalized between BJP, JD(U) and LJP, BJP sacrificed 5 of its sitting MPs, JD (U) with 2 MPs got 17. No one understood the seat-sharing formula. Nitish from the position of a potential future challenger as an alternative of Modi was reduced to a state leader of Bihar.

The election results of Madhya Pradesh, Rajasthan and Chhattisgarh in 2018 were seen by many as the beginning of the end of Modi Rule if not BJP. Congress replaced the BJP and formed a government in these states though not with the majority which had been predicted. The Congress chief minister Kamal Nath and Ashok Gehlot were old hands and it was expected that if not substantial, at least more than 50 per cent seats would be won by the Congress. In the final count, out of the total 54 seats of MP and Rajasthan, the BJP retained its tally of 2014 of 52 seats.

Karnataka state was ruled by the Congress coalition government. BJP had won 17 seats in the 2014 elections and Congress, 9. It was expected that the Congress and JD(S) led by ex-Prime Minister Deve Gowda will stop the march of the BJP but its tally improved to 25. So, the overall result of these 7 states in the 2019 election was that out of 276 seats, they improved it to 247 from 241 in the 2014 elections. BJP got a clear-cut majority of 303 on its own and NDA bagged 353 seats. Six states—West Bengal, Odisha, Tamil Nadu, Andhra Pradesh, Telangana and Kerala—had 164 seats between them that are about 30 per cent of total seats. BJP in 2014 won 7 seats and making 100 per cent gain in 2019 elections, won 14 seats.

After losing power in the state elections held in December 2018, just 5 months before the general elections in the states of Rajasthan, Madhya Pradesh and Chhattisgarh, even BJP supporters were talking of the party returning but with a reduced majority. Gadkari's name started circulating as the likely successor of Modi, as he had more acceptance not only within the party but also with parties sitting on the fence, who could support BJP to form the government. On the performance front, it was difficult to ask the voters for the second term, though the Ujjawala Yojana (distribution of cooking gas to the poor) and construction of toilets under the Swachchata Abhiyan were some successful policies, the hardship due to demonetization was proving to be one single factor to wipe out all the good work done in the past five years. The political scientists sitting in the lab of the BJP were trying to work out a winning formula—the time-tested Hindu-Muslim dispute over construction of the Ram Mandir was in their closet but its effectiveness was always in doubt. Every drug has an expiry and it was doubtful if the earlier mentioned medicine for votes would still work or not.

The Pulwama—Balakot incident came as the wonder drug penicillin with many similarities. Penicillin was invented after years of research and trials in the lab but the Pulwama–Balakot incident happened at the time when political scientists were searching for some new formula for winning elections. Pulwama which was a challenge for the nation was packaged as the wonder formula for winning elections. Nationalism, with the sole patent and proprietary rights with Team Modi, was the sure-shot prescription to work. The journey of Modi from 2014 to 2019 saw a very basic shift in the way he wanted to present himself—he started as *pradhan sewak* and by the time the 2019 elections were announced, Modi transformed himself into the role of *pradhan senapati*. Now, he positioned himself as the protector of the nation, religion, culture and everything '*Bharatiya*'. Now, instead of serving the people, he was going to play the role of the 'protector'. Modi invoked the Pulwama martyrs to seek votes. During the election rally, a common appeal properly wrapped as a war cry was delivered by Modi to the voters—to dedicate their ballot to the valiant soldiers who carried out the air strike at Balakot and to the Pulwama martyrs.

On Valentine's Day, 14 February 2019, a day of celebration of love and affection especially among the urban youth, a young Kashmiri boy of 22 years Adil Ahmad Dar had other plans driven by hate and revenge. Due to snow, the Srinagar—Jammu Highway was closed for two days and vehicle movement was allowed on 14 February. Seventy-eight buses carrying about 2,500 Central Reserve Police Force (CRPF) started from Jammu to Srinagar early morning. The unusually long convoy was moving as per plan. At 3.15 pm in Pulwama district at a place called Lethpora (near Awantipur), Adil Ahmad Dar rammed his four-wheeler carrying explosives in one of the buses of the convoy, killing 40 personnel of the 76th Battalion of the CRPF. The area is a hotbed of militancy. Pulwama is a part of the Anantnag parliament constituency. In the 2019 general election, this was the only constituency where voting was done in three phases owing to militancy. Shortly afterwards, Jaish-e-Mohammad (JeM), a militant organization headed by Masood Azhar, released the video of Adil Ahmad Dar, recorded before the act taking responsibility for this gory act.

Kashmir had witnessed violence at the time of the merger with India had remained more or less peaceful after that. It was only in 1989 when the V. P. Singh government, formed with the support of the BJP, made Mufti Mohammad Sayeed, a Kashmiri politician, the home minister of India. Railway Minister George Fernandes was put in charge to talk to Kashmiri stakeholders including separatists, extremists and even terrorists. The thin line dividing extremists and militants was still visible in Kashmir. George started his job in earnest but few political groups saw this as an end of their long-term political goals in Kashmir which resulted in the unceremonious removal of George and bringing Jagmohan as Governor of Jammu and Kashmir. The exodus of Kashmiri Pundits was during the regime of Jagmohan. At the time of the exodus, the Congress had lost power to V. P. Singh's Janata Dal which was supported by the BJP, so why is the Congress held responsible for this exodus? The valley was disturbed thereafter. Some peace returned around the turn of the century in 2000.

The performance of the BJP in the state assembly elections along with the general elections of 2014 was below par considering the mandate which BJP got with Modi as the prime ministerial candidate. A total of 652 seats in five state assemblies of Andhra Pradesh, Telangana, Arunachal Pradesh, Odisha and Sikkim went for election. BJP won – 4 seats in Andhra, 5 seats in Telangana, 11 seats in Arunachal, 10 seats in Odisha and none in Sikkim making a total of 30 which is less than 5 per cent of the total seats of 652. The election of Jammu and Kashmir is held for a 6-year term unlike the 5-year term for the rest of the Indian states. The term 'national conference government' led by Omar Abdullah was coming to an end in January 2015 and accordingly elections were held in December 2014. The NDA government was well settled and the party had a young and strong president Amit Shah enjoying complete (a better word would be blind) confidence of Prime Minister Modi. Two state assembly elections were held under the stewardship of Amit Shah in October 2014 in the states of Maharashtra and Haryana. In Maharashtra, the decades-long alliance with Shiv Sena was broken. The BJP used to be the junior partner in the state elections, but the new president of the party Amit Shah had different plans. The BJP failed to get a majority on its own. A post-poll alliance with the Shiv Sena was made and for the first time, BJP had their Chief minister Devendra Phadnavis in Maharashtra. The story of Haryana was different. Out of 90 seats, BJP won 47 which was a clear majority. Again, for the first time, the BJP Chief Minister, Manohar Lal Khattar took oath in Haryana. With this background, the Jammu and Kashmir assembly elections were fought. Despite the call given by the separatists to boycott the poll, more than 65 per cent of voters turned out to exercise their right to vote for 87 seats. The Jammu and Kashmir People's Democratic Party (PDP) led by Mufti Mohammad Sayeed emerged as the largest party with 28 seats and BJP, with 25 seats, was the second-largest party. Though both the parties got about 23 per cent votes each, the BJP vote share was fractionally more than that of the PDP. Prime Minister Modi campaigned for the party in the valley, nothing was left uncertain. Sajjad Lone, a known separatist leader who was fighting election from Handwara seat, met Modi before the polls and addressed him as 'Big Brother'. The BJP did not put up any candidate against him. Sajjad won and was subsequently made minister as well.

After two months of discussion, the coalition government of PDP and BJP was formed on 1 March 2015. The oath ceremony in Jammu was attended by the top brass of BJP including Prime Minister Modi and president of the party Amit Shah. The turning point in the militant activity of Jammu and Kashmir was in July 2016 when 22-year-old dreaded militant Burhan Wani, commander of Hizbul Mujahideen was killed. Wani was immensely popular among the youth of Kashmir and was one of the most-wanted militants. The valley had to face violent protests after Wani's death and hundreds of youngsters including Adil Ahmad Dar were a part of these protests. Dar was arrested 6 times between 2016 and 2018 and was bedridden for 11 months due to an injury in the leg by a bullet. Manzoor, a suspected militant killed in June 2016, was his cousin. Dar left his home in March 2018 and appeared on 14 February 2019 as Waqas Commander Dar. The funeral of Dar was attended by thousands as these misguided youth struck a lot of emotional connect with the local population. Sadly, these Kashmiri youngsters born after 1989, have never seen peace. Theirs is a painful story of being born in curfew, living their whole lives through curfews and dying in curfews. The locals believe that one becomes a militant in a police station or an army camp, not inside the four walls of their house. When a militant is killed, two are born. Every time we claim that with the killing of a so-and-so militant, the unrest in the valley has come to rest something new happens. The killing of militants does not bring peace to the valley but it creates a mirage of bravado and heroism and pushes Kashmir into a deeper abyss.

The 14 February terrorist attack on a convoy that killed 40 jawans in Pulwama, Jammu and Kashmir was preceded by a 'massive intelligence failure'. This could deeply embarrass the central government—the Pulwama tragedy was set in an electoral dynamic that was sure to affect the outcome of the general elections. In Pulwama, Narendra Modi found the trigger he needed before the 2019 elections. Modi returned from Uttarkhand in the evening and took control in his hands. Something drastic was required before the opposition could raise the issues of intelligence failure and other lapses of the government. Several questions had no answers—How multiple intelligence agencies failed to answer from where did such huge quantities of explosives come? Even after more than a year of investigation, no one knows the source and origin of these explosives. An unusually long convoy of CRPF men became an easy target. Why were so many vehicles moving together? Why were CRPF men not airlifted? In response to the dastardly terrorist attack, India announced some routine actions against Pakistan like revoking the Most Favoured Nation (MFN) status of Pakistan, increasing import duty on Pakistani goods by 200 per cent. Shakarullah, a Pakistani serving life term in Jaipur jail, was killed inside the jail on 20 February 2019.

As a damage-control exercise and to take away the initiative from the opposition party, Modi came on the crease. When the dead bodies of 40 CRPF were flown to Delhi Prime minister personally received them to pay homage. He did *parikrama* (taking round) of each coffin carrying the body. His ministers were instructed to accompany all the forty bodies to their homes and be present during the last rites. Next came the Balakot airstrike, on 26 February 2019. Twelve Mirage fighter jets of the Indian Air Force crossed the Line of Control (LOC) and dropped bombs on the Jaish-e-Mohammad training camps located in Balakot allegedly killing 300–350 terrorists. Wing Commander Abhinandan Varthaman MIG-21 was hit by a Pakistani missile on 27 February 2019 and was captured by Pakistan. After 60 hours of captivity, Abhinandan was handed over to India on 1 March 2019. Imran Khan announced in the Pakistani parliament that as a peace gesture Wing Commander Abhinandan would be released on 28 February. Based on the Indian dossier, Pakistan arrested 44 suspects including JEM leader Masood Azhar's son Hamad Azhar and brother Abdul Rauf.

In all the political and election rallies mention of Balakot airstrike and '*Ghar mein ghuskar marenge*' (we will hit them inside their house, referring to Pakistan) was the popular rhetoric of Modi. The BJP and Modi conveniently avoided questions on the performance of government regarding agriculture, poverty, employment and economy. Modi and Shah pitched the election as 'Kargil 2.0'. This was a strategy similar to Atal Bihari Vajpayee's. A rather simple and one-dimensional strategy to just plug away at the 'war card' was a tried and tested formula for winning the elections.

Atal Bihari Vajpayee failed to win a confidence vote in April 1999 by 269 votes to 270 (it was not a no-confidence motion of the opposition, the motion was moved by the ruling National Democratic Alliance). He lost the crucial confidence motion by one vote. There are three claimants for that crucial one vote, which was responsible for the fall of the Vajpayee government. On the day of the vote, Mayawati, the Bahujan Samaj Party leader from Uttar Pradesh, met Prime Minister Vajpayee and pledged her support. At the time of voting, she voted against the government. The second is Giridhar Gamang, Chief Minister of Odisha, still, a member of the Congress party in Lok Sabha as per the whip of the party voted against the government. It is debatable that technically it may be right but ethically it was improper to vote being a chief minister. The third was Saifuddin Soz, a member of the National Conference which was part of the Vajpayee government, defied his party and voted against the motion. So even before Kargil, the mood of the nation was in favour of Vajpayee, a victim who was denied a full-term government. He had the nation's sympathy in his favour. Atal Bihari Vajpayee had to fight the Kargil War as a caretaker prime minister in May–July 1999. It certainly helped him win the general elections of 1999 held in September–October but it was not the only factor for his win. In 2019, Team Modi pitched it selection campaign based solely on the theme of nationalism. The performance of the government in its five-year tenure was never discussed. Modi's economic record was his biggest liability in this election—but he managed to over come it. In recent years Prime Minister Modi has built up a tough, muscular image of being more willing to use force and speaking up for India's armed forces. He has assumed a position of near invincibility.

The 2019 elections brought to the surface issues that lie dormant between elections. The political space in India today is crowded with salient issues such as the centralization of power under one hand. The build-up to Modi-2 shows the credibility of institutions such as the CBI, the EC, the RBI, the ED being compromised. There is an attempt to conduct governance through remote control through the judiciary and the media. The blatant use of UAPA (Unlawful Activities Prevention Act), NIA (National Investigation Agency), NSA (National Security Agency), NDPS (Narcotic Drugs and Psychotropic Substances Act), etc. is undermining India's institutions in the process. The autonomy of essential institutions is clearly under question as the Modi government seeks to influence them politically. The party's majority in the Lok Sabha gave it virtual carte blanche to legislate at will. The CBI termed 'a caged parrot' by the Supreme Court many years ago saw one of the greatest intra-departmental rivalries. Dirty linen was washed in the public. The CBI attracted a lot of public attention for the misdemeanour of its past directors, and also due to the alleged discord between its director and special director. Allegations were freely hurled against each other by the top officers of the department forgetting professional work culture and the ethos of the organization. Another independent national body the RBI also was not in full command. Successive governors left their positions midway due to which direction of the money market and the economy took a beating. GDP, which was growing at the rate of 7.4 per cent, dropped to 4.2 per cent in 2019–20 and started shrinking during the Covid-19 pandemic in 2020–21.

The worst victim was the Election Commission of India. The Constitution provided us with an independent Election Commission headed by Chief Election Commissioner (CEC). A docile Commission got its true status and position when T.N. Seshan became CEC. Seshan was appointed in December 1990 and served for six years till 1996. I had the privilege of appearing for a political party along with George Fernandes assisting our counsel Rajiv Dhavan and Gopal Rai. He was blunt, straight forward and ready to listen to your argument if it was logical. He upheld the authority of the commission and invoked fear in politicians for his ruthless approach. He was a no-nonsensical CEC and one who enforced, in his own way, discipline on political parties and contestants. Seshan had unprecedented efficiency in protecting the electoral process. The office of CEC was reinvented and many electoral reforms were made under him—the Voter ID card for all eligible voters was his major contribution. He also enforced a strict model code of conduct. Seshan redefined the role of the Election Commission and made people realize that this is a strong institution provided by the Constitution to have free and fair elections. Sadly, this watchdog of democracy by the 2019 elections was domesticated. The EC's independence, fairness, impartiality and efficiency are perceived to be compromised today. It has become toothless and timid. In this context, we will talk about two events.

In the name of election reforms, the BJP government implemented electoral bonds.[1] It was supposed to bring transparency in the system but it reinforced the opacity of public funding. In reality, the whole scheme of the electoral bond is designed in a way that the party in power only gets the fund. Why these are called bonds is another mystery. The public was misled by the word 'bond' because bonds are issued by the sovereign authority. These are more like the gift cheques or prepaid cards that are often given away as gifts.

Though the scheme says that the identity of the donor cannot be traced,since it is issued only by the State Bank of India and every bond has a unique number, tracking is not difficult. In reality, it is revealed that more than 95 per cent of electoral bonds had gone to the BJP alone. The bond which is in the denomination of Rs 1,000–Rs 1,000,000 is tax-deductible for the donor as well as for the political parties. These bonds can only be encashed by political parties, which had secured at least 1 per cent of the votes polled in the most recent Lok Sabha or state election. They should have filed returns with the Election Commission and Income Tax Department as well. Therefore, it can be said that this scheme is only for big parties. If an individual or a group decides to form a political party with all sincerity and with the noblest of ideas, it would not be eligible to receive money through these election bonds. It is only available to the parties who are the so-called guardians of Indian democracy but do not elect their president democratically. They do not have internal democracy within the party. These big parties support the woman reservation bill for providing 33 per cent seats to women in the parliament but ironically in their party never give tickets to 33 per cent women to fight an election.

On 1 February 2017, as part of the preparation for the 2019 elections, Arun Jaitley presented an electoral bond along with the Annual Budget as part of the Finance Bill in Parliament. The bill was passed as a money bill by the Lok Sabha and was implemented from 1 January 2018. The finance bill is one that draws money from the Consolidated Fund of India. Electoral Bonds have nothing to do with the Consolidated Fund of India. So why was it presented as a money bills is a big question. A money bill must be passed in the Lok Sabha, it is not necessary to get it passed in the Rajya Sabha. In February 2017, the NDA was not enjoying a majority in the Rajya Sabha so Team Modi decided to circumvent the Rajya Sabha by tabling it as a money bill in Lok Sabha. So, a bill which was not a money bill got passed from the Lok Sabha. Five Acts were surreptitiously amended so that electoral bonds could be implemented: (i) the Reserve Bank of India Act—of the RBI Act of 1934 was amended to allow an entity other than the RBI and the union government to issue a bearer bond as the State Bank of India was going to issue these bonds; (ii) the Income Tax Act—Section 13(A) of the IT Act of 1961 (amended in 1995) dealing with the exempted income of political parties was amended so that the donor remained anonymous. Another change was made so that donation over Rs 2,000 could be made by cheque, electronic transfer or electoral bonds. In the first read, it appeared that the government wanted transparency as previously donations up to Rs 20,000 could be made in cash, which means tracking these donors was not possible. Political parties had taken advantage of this clause showing unaccounted money as a donation by making fictitious receipts. Now if the cap was lowered to Rs 2,000 the task of making fictitious receipt was made more cumbersome. The catch was if you received donations through electoral bonds of any amount, even Rs 100 crores or more, there was no need of disclosing the name of the donor in the Income Tax Return; (iii) the RPI Act–Section 29(C) of the Representation of the Peoples Act 1951 was amended. Previously, the stipulation was that for the donation amount of more than Rs 20,000 details of the donor was to be given. Now in the electoral bond, the donor was anonymous and exempted from the requirement of giving their details; (iv) the Companies Act, 1956—Before the company could donate only up to 7.5 per cent of its average profit of the last three years, and must disclose this amount and the beneficiary political party. This act was amended. Now, through the electoral bonds, there is no limit to the amount companies can donate, and the requirement for such firms to have existed for the last three years on a profit-making basis has also been withdrawn. The implication is that now even a loss-making company can give donations through an electoral bond without any limit. The people in power can intimidate any company for donations. The earlier clause of how much a company is donating to which political party was also dropped; (v) the Foreign Contribution Regulating Act (FCRA) 1976 amended in 2010 had closed political funding through the FCRA route. This clause of receiving money through the FCRA was amended and parties were free to take foreign funding but the highlight was that it was implemented with a retrospective date from 1976. The idea was to give relief to the Congress and the BJP, who had violated the law of the land by taking donations through FCRA in the past. A case of violation of the FCRA was pending in the Delhi High Court. This amendment overturned the Delhi High Court order that found both the Congress and BJP guilty of violating the

FCRA. The order was rendered infructuous due to this amendment.

The Election Commission initially vehemently opposed these electoral bonds. They sent their reservations to the ministry of law and challenged the legality of electoral bonds in the Supreme Court. The government gives the logic that they want to protect the right of secrecy of the donor and hence the name cannot be disclosed. The validity of the electoral bond is only fifteen days. If it is not encashed within fifteen days, the bond can only be deposited in the Prime Minister's Relief Fund. Electoral bonds will be available for purchase from the State Bank of India within a designated window of ten days in every quarter of the financial year. So, four windows every year will be opened when the donor can buy the bond. During the general election year (Lok Sabha), an additional window of thirty days will be opened. The Prime Minister Office (PMO), which has nothing to do with the operation of these bonds, intervened several times. The scheme of the electoral bond was launched on 1 January 2018 to come into practice from 1 April 2018. Due to the PMO's intervention, an exception was made and a special window was opened in March 2018. A total of Rs 222 crores was received out of which the BJP's share was a phenomenal Rs 210 crores, about 95 per cent of the total amount received. After the March window, a regular window of ten days was opened in April 2018. The PMO again intervened just before the Karnataka elections and a special window was opened in the succeeding month of May 2018. A regular window was opened in October for the third quarter of 2018–19. Again, the PMO intervened and a special window for receiving electoral bonds was opened in November 2018. An interesting thing happened in May 2018; the Ministry of

Finance was advised by the PMO to consider two bonds of Rs 10 crores each which had expired. According to the regulations if a bond lapses, the money is to be donated to the Prime Minister's Relief Fund. The bond holders had asked the bank to accept the lapsed bonds because they had been deposited within fifteen working days—though the rules say calendar days. The justification tailored by the ministry was it happened because of the ambiguity of fifteen working days or fifteen calendar days. One bond was accepted as a political donation and the other bond went to the Prime Minister's Relief Fund. The choice of PMO was very clear that it preferred the interest of the political party over the PM's Relief Fund.

How the bill was brought up in the parliament on 1 February 2017 raises many questions. Someone in the ministry of finance realized that the consent of the RBI is required; since the RBI Act was also to be amended, for the first time, the sovereign powers of the RBI were going to be changed. In the afternoon of 28 January at 1.45 pm, an email was sent to the RBI to take their (so-called) approval. Twenty-ninth January 2017 being a Sunday, the RBI replied on 30th, that is on Monday morning by way of strong objections. The RBI warned the government about the perils of electoral bonds. But the multiple secretaries in the ministry of finance overlooked it stating the apex bank had not 'understood the proposed mechanism' and since the Finance Bill was already printed, we should go ahead with it. The result was that a bill that was not a finance bill was passed as one and made into a law. Even the objections of the sovereign agency of the country which was responsible for monetary regulation and discipline of the nation were ignored.

The hurry which the government showed in

implementing these electoral bonds is questionable. Concerns and reservations of the stakeholders were ignored by the ruling government. Anonymous electoral bonds can allow funding by dubious companies. We have no law to know whether the money is drug money or it is funded by a shell company or a terror company. In none of the established democracies of the world, such funding through bonds is prevalent. In the USA complete details of the donor including the name of the employer is to be given for all donations received by the political parties above $200. In the United Kingdom, the party has to submit complete details of the donor for donations above £7,500. In India, if the donation comes through electoral bonds, political parties enjoy the privilege of not revealing the name of the donor irrespective of the amount received. The then Chief Justice of India Ranjan Gogoi's observation aptly defines the electoral bond –'If the identity of the donor is unknown, your entire exercise to eliminate black money becomes a futile exercise. Black money only becomes white.'

The line which was well defined in the initial years demarcating party and the government over the period started getting blurred. Now the transformation is complete. There is no difference between party and government. All the ministers, chief ministers and prime minister openly engage themselves for party work and use (or abuse) government machinery for the same. One example will clear the position—elections are now round the year in India in some state or the other. Political bosses involve themselves completely in the campaign. Apart from using logistic support has anybody heard anyone of them asking for a salary cut for the period they are doing party work?

The entry of a shiny new channel NaMo TV has opened the proverbial Pandora's box. Out of this comes questions of ownership, licensing, TRAI regulations, the Model Code of Conduct, and whether the BJP is above all rules. The way NaMo TV was used leaves lots of unanswered questions. Despite repeated complaints, no action was taken by the Election Commission against the channel or against BJP or Prime Minister Modi who owns the NaMo App of which NaMo TV was said to be a part. The channel was launched by the prime minister all of a sudden on 26 March 2019 and went off the air on 17 May after finishing the Lok Sabha campaign. The use of NSS-6 satellite to uplink and downlink the NaMo TV signal without having the necessary licence raised questions on compliance with the Indian Broadcast Law. Despite being a television channel the concerned department which regulates and grants licence turned a blind eye to it. All the major DTH (Direct to Home) operators such as Tata Sky, Videocon and Dish TV aired NaMo TV free of cost. Tata Sky initially termed NaMo TV as the Hindi News Channel and later termed it as a special service. NaMo TV does not have a compulsory security clearance and this makes the enterprise illegal under broadcast laws. It is possibly a first in the history of broadcasting in India that a channel had gone on air without any permission from the government or even applying for it.

The then Governor of Rajasthan Kalyan Singh visited his home town and was caught on camera soliciting support and vote for his son, a BJP candidate. A complaint was made and the note was sent to the president for approval as the incident involved a constitutional post where the sanction of the president was essential. The president's office sat on the file for the entire period of the election. Subsequently, Kalyan Singh retired as governor but to date, no one has heard of any action against Kalyan Singh. The chief minister of Uttar Pradesh Yogi Adityanath was barred from campaigning for three days by the Election Commissioner for violating the model code of conduct. Is it not an irony that holders and custodians of the law were indicted by the constitutional authority for breaking the code? The fine by way of the ban was imposed and he continued to hold the post of chief minister.

Yogi Aditya Nath, chief minister of Uttar Pradesh, was the poster boy of the BJP to address Hindu voters. In the 2017 Uttar Pradesh assembly elections, the BJP had not fielded a single Muslim candidate from any of the 403 constituencies making it amply clear that the politics of majority would be the winning formula. Yogi Adityanath in his role as chief minister is practical and understands the compulsions of administration. But in his avatar as leader soliciting votes for the BJP, he is a hardcore Hindu leader challenging 'their Ali with our Bajrangbali'.

The Congress came out with its manifesto in the first week of April 2019 and talked of NYAY (Nuyuntam Aay Yojana), a minimum income guarantee of Rs 72,000 per annum for 20 per cent of the poorest in the country. They pitched it as a game-changer like MGNREGA (The Mahatma Gandhi National Rural Employment Guarantee Act). The theme of the Congress manifesto was wealth and welfare. The BJP released its manifesto on 9 April 2019 as *sankalp patra* (pledge document). One of the highlights of this document was Prime Minister Modi addressing a letter to 130 crore citizens of India. The document talked of 100 years of celebration of India's independence and to lay the foundation for the same in the next five years' time. One can read between the lines regarding the BJP's intention of ruling the country till 2047.

Modi's strident nationalism as the main campaign plank

seems to have overruled the more pressing economic problems facing voters. The narrative of the 2019 election was conveniently changed by Team Modi from a vote on the five-year performance of his government to nationalism. In Indian elections, hearing the number of times Team Modi uses Pakistan's name, a new observer from some other country would get confused whether it is a cross-border election. On the election management front, Team Modi is miles ahead of any party. Especially, the Congress is nowhere near their booth management and election management strategies. Amit Shah as president of the party put all his resources and it was not done overnight. Preparations started from the day Modi was sworn in 2014. The way one of the charges of corruption in the Rafal deal was deflected needed very deft handling of the issue. This deal was murkier than Bofors. The slogan – '*Chowkidar chor hai*'coined by Rahul Gandhi was cleverly used by Team Modi to its advantage—'*Main bhi chowkidar*'. The nation ultimately believed and voted—There is No Alternative (TNA) factor and Modi won 2019 with a remarkably improved clear majority.

It has to be seen how Modi 2.0 will determine the contours of India's future as a secular republic dedicated to upholding the country's unparalleled diversity and committed to embracing ethnic and religious pluralism.

Notes

1. An electoral bond can be bought by any Indian citizen or company incorporated in India from select branches of the State Bank of India. The citizen or corporate can then donate the same to any eligible political party of his/her choice. The bonds are similar to ban knotes that are payable to the bearer on demand and are free of interest

CHAPTER-4

Jai Shri Ram

Ram Temple Yes, but Whose Ram Rajya – Gandhi's or Modi's

Many think that the demolition of Babri Masjid was state-sponsored and it certainly changed the way India interpreted secularism. A new term that is close to reality is 'emotional truth'. Now the truth is decided by emotions and not by facts and obviously, emotions of the majority will prevail. Post-6 December 1992, infuriated Muslims protested all over India. In the process of keeping law and order under control, the police opened fire at the very outset. Policemen are trained in matters of law and order of the set SOP (Standard Operating Procedure)– *Boli-Danda-Goli*. *Boli*—Talk to people, cajole, threaten, and in this process commonly used procedure is verbal abuse. Even society discounts the abusive tongue of the police personnel with the logic that in course of their duty they are supposed to abuse and which becomes their habit. *Danda*—The majority of the policemen carry sticks with them which are also a symbol of their authority. Lathi charge is also very common when the policemen are handling protestors. *Goli*—to shoot is the last resort mostly in cases of self-defence. In recent times, between *danda* and *goli*, one more procedure has crept in—the use of water cannon and rubber bullets. It is estimated that more than 1,000 lives were lost, mostly Muslims, when they protested against the destruction of the Babri Masjid. One grievance which the minority had was that when the disputed structure was being razed to the ground, not even one *danda* was raised, and when they protested, the police resorted to *goli*.

The protest was pretty widespread. In Maharashtra, Bal Thackeray was in command and he claimed that the final assault on Babri Masjid was by Shiv Sainiks of Maharashtra. In Maharashtra, the death toll was 259. In Gujarat, 246 people, mostly Muslims died. Shops were looted in the area where prosperous Muslims lived and the army was summoned. Though the epicentre, Uttar Pradesh surprisingly remained calm and only 201 lives were lost, Kanpur and Varanasi had some rumbling but was contained. One reason for this calm could be the imposition of President's Rule and removal of the BJP government. This gave the authorities more freedom to tackle the unrest. In Bhopal, sweets were distributed and crackers were lit after the demolition. The BJP government remained a mute spectator and Chief Minister Sunder Lal Patwa acted only when it became apparent that the Centre might dismiss his government for non-action. The toll in Madhya Pradesh was 120 dead. Assam had 100 deaths and immigrants from Bangladesh targeted the Hindus and the temples. Chief Minister Saikia kept on demanding extra paramilitary forces. In Karnataka, 60 people died. The rioting was localized in Muslim-dominated areas like Shivajinagar in Bangalore.

Karnataka had an acute shortage of paramilitary forces. In Rajasthan, Bhairon Singh Shekhawat was the only BJP chief minister who acted promptly. He called the army in 7 towns, imposed curfew in 8 towns and thus the death toll was restricted to 48. West Bengal with the communist government in place had 32 deaths. The state of affairs was aptly described by a local newspaper –'Not a very bad situation but badly managed one'. Laloo Prasad Yadav, who had an image of a happy-go-lucky person was one of the best chief ministers who acted firmly to manage riots. Twenty-four people died in Bihar, out of which only 9 died in police firing. Laloo withdrew armed security cover from VIP duties to give additional strength for law enforcement. The MY (Muslim-Yadav) factor could have been one of the reasons for this prompt action. It was his base vote bank; as a result, the Muslims felt more secure. Kerala had 12 deaths but remained peaceful. ISS head Abdul Nasser Madhani was not arrested as he remained silent. The BJP called for a bandh on 9 December 1992 which resulted in 4 deaths. Andhra Pradesh was also credited for keeping the death toll contained to 12 and the main reason for this was the freehand given by Chief Minister Vijay Bhaskar Reddy to the police to deal firmly with the situation. Muslims in Tamil Nadu showed remarkable restraint and the death toll was only 2 and that too in the district of Tirunelveli.

India slowly limped back to normalcy barring Mumbai where murders, arson, police firings and riots between two religious communities kept on happening. This left 900 dead and by the end of January 1993, it looked like that the city was back to normal. The years 1992 and 1993, when the country's secular foundations were being challenged, also witnessed the entry of an actor in Bollywood who became the second superstar after Rajesh Khanna. He was Shah

Rukh Khan, who became a phenomenon in the years to come. His debut film *Deewana* in 1992 got him a Filmfare award for the best male debut. In these two turbulent years, this actor from Delhi with no connection or mentor in the film industry gave nine box-office hits (commercially successful)—*Deewana, Chamatkaar, Raju Ban Gaya Gentleman, Dil Ashna Hai, Maya Mem Saheb, Pahla Nasha, King Uncle, Bazigar* and *Darr*. The first and last film of this list got him Filmfare awards for Best Male Debut and Best Actor respectively. The purpose of sharing this information is to understand that despite communal riots, the masses were not divided into different religious groups. Today it is very common to hear appeals from groups to boycott films of a particular community. The political strategists and vote managers took the time to widen this divide. In today's world, actors, artists, writers, activists, social workers, teachers, universities are branded as national and anti-national because they are from a particular community.

The Maharashtra government appointed sitting High Court judge, Justice B.N. Srikrishna as a one-man commission to look into the Bombay riots. Justice Srikrishna by birth is a Kannada, born and brought up in Mumbai. He was a postgraduate in Sanskrit, Indian aesthetics and had a diploma in Urdu. The commission's scope of inquiry was later enlarged to probe the Bombay blast of March 1993. The commission in its finding stated that the political leadership and police were complicit in their conduct during December and January 1992–93. The report criticized the role of the Congress and the BJP both but blamed inciting and organizing communal riots squarely on the Shiv Sena and its leader Bal Thackeray resulting in the deaths of many Muslims. Manohar Joshi, the Shiv Sena chief minister in 1998, while presenting the report in the Maharashtra assembly, rejected its finding calling it pro-Muslim and anti-Hindu. Former Shiv Sena MP Madhukar Sarpotdar was sentenced for his role in the Bombay riots in 2008, He got bail and died in 2010 without serving his sentence. Justice Srikrishna became Chief Justice of Kerala High Court and retired as a Supreme Court Judge. He headed many commissions and committees, such as the Sixth Central Pay Commission, the Madras High Court Riots Commission, the Committee on Separate Telangana, the Committee on data protection, etc. As scores of commission and inquiry reports were filed, the fate of Srikrishna's findings was decided the day it was appointed. What was the purpose of these commissions/enquiries/committees/investigations/SIT etc., when no future corrective action was to be taken? It seems it is used by successive political leadership just to address the immediate public rage and emotions knowing it very well that no one is interested in long-term solutions.

Like the Indian political system, the Mumbai underworld was also changing. Religion had no place in the criminal world and most of the criminals/mafias/dons, the epitome of secular brotherhood, was also changing. The Mumbai underworld, which used to control smuggling of the Indian subcontinent post-liberalization, was out of a job as anything and everything was available in India. The demolition allowed neighbouring Pakistan to take revenge on the wounds of Bangladesh which had still not healed. Dawood Ibrahim had taken refuge in Pakistan and he was more than ready to oblige his new masters which brought him not only money but an opportunity to establish his grip on the crime world of Mumbai. Dawood became the champion of the Muslims and decided to avenge the fall of the Babri mosque. He wanted to show the world that he had taken revenge for the injustice done by the demolition.

On 12 March 1993, twelve bombs exploded in different parts of Mumbai. Two hundred and fifty-seven people were killed and more than 713 were injured. Some documents write that about 320 people were killed but they add about 60/70 people who died in the Kolkata bomb blast on 16 March 1993.[1] The Kolkata and Mumbai blasts had no connection. In Mumbai, the blasts occurred between 1.30 pm to 3.40 pm at important crowded places like Hotel Sea Rock, the Air India Building, the Mumbai Stock Exchange, etc. Sharad Pawar had just taken over from Sudhakarrao Naik as Chief Minister of Maharashtra on 6 March 1993 and managed to control the subsequent unrest/riot/ backlash of the Mumbai blast. The chief minister's office told that the blasts were not at 12, but 13 places. They named the Tamil Tigers as possible suspects behind the blast. Many years later, Sharad Pawar confessed that he purposely named the imaginary 13th blast in a Muslim Area and named the Tamil Tigers as suspects to prevent a Hindu backlash.

The Dawood gang was also divided into communal lines. It was split into Hindu and Muslim groups. When Dawood positioned himself as a champion of the Muslim cause, his long-time associate Chhota Rajan left him. Chotta Rajan then took up the role of a 'Hindu protector'. The subsequent investigations revealed that the Memon brothers, who were the key persons of Dawood had planned, recruited, trained and executed the Mumbai bomb blasts. Mumbai Police caught Gul Noor Mohammad Sheikh (Gullu) on 9 March 1993. He was one of the many enrolled by Tiger Memon to carry out the blasts. It is said that Gullu, after returning from training in Pakistan, developed cold feet. On the insistence of his mother, he got himself arrested for a petty offence to avoid participation in the main act of terror. The original plan was to attack several places all over India in April 1993 during the Shiv Jayanti celebrations, but it was advanced to 12 March 1993 due to two reasons—one was the arrest of Gullu due to which Tiger Memon's apprehension was that he might spill the beans. The second reason was that Dawood wanted it in the holy month of Ramadan and on a Juma (Friday). About 129 people were accused, many of them eluded arrest including Dawood and Tiger Memon; the TADA (Terrorist and Disruptive Activities [Prevention]) Court found 100 people guilty which included landing agents who organized the landing of arms and ammunition, bomb planters, custom officials, policemen and other co-conspirators. The most famous accused was the Hindi film star Sanjay Dutt. Twelve accused got the death penalty, 20 life imprisonment, a few got small punishments and 23 were acquitted. The Supreme Court on 2 March 2013 confirmed the death sentence of Yakub Menon and commuted the death sentence to life imprisonment in 10 cases. Yakub Menon was hanged on 30 July 2015 in Nagpur Central jail. Mohammed Iqbal died while in prison.

Sanjay Dutt was arrested on 19 April 1993 and got bail only after 18 months after his father Sunil Dutt, MP knocked on all the doors to get him released. It is said that ultimately it was Bal Thackeray who got him bailed out. The TADA Court found him guilty of illegal possession of fire arms but acquitted in charges of conspiracy. His six-year sentence was reduced to five years by the Supreme Court, which Sanjay had to serve.

The city of Mumbai again witnessed a terrorist attack sponsored by Pakistan and Dawood in November 2008 (commonly referred to as the 26/11 attack). Ten Lashkar-e-Taiba members entered Mumbai via sea route and attacked Taj Hotel, Bombay VT Station, Best Bakery, etc. killing 164 and injuring 308. One of the terrorists Ajmal Kasab was caught alive. India gave him a fair trial and after four years, Kasab was hanged in Pune's Yerwada Jail on 21 November 2012. As per the procedure, the official letter intimating his death was sent to Pakistan which the Pakistan government refused to accept. The same was then faxed to Pakistan authorities. The intimation was also sent to his family by courier to Kasab's address in Pakistan.

The demolition of the mosque left an indelible scar on far-away Mumbai. The city witnessed a traumatic period from 6 December 1992, when the Babri mosque was demolished, to 12 March 1993, when serial blasts rocked Mumbai and 2008 when Bombay the city which never sleeps came to a standstill due to the 26/11 massacre. In 2008, it witnessed a siege for a few days which changed the city's cosmopolitan character forever. The year 1993 turned out to be the city's watershed year, one that scarred Mumbai deeply and viscerally. The city has never been the same since. Bombay, now Mumbai, has since been a communally ghettoized city whose glitzy commerce and swanky metros barely mask the social divisions of the 1990s.

Now we turn back to the legal dispute about ownership of the Ram Janmbhoomi land or title suit that started about sixty years ago and reached a conclusive stage in the Lucknow Bench of the Allahabad High Court. After listening to all the parties, a bench of three judges comprising Justice S.U. Khan, Justice Sudhir Agrawal and Justice D.V. Sharma reserved the judgement on 26 July 2010. A High Court order running into 800 pages was delivered on 30 September 2010. The opening lines of the judgement were—'Here is a small piece of land (1500 square yards) where angels fear to tread. It is full of innumerable land mines. We are required to clear it. . . . Accordingly, herein follows the judgement for which the entire country is waiting with bated breath.'The majority judgement of 2 : 1 divided the disputed land of 2.77 acres into three equal parts. One part was given to Suni Waqf Board, one part to Nirmohi Akhara and one part to the party for 'Ram lalla'.

Liberhan Commission was appointed on 16 December 1992. Justice Manmohan Singh Liberahn was assigned to probe the demolition of Ram Janmabhoomi–Babri Masjid structure and submit its report within three months. It became the longest commission of enquiry with 48 extensions. It submitted its report on 30 June 2009 after 17 years. It spent an estimated Rs 8 crores as direct expenses. Liberhan Commission came down heavily on mixing politics and religion. In the 1,029 page-report, it has recommended making a law so that exemplary punishment is given for misusing religion to acquire political power. The inter-mixing of religion and politics is dangerous and has disruptive potential. The Commission further stated that the demolition of Babri Masjid was planned and systematic. The Liberhan Commission while recommending measures has mentioned in its report:

> 172.16 – The next logical conclusion must therefore be that a government which is formed on the premises of religion or which has religious issues, on its political agenda must also be barred. A government which is formed by professing its support to a particular religion or which has a religious issue or purpose as its stated agenda must therefore fall foul of the explicit and implicit prescriptions of the Constitution.

The Liberhan Commission clearly stated that the events of 6 December 1992 leading to the demolition of the structure were 'neither spontaneous nor unplanned'. The commission recorded statements of the elite group of the Indian power structure, such as P.V. Narasimha Rao, V.P. Singh, S.B. Chavan, Advani, Mulayam Singh Yadav, Kalyan Singh, Arjun Singh, K.S. Sudarshan, Vishnu Hari Dalmia, Ashok Singhal, Uma Bharti, Mark Tully and some top bureaucrats. Around 100 witnesses were examined. In 2015, the Supreme Court intervened on the petition alleging that with a BJP government in power, the CBI would not effectively pursue charges against the top leadership of the BJP including Lal Krishna Advani, Murli Manohar Joshi, etc. This was because the CBI's handling of the case has always depended on which political party was in power at the centre. The CBI could be misused by the ruling party and the prosecution of senior BJP leaders could be partial. A special CBI Court was formed clubbing cases going on in different courts into one consolidated case naming the special CBI case as 'Ram Janm Bhoomi Prakaran'. The Supreme Court directed for the case to be heard daily and judgement to be pronounced within two years.

The High Court order of splitting the disputed land into three parts was challenged in the Supreme Court in December 2010. The Supreme Court in May 2011 stayed the division of land as decided by the High Court. Chief Justice Ranjan Gogoi assumed charge of Chief Justice of India on 3 October 2018 and soon announced that the Supreme Court in a time-bound period would listen and conclude the case of Ram Janambhumi. Chief Justice of India Gogoi was scheduled to retire on 17 November 2019. The five-judge bench comprising Justice Ranjan Gogoi,

Justice Arvind Bobde, Justice D.Y. Chandrachud, Justice S. Abdul Nazeer, and Justice Ashok Bhushan heard the case on a day-to-day basis from 6 August to 16 October 2019 and pronounced unanimous judgement on 9 November 2019.

The main points of the judgement were as follows—

- A trust with a board of trustees was to be created within three months by the government and the entire 2.77 acres of disputed land was to be transferred to the trust;
- Five acres of land was to be allotted in Ayodhya as an alternative site for construction of a masjid;
- The demolition of the Babri Masjid and the 1949 desecration of the Babri Masjid violated the law.

In December 2019, petitions seeking review of the judgement were dismissed by the Supreme Court.

The Supreme Court judgement led by Chief Justice Gogoi will always be questioned as after retirement he was nominated to Rajya Sabha in March 2020. This was severely criticized not only by the public at large but by the legal fraternity as well. Gogoi was part of several judgements and decisions that were criticized because of his post-retirement Rajya Sabha seat. Starting with the Ram Janambhumi case, CJI Gogoi sought to end a decades-old dispute over the ownership of a plot in Ayodhya. The court gave the judgement that demolition was illegal but still handed over the rights to one aggrieved party. The judgement is severely criticized for preferring an imaginary, hypothetical peace over the injustice suffered due to the demolition of the mosque. The Triple talaq and Sabrimala verdicts were also linked with the appointment. Following the Modi government's decision to scrap Article 370, Gogoi came in for criticism. The way the government enforced the abrogation of Article 370 in Jammu and Kashmir was seen as a blatant misuse of power and the top judiciary not only remained a mute spectator but the aggrieved parties were denied a fair hearing too. Gogoi is also criticized for laying too much emphasis on the process rather than adjudicating the case. The Supreme Court which is supposed to be transparent and is the highest and last hope for the common man started a new practice during Justice Gogoi's tenure. The sealed-cover doctrine gained prominence during the tenure of former Chief Justice of India Ranjan Gogoi. The court asked for information in sealed covers for the cases which were sensitive and which affected common citizens–electoral bonds, the CBI Director Row, the Rafael case, etc. Transparency and accountability form the core of India's legal system. Justice should be seen as being delivered. In such a system why did a court which adjudicates the cases based on facts want to keep certain facts out of the purview of a common man?

The treatment given to some of the independent-minded judges of the High Court speaks volumes about the independence of the judiciary during Justice Gogoi's time. Justice Kureshi, the seniormost judge of the Gujarat High Court was recommended by the collegium to be appointed as the Chief Justice of Madhya Pradesh High Court. The collegium was headed by CJI Gogoi. The government sat on the decision for months. This kind of 'unexplained' in action on the part of the centre is viewed as an attack on the independence of the judiciary and diminishes the supremacy of the judiciary. Later, on the advice of the government, the same collegium transferred him to Tripura High Court. In 2010, Justice Kureshi as a sitting High Court Judge of Gujarat had sent Amit Shah to police custody in the Sohrabuddin encounter case. The Chief Justice of Madras High Court V.K. Tahilramani was transferred to the Meghalaya High Court. Not only was her request to reconsider her transfer turned down but after her resignation, an enquiry was instituted against her. As Justice of Bombay High Court in 2017, Tahilramani had upheld the convictions in the brutal Bilkis Bano gang rape case during the Godhra riots. The case was transferred from Gujarat to Maharashtra to have a fair trial. Chief Justice Gogoi got involved in another serious controversy when a woman employee posted at his office complained that she had been sexually harassed by him. She also sent an affidavit to twenty-two judges of the Supreme Court alleging sexual harassment by Justice Gogoi. The case was probed by the house committee of the Supreme Court instead of an independent committee as provided by the law. Justice Gogoi was given a clean chit in a month. Navigating this judicial process became more traumatic for the victimized woman when she was suspended. Travesty of justice was when she was reinstated with a clean chit after the retirement of Justice Gogoi. This is a bizarre and curious case where the victim and the accused both got a clean chit. We do not have an answer to the question, 'How to guard against the guardian?'

The nomination of Justice Gogoi is justified stating that another former Chief Justice of India, Rang Nath Mishra also became a member of Rajya Sabha in the 1990s. Justice Mishra retired in 1991 and after several years joined the Congress party. He fought elections for the Rajya Sabha in 1998 as a Congress candidate from Orissa and got elected. So, he was an elected member, not a nominated member. The best part is as per Schedule 4 of the Constitution, the President nominates twelve persons of eminence who have contributed in the field of art, literature, science and social service. Justice Gogoi's contribution to these fields is a matter of research!

The Prime Minister of India Narendra Modi announced in the parliament on 5 February 2020 that in line with the judgement of the Supreme Court a trust was established by the central government—Shri Ram Janmabhoomi Teerth Kshetra.The trust has fifteen trustees out of which nine are permanent and six are nominated or ex-officio. The disputed land of 2.77 acres as decided by the Supreme Court is transferred to the trust. Another 67.70 acres of land acquired earlier by the government is also transferred to the trust. The trust elected Champat Rai of Vishwa Hindu Parishad as General Secretary and Swami Govind Dev Giri as a Treasurer.

The nine permanent members of the trust are:

Govind Dev Giri—born in a Brahmin family and is known for his discourse on the Bhagvat Gita. He is based in Pune.

Vimalendra Mohan Pratap Mishra—is from the Ayodhya princely state. He is the patron of the trust of Ramayan Mela inspired by Dr Lohia. When the old idol went missing, the replaced idol of Ram *lalla* was provided by his family on 6 December 1992. Vimalendra unsuccessfully contested the 2009 Lok Sabha election on a BSP ticket.

Dr Anil Mishra—RSS Prant Karyawah (executive head) is a local practising homoeopath doctor born in Ambedkarnagar.

Mahant Dinendra Das—The only representative of saints and sadhus of Ayodhya, Mahant Dinendra Das is from Nirmohi Akhara, one of the parties in the dispute.

Vasudeva Nand Sarswati—is nominated in the trust as the Shankaracharya of *Jyotish Peeth.* His claim as Shankaracharya of Jyotishpeeth is vehemently opposed by Swaroopanand Sarswati of Sharda Peeth and Jyotishpeeth, 'I am the Shankaracharya of Jyotish Peeth. The Prime Minister by nominating another person as Shankaracharya of Jyotish Peeth has disobeyed the Supreme Court which even refused to consider Vasudevanand a sanyasi.'

Swami Paramanand Maharaj—is the head of Akhand Ashram, Haridwar. He has written more than 150 books on 'Vedant'.

Swami Vishwa Prasan Tirth Maharaj—is the head of Pejawar Math in Karnataka.

K. Parasaran—was born in 1927. At the age of 92 years, he was leading the Hindu side of the Ram Janmbhumi case in the Supreme Court. He is the former Advocate General of Tamil Nadu, Solicitor General of India, Attorney General of India and Rajya Sabha Member. He was appointed as the first trustee. The trust was registered at his home address in Delhi.

Kameshwar Chaupal—served as Zila Parcharak of RSS and then as an office-bearer of VHP, Chaupal laid the first brick of the foundation stone of the Ram Janmbhumi Temple on 9 November 1989. This Dalit leader from Supaul, Bihar contested elections thrice on a BJP ticket—the 1991 Lok Sabha elections from Rasada, the assembly elections in 1995 from Begusarai, and again the 2014 Lok Sabha elections. He lost all the elections. He became a member of the Bihar Legislative Council in 2002.

The six nominated members of the Trust in August 2020 were as follows:

Mahant Nritya Gopal Das—He was one of the accused in the Babri Masjid demolition case. He was associated with the Ram Janmbhumi movement since 1984. He headed the *nyas* at the time of the court order and was upset when his name was not in the first list of the nine trustees when the trust was formed in line with the court order. He was later made the president of the trust.

Champat Rai—He is a Vishwa Hindu Parishad activist and is currently the International General Secretary of VHP. He is the General Secretary of the trust.

Nripendra Mishra—He is an alumnus of Allahabad University and 1967 batch IAS of the UP cadre; he was the principal functionary of the PMO during the Modi-1 regime from 2014 to 2019. He was nominated as the member and Chairman of the Construction Committee.

Gyanesh Kumar—He is an IAS officer. As per the provision of the Trust, representation is needed from the Ministry of Home, Government of India. He is the Additional Secretary–Home, therefore, he is a member of the trust.

Awaneesh Awasthi—He is an IAS officer and holds the post of Additional Chief Secretary (Home). He is the most powerful bureaucrat in Yogis administration and is the representative of the state government.

Anuj Kumar Jha—He is an IAS officer and holds the post of the District Magistrate of Ayodhya.

The trust formed as per the judgement of the Supreme Court will drive the construction of Ram Mandir (temple). Out of the total fifteen members of the trust, twelve are Brahmins. The moot question is—Are we building a society where all are equal without caste, creed, colour and gender? Ram belongs to all so why was representation not given to all the castes. In 'Ram Rajya' it is important to include the Shudras and Dalits. The absence of women in the trust reflects the mindset of society towards half of the population (*aadhi abadi*). Another provision is that the district magistrate of Ayodhya will be the ex-officio member of the trust provided he is a Hindu. If he is not a Hindu, then his deputy would be the ex-officio member provided he is a Hindu. If the trust was created by a private individual or institution, then any clause kept by them would have been accepted and no one would have pointed a finger at them. But if the government, on the advice of the court, puts such clause then it is deplorable. Last but not the least, the central government and the state government representative has to be an IAS officer. Officers of other all-India services are not qualified to be a part of the trust. This clearly shows a bias towards the IAS.

It was decided to do the *bhumi pujan* (worshipping of the land) of Ram Janm Mandir once again on 5 August 2020. In the year 1989, VHP was putting pressure to do the *shilanyas* at the disputed plot no. 586. The government wanted *shilanyas* on plot no. 576 which was located seven yards away from the disputed site. This plot was leased to Ram Kripal Das and he had given his consent for plot no. 576 to be used for *shilanyas*. The state government went to the High Court on 6 November 1989. The court upheld the interim order that the land is disputed and no construction will be allowed. Narain Dutt Tewari, who had earned the nickname of 'New Delhi Tewari' as he was always seeking the advice of the central leadership for even trivial matters, was reluctant to go against the orders of the High Court. On 6 November 1989, instead of going to the High Court, the matter was settled in the ashram of Devraha Baba in Brindavan. Rajiv Gandhi sought the advice of Devraha Baba in this matter. Devraha Baba consulted Shish Chand Dixit who was the retired IPS officer of the UP cadre. Shish Chand Dixit was the chief negotiator. The VHP told the prime minister to go ahead with the *shilanyas*. He also advised not to shift the place of the *shilanyas*. Finally, on 9 November 1989, *bhumi pujan* and *shilanyas* were performed. *Bhumi pujan* was done by Swami Vam Dev, Vastu Puja by Mahadev Bhatt and Ayodhya Prasad, the first ground breaking was done by the spade of Mahant Avaidyanath and the first brick was laid by Kameshwar Chaupal.

The date 5 August is important for the Modi government as just after the commencement of the second innings, the Modi government scrapped Article 370 in Jammu & Kashmir relegating its statehood to union territory status. In India, we believe in auspicious and inauspicious *muhurt* (time) not only for starting any auspicious work but even in our day-to-day lives. In India, *rahukalam* (a particular time every day during which the start of new work or commencing a journey is avoided) is followed strictly by many Indians not only in India but even by those who live abroad. The launch of a rocket or any spacecraft in India invariably is preceded by *puja* after calculating the auspicious time. Even Defence Minister Rajnath Singh while taking the delivery of the ultra-modern Rafale fighter planes from France performed a small *puja*. Indians by nature and custom follow a good and bad time matrix while laying the foundation stone of even a house. The foundation ceremony of Ram Mandir which is the dream of Hindus for the last 500 years as propagated by the saffron brigade was supposed to be started at the best time as per the calculation of the Hindu calendar. The period of monsoon is called *chaumasa*. It starts from *devshyani ekadashi* of *shukl paksh*a of *Ashadh mas* and ends on *devshtauni ekadashi* of *shukl* *paksha* of *kartik mas* (roughly starting from July to October, fifteen/twenty days plus-minus every year as per the Hindu calendar). During these four months, it is believed that Hindu gods go for a long rest and sleep and no pious and auspicious acts, events, marriages or ceremonies are performed during this period. The rituals and traditions of Ayodhya are closer to eastern Uttar Pradesh society and 5 August 2020 happened to be *dwitiya* (day two) of *Bhadrapada* month of the Hindu calendar and especially on this day, any auspicious ceremony is prohibited.

Another act of Modiji doing the Ram Mandir Nirman *puja* himself was not in line with the Hindu tradition. Any auspicious religious work is to be done with husband and wife together. If a man is married then he cannot sit alone for the puja or any other ritual. Modi had left the column on the marital status blank in four assembly polls but in the 2014 general elections declared Jassoda Ben as his wife. If the wife is alive, then performing the ritual without her is not in order. The importance of the wife to sit for such rituals can be substantiated by two examples of Lord Ram and Sita. At the time of performing the *puja* at Rameshwaram, Ravan being the most learned pandit (priest) was requested to be the priest for Ram to which he agreed. The story says that he brought Sita with him to be by the side of Ram because according to the Hindu scriptures, the rituals are not complete without the wife. The second instance is when Ram was performing the Ashvamedh *Yagya*, Sita was needed by his side. Since Sita was staying away from Ram, scholars suggested that Ram should remarry so that the new wife can sit with him for the rituals. The proposal was vehemently opposed by Ram on the ground that he was already married and his commitment was only towards his wife Sita. As a stop-gap arrangement in the absence of

Sita, a gold statue of Sita was placed beside Ram and puja was performed. Narendra Modi performing puja at Lord Ram's temple without his wife was certainly not as per Hindu tradition.

The President of India as the first citizen of the country was the rightful person to perform the puja. Depriving him to do the puja is not taken up very well by the deprived section of the society from where the president hails. Inviting only the RSS head, Mohan Bhagwat to share the stage reduced the entire Ram Janambhumi *puja* as an event of the saffron brigade instead of being a huge event for the nation as a whole. The celebration at the time of the Covid-19 pandemic, when people are struggling for basic life needs and China knocking at the doors was also not the best of decisions to cherish. The ceremony marked the complete disappearance of the line of separation between religion and the state.

The final verdict of the special CBI court on 30 September 2020 confirmed the direction of the new path along which our country is now progressing. A total of forty-nine FIRs were lodged in December 1992 after the demolition out of which forty-eight were of cognizable offence. The FIR named Advani, Murli Manohar Joshi, Uma Bharti, Mahant Avaidyanath, Vishnu Hari Dalmia and Ashok Singhal for making speeches leading to the demolition. The case was handed over to CBI on 27 August 1993 and a joint charge sheet was filed on 5 October 1993 naming 40 persons as accused. In 2001, the conspiracy charge against Advani, the then Home Minister of India and others were dropped by the Special CBI Court. The same was upheld by the Allahabad High Court in 2010. On 19 April 2017, a bench of the Supreme Court of Justice P.C. Ghosh and R.F. Nariman reversed the judgement restoring criminal conspiracy charges against Advani and others. While ordering for a time-bound trial to be completed within two years the bench observed—'In the present case, crime which shakes the secular fabric of the Constitution of India have allegedly been committed almost 25 years ago.'

The special CBI court judge Surendra Kumar Yadav was due to retire on 30 September 2019, several extensions including service extensions of judges were made by the apex court. In the verdict of 9 November 2019 by which the disputed site was given for the construction of the Ram mandir, the five-judge bench of the Supreme Court has observed—'The destruction of the mosque and the obliteration of the Islamic Structure was an egregious violation of the rule of law. 'The Liberhan Commission has already observed the conspiracy theory in the demolition of the structure. After 28 years, all the living 32 accused of the Babri Masjid demolition case were asked to be present on 30 September 2020 in the special court of the CBI. Twenty-six were present, Advani and Murli Manohar Joshi on the ground of advance age and Uma Bharti who was in hospital were exempted. All the thirty-two accused were acquitted; according to the verdict, the demolition was not pre-planned and persons accused of demolition were—'trying to stop the mob and not incite them'. The court said that it cannot probe the authenticity of the audio-video evidence provided by the CBI. So, in the end, **one can say Babri Masjid was not demolished**.

The recent incidents of our land brought cheers to a substantial section of our society but only time will tell if this path leads us to become *vishva guru*. I can only wish the nation moves from 'Jai Shri Ram' which is being used like a war cry these days, to 'Jai Sia Ram', the sound of peace and tranquillity for all.

NOTES

1. On the night of 16 March 1993, a stock of explosives which Rashid Khan was gathering, accidentally blew up in Bowbazar Area in Kolkata. Rashid was planning bomb blasts at different places in Kolkata on the lines of the Mumbai blast.

Index